Target Corinth Canal
1940–1944

To the memory of Alex Stratoudakis
and Mike Cumberlege and his companions.

Target Corinth Canal
1940–1944

*Mike Cumberlege and the Attempts
to Block the Corinth Canal*

PLATON ALEXIADES

Pen & Sword
MILITARY

First published in Great Britain by
PEN AND SWORD MILITARY
an imprint of
Pen and Sword Books Ltd
47 Church Street
Barnsley
South Yorkshire S70 2AS

Copyright © Platon Alexiades, 2015

ISBN 978 1 47382 756 1

Printed and bound in England by
CPI Group (UK) Ltd, Croydon, CR0 4YY

Typeset in Times by CHIC GRAPHICS

Pen & Sword Books Ltd incorporates the imprints of Pen & Sword
Archaeology, Atlas, Aviation, Battleground, Discovery,
Family History, History, Maritime, Military, Naval, Politics,
Railways, Select, Social History, Transport, True Crime,
Claymore Press, Frontline Books, Leo Cooper, Praetorian Press,
Remember When, Seaforth Publishing and Wharncliffe.

For a complete list of Pen and Sword titles please contact
Pen and Sword Books Limited
47 Church Street, Barnsley, South Yorkshire, S70 2AS, England
E-mail: enquiries@pen-and-sword.co.uk
Website: www.pen-and-sword.co.uk

Contents

Acknowledgements

The author is grateful for the assistance of:

Marcus and Maria Cumberlege
Eunice Cumberlege-Ravassat
The late Major Michael Ward OBE
Robin d'Arcy Ward
The late Dr Alexandros and Chrys Stratoudakis
Kostas Thoctarides
Caterina Callitsis
Rear Admiral Ioannis Maniatis (Retired)
Rear Admiral Giuliano Manzari

Ian Frazer
Professor André Gerolymatos
Robert Hall
Petros and Aline Haritatos
Alan Harris
George Karelas
Dr Steven Kippax
Robin Knight
Myrto and Heinz Larsen
Paul R. London
Gilbert Mangerel
Panayotis Manzaris
Jean-Pierre Misson
Alan Ogden
Bill Rudd
Ioannis Sambanis
Francis Suttill
Sir John Weston

At the *Archiv Gedenkstaette-Sachsenhausen*:
Monika Liebscher and Barbara Müller

At the Benaki Museum (Athens):
Maria Dimitriadou and her staff

At the British School at Athens (BSA):
Amalia Kikassis

At the Sedbergh School (Cumbria):
Katy Iliffe

At the Hellenic Naval Archives:
Rear Admiral Athanasios Panogoulos
Captain Spiridon Mimikos
Sub Lieutenant Panayotis Gerontas
Warrant Officer George Mastrogeorgiou

Staff at the National Archives (TNA, London)
Staff at the National Archives (NARA, Washington)
Staff at the Imperial War Museum (IWM, London)

At the *Ufficio Storico della Marina Militare* (USMM, Rome):
Capitano di vascello Francesco Loriga (Capo Ufficio Storico)
Capitano di vascello Giosuè Allegrini (Capo Ufficio Storico)
Capitano di fregata Domenico Rotolo (Capo Sezione Archivio)
Capitano di fregata (Stato Maggiore) Ennio Chiffi (Capo Sezione Archivio)
Professore Marco Cormani
Franco Senatore
Rita Micheli
Romeo Perini
Primo Maresciallo Vincenzo Fiorillo (Capo Fotografo)

Staff at the *Ufficio Storico dello Stato Maggiore dell'esercito* (Rome)

and the following individuals:

David Asprey
Andrzej Bartelski
Yehuda Ben-Tzur
Jordi Comas
Brian Corijn
Francesco de Domenico
Theodor Dorgeist
Dimitrios Galon
Mark C. Jones
Francesco Mattesini
Bernard O'Connor

René Stenzel
Paul H. Silverstone
Michel-Charles Tadros

My wife Viviane for her patience.

The maps are made by Robert E. Pratt

At Pen and Sword: special thanks to Henry Wilson, Richard Doherty, Matt Jones and Sylvia Menzies-Earl.

The author can be reached at:
palexiad@sympatico.ca

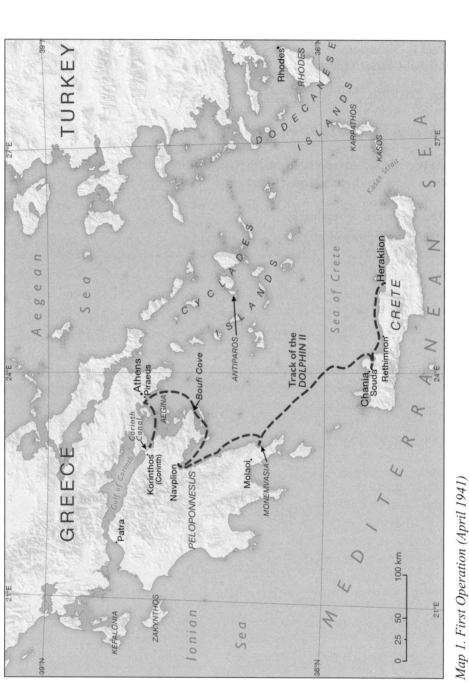

Map 1. First Operation (April 1941)

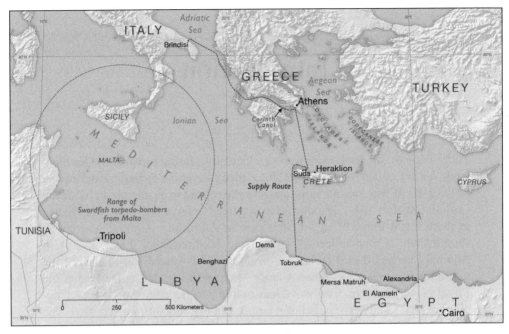

Map 2. Axis Supply Route via Corinth Canal

Map 3. Second Operation (March 1943)

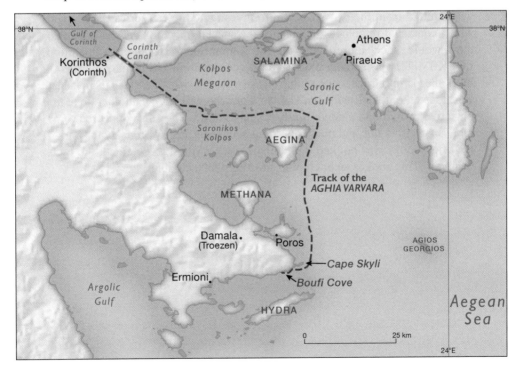

Introduction

The making of this book came quite accidentally. During a visit at the National Archives in London, I was researching Allied submarine operations during the Second World War, when I came across a file related to an attempt to block the Corinth Canal in 1941. The operation appeared to have had some importance as there was a flurry of signals between the Admiralty, Admiral Andrew B. Cunningham, Commander-in-Chief of the Mediterranean Fleet, and Rear Admiral Charles Edward Turle, the Naval Attaché in Athens. The man entrusted to this mission was a Lieutenant Claude Michael Bulstrode Cumberlege of the Royal Naval Reserve. The story had nothing to do with the object of my research, but I had never heard of it before and my curiosity was aroused. The story appeared interesting but things might have stood there when, by sheer coincidence, the same afternoon I stumbled upon a file about Operation LOCKSMITH.

Allied submarines had carried out many special operations landing spies or saboteurs behind enemy lines. In their patrol reports, these operations were often described very briefly and for security purposes, even the location of the landing was omitted from their log. I began to investigate the HS series (SOE files) which contained references to some of the special operations in the hope that they would shed more light on the submarine movements. Operation LOCKSMITH was another cloak and dagger operation and its purpose was to block the Corinth Canal once again! The year was now 1943 and the team leader was none other than Lieutenant Cumberlege who was having another go at the objective, which had eluded him two years before. The story appeared to be quite an exciting one and many questions remained unanswered. By the end of the afternoon, I was hooked and embarked on a quest to elucidate the facts behind it. This book is an attempt to shed light on a complex story.

Montreal
July 2013

Prologue

Friday, 30 April 1943. On the Russian front, the Germans are still reeling from their defeat at Stalingrad and in a few days the Führer will discuss with his General Staff the means of redressing the situation by attacking the Kursk salient. Within a few weeks, the U-boats of Admiral Dönitz will be defeated in the Battle of the Atlantic. In the Pacific Theatre, the US Navy has been bruised at Guadalcanal but emerged victorious and the Empire of Japan is now on the defensive. Admiral Yamamoto has just been killed when his plane was ambushed by American fighter planes over Bougainville.

The war in North Africa is entering its final stage; the Allies are poised to capture Tunis, the last Axis stronghold on the continent. The tide of the war is turning. Already plans have been drawn to invade Sicily and deception operations are being carried out to draw away Axis forces by leaking that the main landings will occur in Sardinia or the west coast of the Peloponnese.

Somewhere on the north-east coast of the Peloponnese, four commandos are putting on their uniforms and gathering a few personal belongings. At dusk they walk to a beach where they are to be picked up by a submarine.

The four men are: Lieutenant Claude Michael Bulstrode Cumberlege DSO RNVR, the radio operator Sergeant Thomas E.V. Handley, Rhodesian Company Sergeant Major James Cook Steele and Czech Corporal Jan Kotrba, and they have been sent by SOE to occupied Greece on a sabotage mission to block the Corinth Canal.

One hundred and seven days ago, they were brought to the same spot by another submarine. The mission is now terminated and they are going home. It had gotten off to a bad start. The day after their arrival, their main contact in Athens, Major Ioannis Tsigantes, was killed in a shootout with the Italian police. The Gestapo has been hot on their trail ever since. A few weeks earlier, in the same area, a radio set and their code books were seized by the Germans following a gunfight in which Cumberlege and Handley barely escaped with their lives. They had managed to rejoin their two colleagues already established at Damala, Troizina, a few miles to the west. In this village, they had set up their second transmitter and contact with their headquarters in Cairo was renewed.

They have now been informed that they are no longer needed in Greece and that a submarine has been sent to fetch them and will wait for them for two consecutive nights starting on 29 April.

The area is sparsely populated, almost deserted, but on the beach they are joined by a party of Greeks who are anxious to be evacuated. Some of them wish to join relatives in Egypt, others to enrol in the Greek Armed Forces in the Middle East. Curiously, their friend Dimitrios Sambanis who lives in a house on a nearby beach has declined to join them as he feels indisposed.

During the day they could clearly see the island of Hydra across the channel but now the night is very dark and the sea is rough.

The submarine has failed to show up the first night and, with increasing anxiety, they scrutinize the darkness for any sign of it. Finally, at about 2130 hours, a light is seen flashing but they cannot make out the signals. They answer with a torch and wait for the submarine to send a boat but it is not forthcoming. This is rather odd as a submarine on a special operation is usually equipped with a folbot (kayak) favoured by commandos and other SOE operatives. Perhaps the rough seas prevented them from using it. The lights keep on flashing but Cumberlege is apprehensive and hesitates. None of the four men speaks Greek but the Greeks sense their uneasiness. After about two hours, the four commandos decide to chance it; they take to a rubber dinghy and begin paddling towards the flashing light. The Greeks wisely refuse to join them. Suddenly the four men are illuminated by searchlights; there is a burst of machine-gun fire followed by shouts in German.

The game is up.

Chapter 1

Greece and the Corinth Canal

Paul the Apostle founded one of the earliest churches in Corinth and it is there that he is reported to have written the two letters known as the 'Epistles to the Corinthians' which are incorporated in the New Testament. But outside Greece the average person has never heard of the Corinth Canal, and few are aware that it was the focus of so many attempts to block it during the Second World War. History books have ignored these episodes and none of our heroes have left a memoir. Canals have always been an asset to their country and a good source of revenue, but they can also attract the unwelcome attention of foreign powers as they have often been strategic objectives.

We are told that the origin of the Corinth Canal dates at least back to 602 BC when Periander, tyrant of Corinth, tried digging one across the isthmus which links the Corinth and Saronic Gulfs. It separates the Peloponnese peninsula from mainland Greece. For the navigator in the Ionian Sea, it provides a quick access to Piraeus and the Aegean. The canal allows shipping to avoid the circumnavigation of the Peloponnese and the dangerous areas around Cape Matapan (Matapas) and Cape Malea.

Because of the cost involved, this first attempt came to naught. Periander was more successful in his construction of the Diolkos, an elaborate system which allowed vessels to be dragged across overland. In his *History of the Peloponnesian War* (431-404 BC), Thucydides writes that the Lacedemonians sent twenty-one ships over the isthmus to help the defection of Khios from its alliance with Athens. This challenge to the Athenian naval supremacy would lead to their eventual defeat. The Diolkos was an innovative concept for the times. The Corinth canal project was undertaken at various times by kings or emperors but the magnitude of the task proved formidable. Suetonius tells us that Emperor Nero ordered the digging of the waterway and even exhorted his Praetorian Guard to help with the project. He himself removed the first basket of earth but his assassination interrupted the enterprise.

At the end of the nineteenth century, modern digging equipment had overcome the obstacles of Suez and Panama and this time the Corinth project was successfully tackled and completed in 1893. At that time Greece had been an independent country for barely three score years. The canal was a great achievement and a symbol of the modernization of the country after more than three centuries of Turkish occupation which had left it devastated and prostrate. The canal is 6,343 metres long (3.94 miles), has a maximum width of 21.3 metres (70 feet) at sea bed and a depth of 8 metres (26 feet). It crosses the Isthmus of Corinth, which, at its highest point, is 80 metres (260 feet) above sea level. Its vertical cliffs are a testimony of the power of Man over Nature. Even the blasé tourist of today cannot fail but be dazzled by this cleft in the isthmus. The traveller saves as much as 185 nautical miles by using it instead of taking the route around the Peloponnese. At first glance this seems to be dwarfed by the Suez and Panama Canals, which can save thousands of miles, yet in the Second World War, this strategic shortcut to the Aegean would take an importance disproportionate to its size.

Greece was occupied by foreign armies in both world wars. This statement is not altogether true since in the Great War half of Greece was on the side of the Allies, who had landed at Salonika, and the other half was resolutely against them. But to claim that the possession of the Corinth Canal caused the occupation of Greece is certainly an exaggeration. It certainly did not prove to be a curse as the Suez Canal sometimes was to its local population.

Despite its long tradition of democracy, Greece had been ruled by kings since 1832, first with Otto of Wittelsbach and then, from 1863, by the house of Schleswig-Holstein-Sonderburg-Glücksburg, which had taken over with George I, who ruled until his assassination by an anarchist in 1913. His eldest son succeeded him and took the title of Constantine I. His reign had auspicious beginnings, as he led his armies in the Second Balkan War which doubled Greek territory. But his popularity was soon put to the test. At the start of the Great War Greece attempted in vain to maintain its neutrality. The new king leaned heavily towards the Central Powers, Germany and the Austro-Hungarian Empire. He could hardly be blamed for that; after all his ancestors were Germans and his wife, Queen Sophie, was the Kaiser's sister. But Germany had allied itself with Turkey, the hereditary enemy, and this did not go down well with the majority of Greeks.

Greece had nothing to win from such an alliance; most of her coveted territories were in Turkey. The dream of recovering Constantinople, the *'Megali idea'* (Great Idea), was not far from every Greek politician's mind and might only be attainable by allying themselves with the powers of the Entente. Russia and Serbia, bastions of the Orthodox faith, had allied themselves with France and Great Britain, and to fight them would have been abhorrent to the majority of Greeks. It was not surprising that a large element of the population, led by the charismatic Prime Minister Eleftherios Venizelos, would be at odds with their king. Venizelos was unflinching in his conviction that the Western powers would prevail and advocated an alliance which was resisted by the king. The Anglo-French ill-fated expedition in the Dardanelles and the subsequent landing at Gallipoli put a great strain on the neutrality of Greece. Nor were the Greeks indifferent to the fate of the Serbs who were fighting the Bulgarians and the Austro-Hungarian Empire.

By December 1915 the Serbian Army, after having put up a fierce resistance, was exhausted and in full retreat through Albania. Italy had joined the Allies' side; the French had occupied Argostoli on the island of Cephalonia to close the Adriatic and bottle up the Austrian Navy. They wanted to evacuate the Serbian Army to Salonika where they had taken a foothold the previous October and were fighting Bulgaria. Political pressure was exerted to use the Corinth Canal, as the trip around the Peloponnese would expose the French transports to the threat of lurking German U-boats. This was opposed by the King of Greece. Allied heavy-handedness had begun to alienate a number of Greeks and Prime Minister Venizelos had to resign.

Prime Minister Skouloudis was appointed by King Constantine and bent on preserving Greek neutrality at all cost. He even threatened to blow up the Corinth Canal.

Flying his flag on the brand new battleship *Provence*, Vice Admiral Dartige du Fournet led an Allied squadron to Piraeus and threatened Athens with its guns. The French admiral had supervised the transfer by sea of over 100,000 Serbian troops from Corfu to Salonika around the Peloponnese, bypassing the canal. Austrian and German submarines appear to have been singularly ill-informed as the operation was completed without a single casualty. The Allies were building up their strength in Salonika to attack Bulgaria which was believed to be a weak ally of Germany. The French admiral had come to the conclusion that the Corinth Canal could be bypassed and Allied troops landed instead at Itea in the Gulf of Corinth. From there they could be transported by railway to their destination but this could only be done with the permission of the Greek government. At Salonika, the occupation by Allied forces had been viewed by Greeks with mixed feelings. While republicans looked upon it favourably and were eager to join the fight on the side of France and Great Britain, the king and his partisans resented this intervention, which was seen as an infringement of Greek sovereignty. In August 1916, the gulf between royalists and Venizelists deepened when pro-Venizelist officers staged a coup in Salonika and soon Venizelos was at the head of a provisional government in northern Greece. This was the beginning of the 'Great Schism' between royalists and republicans and it would divide Greece for the next decades.

On 1 December, Venizelos and the Salonika government declared war on Germany and Bulgaria. The next day a mixed force of French, British and Italian troops, numbering about 2,500 men, landed in Piraeus in the belief that it could force the king to make concessions. The Allied contingent came under heavy fire from Greek forces loyal to the king and was forced into a humiliating retreat after suffering sixty killed and 167 wounded. This would be known as the 'guêt-apens d'Athènes' and sometime referred to as the 'Greek Vespers'. The future dictator Ioannis Metaxas was one of the royalist officers involved in this resistance and the opportunity was taken to manhandle and jail Venizelist sympathizers in Athens. Admiral Du Fournet had to be recalled to France.

The success of the royalist cause was short-lived for, despite their promises of aid, the Central Powers were helpless to intervene and take advantage of the situation. Eventually the Allied fleets, which ruled the Mediterranean, were able to exert a pressure which the seafaring Greeks were unable to resist. King Constantine I was forced to abdicate on 15 June 1917. His youngest son, Alexander, who was considered pro-Entente, replaced him. The King, Metaxas and many royalist sympathizers were exiled. On the Salonika Front, despite a long and protracted campaign, the Allied forces eventually prevailed; Bulgaria was forced to surrender and Hungary was on the brink of collapse when the Armistice intervened. Everything appeared to have justified the Venizelist action and large chunks of territory were gained by Greece, making the '*Megali idea*' an attainable goal. But due to short memory, war weariness, or perhaps to the abuse of power that is so often seen when opposition is eliminated, the Venizelists lost the election in 1920. King Alexander had died by a freak accident – a monkey bite – and this paved the way to a return of King Constantine I.

Turkey had long been described as 'the sick man of Europe' and had hitherto survived many disastrous wars but the Great War was to prove the death knell of the Ottoman Empire. At the time of the Italo-Turkish War of 1911-1912, the Italian Army had occupied Libya and the Dodecanese Islands. The end of the Great War witnessed dissension between the Allies as they coveted the former Ottoman possessions. Greece had hoped to recover the Dodecanese Islands, as the majority of their population were of Greek descent, but this was to be denied at the peace conference. The islands would remain an Italian colony until the end of the Second World War. Cyprus had been ceded by Turkey to Great Britain and remained firmly in her possession. It was also known that the Italians had their eyes on Smyrna, a predominantly Greek city in Turkey. The secret Sykes-Picot Agreement of 1916 had already divided the Arab World, save for Arabia, between Great Britain and France. The Greeks also feared that the Russians might snatch Constantinople from their hands, an old dream of the Tsars, but the Russian Revolution and ensuing civil war diverted their attention at this critical time. Greece appeared to have a free hand and invaded Turkey in an ill-fated attempt to recover Anatolia. The royalist generals proved to be incompetent and were defeated by Kemal Attatürk in 1922, putting an end to the '*Megali idea*'. The new Turkish Republic recognized the Italian occupation of the Dodecanese.

This defeat appeared to spell the doom of the royalist faction, with King Constantine I abdicating a second time and Venizelos returning to Greece and being elected prime minister again. To universal surprise, he achieved reconciliation with Turkey and a massive exchange of population followed.

In 1932 Venizelos lost the election as the Great Depression had deeply affected Greece. Royalists were again managing to make inroads in Greek politics. In 1935 an attempted coup by Venizelist General Plastiras to restore the Republic failed. King George II acceded to the throne; Venizelos was forced into exile, his sympathizers were persecuted and some of his most important supporters executed. The Greek Army was purged of its republican officers. On 4 August 1936, the dictatorship of General Ioannis Metaxas was established with the king's approval and it was patterned on Italian fascism.

Yet relations between Italy and Greece had been uneasy since the Corfu incident. The rise of Italian fascism had led to expansion demands and Italian forces briefly occupied Corfu in 1923. The island was strategically important as it could give Italy control of the Adriatic. Pressure from the League of Nations forced the Italians to withdraw but the incident was bitterly remembered in Greece. Greek aspirations that the Dodecanese Islands with a predominantly Greek population would be restored to Greece had come to naught.

The advent of Nazism in Germany with Hitler's insatiable demands and unrelenting drive to undo the Treaty of Versailles, coupled with the expansion of Fascism, reflected by Italy's invasion of Abyssinia, did not bode well for the Western democracies. Their societies were uncertain if the threat from the extreme right was a lesser evil than communism. Germany had annexed Austria and, following the Munich agreement, had occupied part of Czechoslovakia. The Spanish Civil War became a confrontation between fascism and the democracies but the influence of the communist faction in the Spanish Republic was on the increase with the Soviet Union openly on their side while the Western democracies vacillated and did nothing. The forces of General Franco ultimately prevailed, thanks to an important contribution from Italy and, to a lesser extent, help from Germany. In April 1939, with the victory of fascism in Spain barely consecrated, Italian troops occupied Albania with little resistance, King Zog fled to Greece and the country was incorporated in the Italian Empire. The presence of an Italian army across the border did nothing to reassure the Greek government.

The following month Italy joined Germany in the Pact of Steel but the Duce had made it clear that his country would not be ready for war before 1942 or 1943.

During the summer the British and French governments attempted half-heartedly to enlist the support of the Soviet Union in the hope that Germany might be dissuaded from invading Poland. The German-Soviet pact took everyone by surprise and within days the invasion of Poland followed. The belief that this war could be contained quickly evaporated when Great Britain and France declared war on Germany.

Italy ought to have joined Germany's side but clearly the promise made by the Führer that Germany would not go to war before 1942 made her adherence to the Pact of Steel questionable and she remained neutral. The Mediterranean was an oasis of peace—for the time being. British and French warships were busy hunting German merchant ships which were scrambling to reach the nearest neutral ports. If the Corinth Canal could be used by the Germans to move from the Aegean to the more friendly ports of neutral Italy, this was not without its drawbacks. Passage of enemy ships could easily be monitored by the British or French naval attachés and reported to the contraband patrol. Interception could then be made and the ship brought to Malta or Bizerta.

On the eve of the war, the canal had a yearly average of 8,600 ships of a net tonnage of 2,649,000 tons. The largest ship to have used the canal was reported to have been the passenger/cargo ship *King Alexander* (11,415 grt, 1897) of the M. Embericos Line but most ships using it were of small and medium sizes and serviced the Aegean. The canal was owned by the *Nouvelle Société Anonyme du Canal de Corinthe* with a capital of 1,750,000 drachmas and 10,000 shares with a nominal value of 25 drachmas each. The society was a private enterprise with 60 per cent of shares held by French interests and 40 per cent held by the National Bank of Athens. The director general was the engineer Costantino Skeferis.

The canal was especially beneficial for Italy. It allowed for faster communications with its Dodecanese possessions. On 22 January 1940 the Italian submarines *Squalo*, *Santarosa* and *Narvalo* passed through the canal on their way to Leros. However, once the war started in the Mediterranean, Italian warships avoided its use for security reasons.

On 26 January 1940 an Anglo-Greek trade agreement was signed in London, with a view to limiting the trade between Greece and Germany. One of the clauses was that the United Kingdom would purchase the yearly chrome production, up to a maximum of 55,000 tons. Chrome was essential for the German military industry. In addition, the Hellenic merchant fleet was the world's seventh largest with over 500 ships and most of these were chartered by Britain with the Greeks heavily dependent on this source of income. The question of a naval base in the Aegean to exercise contraband control was raised. At that time, the Greek delegation was not ready to discuss the matter, as it would be a breach of their neutrality. Admiral Cunningham, Commander-in-Chief of the Mediterranean Fleet, suggested that an anchorage might be a substitute for a base and could be done with a ship such as HMS *Vandyck* acting as a floating base.

When the war with Italy started in June 1940, the oiler *British Union* was sent to Monemvasia (east coast of the Peloponnese) to refuel British destroyers escorting Mediterranean convoys. The Greek government requested her immediate departure but she was just moved to another anchorage. She was finally withdrawn after she was unsuccessfully bombed by Italian aircraft on

12 July, as was the Greek destroyer *Hydra* which had gone to investigate. In the eyes of the Italian government, this only fuelled speculations that collusion existed between Greek and British naval authorities.

The interdiction of traffic with Germany from the Black Sea was sought, especially during the winter months when the Danube froze. For some time, Section D (D for Demolition) of MI6 had studied the possibility of blocking the Iron Gates of the Danube by sabotage. If this was achieved, oil from Rumania or the Soviet Union, chrome and other commodities could be prevented from reaching Germany and an increasingly hostile Italy. Only the sea route through the Bosphorus, Aegean and the Corinth Canal would be left open and this could be disrupted by an Anglo-French Contraband Control. The Germans actually initiated the first naval sabotage operation in this theatre when the British transport *Tintern Abbey* had brought two motor-boats to Bourgas to be used on the Danube by the naval attaché in Bucharest. On her return voyage *Tintern Abbey* was rocked by an explosion after reaching Limni Euroea on 29 January 1940. The vessel required eight days of repairs at Piraeus where an investigation revealed that a time-delay bomb had been placed in a barrel of strawberry pulp loaded at Bourgas. An appropriate response had to be found.

Great Britain occupied the two main accesses to the Mediterranean, Gibraltar to the west and the Suez Canal to the east. Although Egypt had acquired its independence since 1922, she was still under a de facto occupation by British troops. The island of Malta had a strategic position in central Mediterranean but its proximity to Italian air bases made its survival in war questionable; Alexandria had replaced it as the home of the Mediterranean Fleet under Admiral Cunningham. France had colonies in Morocco, Algeria, Tunisia and Syria.

By the spring of 1940 the phoney war had ended with the German invasions of Denmark and Norway. A month later it was the turn of the Low Countries and the Battle of France had begun. Prior to this, France and Great Britain had tried to intervene in the Balkans. French General Weygand had attempted to organize a Balkan Alliance. His intention was to threaten oil supplies to Germany by bombing the Baku oilfields in Soviet Russia. This folly, typical of the last days of the French Third Republic, was never implemented. The British government, more realistically, was working to form a defensive alliance of Balkan States, in particular with Greece, Turkey and Rumania. It could act as a shield to their Middle East interests. The German breakthrough at Sedan forced the recall to France of General Weygand and the British efforts failed to crystallize.

By the end of May, the Allied armies were encircled at Dunkirk and the war seemed lost. For the Duce, the temptation was too great and, at midnight on 10 June, Italy was at war with Great Britain and France. Within two weeks, France had signed an armistice. The balance of power appeared to have shifted in the Mediterranean.

Chapter 2

The Navy and the Mediterranean 1940

For the *Regia Marina*, the Royal Italian Navy, the war had come at a most inopportune time. Italian fuel reserves were short; the war in Abyssinia and the involvement in support of the nationalists in the Spanish Civil War had reduced stocks of ammunition. The naval war was still thought of in terms of battleships, the capital ship of the time; the value of the aircraft carrier had not yet been fully recognized. For Mussolini, Italy was an unsinkable aircraft carrier and there was no need to build one. Reality would prove otherwise. At the start of the war, the combined navies of Great Britain and France could muster twenty-two capital ships; Germany had only two battle-cruisers and three armoured ships commonly known as pocket battleships. By the time of the invasion of Norway, the Royal Navy had lost the aircraft-carrier *Courageous* to the German submarine *U-29* and the battleship *Royal Oak* torpedoed by *U-47* at her anchorage in Scapa Flow while the German Navy had lost the pocket battleship *Graf Spee*, scuttled off Montevideo after the Battle of the River Plate.

The mere presence of a battleship could be counted upon to tilt the strategic situation in one way or the other. True, the Norwegian campaign had demonstrated the fallacy of this assumption but few admirals were ready to accept the fact that the era of the big gun was over. The previous April the British Home Fleet, faced by continuous attacks from the Luftwaffe, had to withdraw although it suffered only light damage.

In June 1940 Italy had only two old but modernized battleships immediately available. The modernized battleships were faster than the British battleships of the same period but their guns were of a smaller calibre (12.6-inch versus 15-inch) and their broadsides barely half of their British counterparts. However, two more battleships were in the process of being modernized and two new battleships, armed with nine 15-inch guns, would be available by the end of the summer and would redress the situation. Despite these shortcomings, the *Regia Marina* was a formidable force. Its strength was approximately equal to the French fleet and both shared the fourth rank in world power, after the British, United States and Japanese navies. Its submarine force was the second largest in the world and Italy had built a large number of fast motor torpedo boats (known as *MAS* for *Motoscafo Armato Silurante*), which, on paper at least, could create havoc in enemy fleets. But this did not deflect from the fact that Britannia ruled the waves and, even if local superiority could be achieved, it could only be a question of time before British sea power would prevail.

Yet, if the Allies appeared on paper to have an overwhelming strength in battleships, they had failed to prevent the Germans from seizing Norway. German air power had managed to neutralize the Royal Navy. Other factors had contributed to reduce the disparity in strength. The German strategy of ocean raiding by the pocket battleships had caused the dispersal of her enemies' naval forces. Worse, Italy's attitude though neutral at the time, had become increasingly hostile and had forced the Allies to send several battleships to the Mediterranean to act as a deterrent.

The Germans were certain that the use of their Enigma coding machines made their communications secure and could defeat any attempt by the enemy to decipher them. Events would prove this confidence to be misplaced and already in May 1940, thanks to Polish and French Intelligence who had laid the groundwork, British Intelligence had made operational use of its first intercepted signals or *sigint* (signal intelligence). These signals, initially known by the code name of HYDRO, shortly after changed to ULTRA, would play a decisive part in the war.

When, on 10 June 1940, Italy entered the war, the disparity in battleships appeared to put her navy in a hopeless situation and no aggressive action was undertaken, save for the deployment of over fifty submarines in the Mediterranean and the Red Sea while extensive defensive minefields were being laid to protect her shores. With over 2,000 miles of coastal lines to defend in Italy alone and many more when her colonies in Africa were added, the *Regia Marina* had a monumental task ahead. *Supermarina*, the Naval High Command, was subordinated to the *Comando Supremo* which was dominated by the Italian Army. The Italian Navy's most important objective was to keep communication lanes open with Libya. The colonies in East Africa were now cut off from the Motherland by the closure of the Suez Canal with little hope of help. The position of the Italian Army in North Africa appeared precarious as it was threatened in the west by French forces in Tunisia and to the east by the British Western Desert Force in Egypt. The French Navy had five battleships in the Mediterranean, four of them based at Oran while the Royal Navy had the battleship *Resolution* at Gibraltar, joined on 23 June by the battle-cruiser *Hood*, the largest warship in the world, and the modern aircraft carrier *Ark Royal*. They would soon form Force H and within days would be reinforced by the battleship *Valiant* fresh from operations off Norway. At the other end of the Middle Sea, the British Mediterranean Fleet was under Admiral Andrew B. Cunningham, affectionately known to his entourage as 'ABC'. It was based at Alexandria and could deploy two battleships, *Warspite* and *Malaya*, with the aircraft carrier *Eagle,* reinforced by the French battleship *Lorraine*. Another battleship,

Ramillies, was completing refit and could be made available within a short time. The first action of the war in the Mediterranean involving battleships was the bombardment of Bardia (Libya) by *Lorraine* on 21 June but, the following day, the French agreed to an armistice and suddenly the Royal Navy was deprived of the support of their five battleships and, although it kept its preponderance, the margin had now narrowed.

The Royal Navy had started the war with the conviction that the submarine threat had been mastered by the use of Asdic (now better known as Sonar), which would detect enemy submarines and hunt them to their destruction before they could create much damage. The reality was to prove otherwise and German U-boats had already sunk some 850,000 tons of shipping by the time Italy had entered the war.

The hope that the Italian submarine fleet could redress the situation vanished when, within three weeks, they had lost ten of their number while sinking only a tanker and an old light cruiser. Although the Asdic threat was known in Italian circles, its true effectiveness was still unknown and the losses were attributed to the clear waters of the Mediterranean and the Red Sea which allowed an aircraft to spot a submarine when it was at a depth of 40 metres (130 feet) or even more.

On 3 July 1940, Force H shelled the French Fleet at Oran to prevent it from falling into German hands; there was heavy loss of life. If the Führer and the Duce had believed that the war was won, there was now no doubt that Great Britain would fight on.

Six days later, the Mediterranean Fleet engaged the Italian Navy at the inconclusive Battle of Calabria, known in Italy as Battle of Punta Stilo. Admiral Cunningham could field three battleships armed with 15-inch guns and an aircraft carrier, HMS *Eagle*, to the Italians' two battleships armed with 12.6-inch guns. After a long-range exchange of fire–with little damage on either side– the Italian warships wisely withdrew. The Italian Air Force showed little discrimination by bombing its own ships as well as the enemy's.

By October 1940, it was evident that the war would be long and that the Luftwaffe had failed to win the Battle of Britain. There was no hope of relief to the Italian possessions of East Africa unless the Suez Canal was seized. The Duce had urged Marshal Graziani to occupy Egypt and the situation in Libya had improved since the threat of a French invasion from Tunisia had been removed. But Italian troops lacked mechanized transport and were poorly armed and the Marshal resisted several orders to advance. The invasion of Egypt finally got underway in September 1940, Graziani proved overly cautious and his forces stopped eighty miles short of Mersa Matruh. This sleepy little town had a small harbour and an airfield and its capture was essential if the Italian Army was to advance to the Egyptian Delta.

For the British Admiralty, there was some anxiety that Greece might tolerate an Italian occupation of Crete, which would have seriously threatened the naval situation in the Eastern Mediterranean. Italian ships did make occasional use of the Corinth Canal, but events were soon to prove that collusion between Greek and Italian forces was not to be feared.

The Italian armed forces and the Italian industries were heavily dependent on oil imported from Rumania. Modern motorized armies required large quantities of fuel to move. At that time it was not known that the Libyan colony had immense reserves of oil. During the Desert War, when oil was found occasionally seeping in water holes, it was believed that the enemy had fouled the water on purpose. This was a cruel irony, considering that the Italian Navy and merchant fleets would bleed to death to bring oil to Libya.

The Corinth Canal on the Agenda
Early in the war, British Intelligence had already studied the possibility of preventing oil from the Soviet Union from reaching Germany through the Danube waterway. Since oil from Rumania was routed to Italy via the Aegean Sea, the blocking of the Corinth Canal appears to have been a logical enterprise. The idea seems to have first been suggested by Admiral Cunningham in June 1940 as every means of weakening the enemy had to be sought. The Commander-in-Chief of the Mediterranean Fleet expressed the wish that it should be carried out as soon as possible but was fully aware of the political repercussions. The suggestion was transmitted to London through Major George Taylor on 27 June. On the other hand, it was reported that General Archibald Wavell, the Commander-in-Chief Middle East, was 'not directly interested' but would not oppose it; later he would prove more reticent. The following month, Cunningham signalled to the Admiralty that the only effective way of dealing with the canal was to block it with or without the connivance of the Greek government. He suggested that aircraft might be used to lay mines in it. By early August, Wavell was openly opposed to the project, describing it as 'politically undesirable'. According to Ian Pirie, who was a member of the D organization (sabotage), London was not receptive to the idea either; the Italians did not seem to be making much use of the canal and the Foreign Office did not want to stir up trouble with the Greeks. As of 2 August 1940, no Italian tanker from the Black Sea had used it since the beginning of the war. It was, however, accepted that when the Danube would freeze in winter this would bring an increase in canal traffic. In fact, the war with Great Britain had caught the *Regia Marina* by surprise and they were beginning to test cautiously the limits of British sea power.

Cunningham insisted that the operation be carried out and Admiral Godfrey, Director of Naval Intelligence, was enlisted to give his opinion.

On 15 August the Italian submarine *Delfino* sank the Royal Hellenic cruiser *Helle* at anchor at the island of Tinos; a flagrant breach of Greek neutrality. The same day Godfrey wrote a memorandum on the possibility of blocking the canal and proposed four options:[1]

1. Laying magnetic mines by aircraft but political repercussions had to be considered.
2. Causing a landslide into the canal by mining the sides, a difficult operation to carry out in complete secrecy, as it required a large quantity of explosives.
3. Blowing up the bridge, which could be easily done but the obstruction could be removed fairly quickly.
4. Sabotaging a large ship which could be caused to blow up in the middle of the canal, preferably a Greek or neutral ship, the sinking could be attributed to an accidental 'boiler explosion'. This could block the canal for several weeks and salvage work could be impeded through bribery.

Godfrey considered that blocking the canal might induce Italy to deliver an ultimatum to Greece and perhaps invade her, concluding that this 'would not advance our cause at the present'. He suggested waiting until Italy was heavily involved in Egypt, an invasion of this country appeared to be imminent, or that the Albanian revolt would assume such proportions that the Italian Army would be reluctant to get involved in Greece. The Director of Plans, Commander Charles Saumarez Daniel, concurred: 'it is of great importance to avoid action likely to lead to war between Italy and Greece at the present time. The staging of the blocking incident will therefore require most careful handling.'

Certainly British planning took some inspiration from the attempt to block Zeebrugge during the Great War and later in this war it was revived in a similar form during the raid on St Nazaire. Churchill had even advocated blocking Tripoli harbour by sacrificing an old battleship and had only been dissuaded by Admiral Cunningham with great difficulty. In 1940, the Royal Navy could not embark openly on an operation that would threaten Greek neutrality. True, it had attempted to test Norwegian neutrality when mines were laid within her territorial waters on 8 April 1940 but, at the time, it had been concluded that the Norwegians would not resist an Anglo-French invasion. The German invasion of Norway, which by sheer coincidence occurred the next day, prevented a test of this strategy.

To block the Corinth Canal could be very counter-productive. It could push Greece into the Axis camp and an enemy occupation of Crete could threaten the British position in the Eastern Mediterranean. Using a blockship to interrupt the Corinth Canal traffic could only have been staged during the period of Greek neutrality and it would have to look like an accident. This could only be achieved through an undercover organization such as SOE.

Chapter 3

SOE in Greece

For the British Secret Service, Greece had already been a fertile ground for Intelligence operations. During the Great War it had been heavily involved in cloak and dagger operations while Greece was neutral. Following the Gallipoli adventure, various deception schemes had been directed towards the Turks, such as bogus landings to induce them to strip away some of their troops from the Dardanelles sector. In Athens, British and French intelligence services co-operated closely to counter German propaganda; not an easy task when King Constantine I, whose wife Queen Sophie was the sister of the Kaiser, did not hide his great sympathies for the Central Powers.

The writer Compton Mackenzie, who was posted in the Greek capital during the Great War, published a vivid account of his tribulations as a secret agent. His books contravened the Official Secrets Act and he was threatened with jail, eventually settling the whole affair by paying a fine.

British foreign policy had vacillated in the early months of the war. It was not keen on attacking another European dynasty for the benefit of Venizelos, the popular prime minister known for his Republican sympathies, who might spearhead another revolution. Mackenzie initially had been leaning towards the Greek monarchy but had with time realized that Venizelos was the true ally of European democracies and became a staunch defender of the Greek statesman. These problems would be replicated in the Second World War with serious consequences. The quagmire of Greek politics would cause headaches to more than one British diplomat.

In the early months of the war, the performance of the British Intelligence Service had been left wanting. In November 1939, two of its agents stationed in the Netherlands, Major Richard Henry Stevens and Captain Sigismund Payne Best, were abducted to Germany after they naively fell for a ploy by the *Sichertheitdienst* (Security service led by Reinhard Heydrich) in what was to become known as the 'Venlo Incident'. Best will figure later in our story. In 1938, a new section of the Intelligence Service had been created to deal with sabotage; this was Section D (for Demolition). In the spring of 1940 an attempt to sabotage the iron ore facilities in Sweden failed miserably and proved to be an embarrassment for the Foreign Office.

In July 1940 Prime Minister Churchill, dissatisfied by the way the Secret Service had so far operated in the war, ordered the creation of a new secret organization on the same line as the Secret Intelligence Service (SIS, also known as MI6) with the instruction to 'set Europe ablaze'. This organization would be known as SOE (Special Operations Executive) and with the whole of continental Western Europe now in Axis hands, or at least under its influence, it was hoped to organize local resistance and create sabotage behind enemy lines. The organization was put under the control of a cabinet minister, Hugh Dalton of the Labour party. This was not without its reasons; Churchill felt that resistance to Nazism in occupied Europe might be more readily revived in left-wing organizations. It would also plant the seeds of discord in the traditional Intelligence Service, which espoused more conservative values and had spent more time in the 1930s spying on communist organizations than any other potential enemy. Its headquarters were located in London, at 64 Baker Street. It was not long before SOE personnel would be referred to as 'Baker Street Irregulars' in a nod to Sherlock Holmes.

In its early days, SOE was formed of three divisions:

- SO1 in charge of propaganda (aka PWE for Political Warfare Executive); it took over from Electra House (EH), a propaganda department of the Foreign Office.
- SO2, which absorbed two former SIS departments MI (R) – guerrilla warfare – and Section D (sabotage). SO2 would later be referred to as the general term for SOE.
- SO3 in charge of planning.

The new organization was formed with amateurs and frowned upon by its sister service, the Secret Intelligence Service, but this was to be expected and inter-service rivalry would remain high throughout the war. It was not possible to define clearly their respective areas; if SIS's task was to collect intelligence, SOE by its very nature involved work behind enemy lines and was also in a position of collecting information. Sometimes the information received by these two different sources could be contradictory and lead to friction. In theory, agents recruited by SOE had to be screened by SIS; in practice this could not always be done and would lead to suspicion and accusations. SOE agents were supposed to be apolitical and most of them were military men, ill-prepared to deal with the subtleties of Greek politics, a formidable task even in ordinary circumstances. Later, a further complication was caused by the introduction of a third organization, MI9, created to organize and facilitate the escape of British troops caught behind enemy lines.

Dalton was fortunate in his selections of the indefatigable Sir Frank Nelson as executive director and Lieutenant Colonel Colin Gubbins as Director of Operations. The latter was immediately promoted to brigadier. Gubbins had distinguished himself at the head of the independent companies which had fought rear-guard actions in northern Norway. One of the few British Army officers to come out untarnished from the Norwegian campaign, he would bring legitimacy to the budding organization. Unfortunately, Gubbins was more at ease in dealing with situations in Poland, Norway or France and showed little interest in the Balkans.

Perhaps the most serious problem faced by SOE was the recruitment of personnel, which, by its very secrecy, it could not do openly. This had to be done discreetly with the results that only few valuable men were available and regular officers from the armed services rarely joined.

In fact, the organization was so secret that when Captain (later Major) Michael Ward joined it in 1943, he was not even aware of its existence. He carried out a clandestine mission in occupied Greece and was stationed in Athens at the end of the war. While put in charge of closing the SOE accounts in Greece, he would try to find out the fate of the four commandos of the Corinth Canal operation.

SOE Middle East and Balkans was run from Cairo. Its exact territory limits would be elastic as the war went on. Remoteness from the parent office led it to act almost independently. This autonomy was not viewed with benevolent eyes by the controllers in London and much criticism would be levelled at its personnel. London appeared to have been hardly aware of the difficulties faced by its Cairo station and it was often suspected that the personnel were spending most of their time at the Gezirah Sporting Club or sipping oriental coffee at Groppi's. As the Cairo organization grew rapidly in size, finding proper cipher clerks became difficult and communications were often backlogged, drawing the wrath of the London staff, which wrongly assumed that it was being deliberately snubbed or ignored.

SOE in Cairo (or MO4 as it would become known) was initially in the hands of Colonel George A. Pollock, a lawyer by profession, supported by Majors R.C. Searight and George Taylor. Its headquarters were located in Rustum Buildings on Salamlik Street in Garden City. It was not difficult to find, as all local taxi drivers knew it as 'secret building'—so much for secrecy.

The organization would have a turbulent history, as Terence Maxwell would replace Pollock in the summer of 1941. In turn, Maxwell would be replaced by Lord Glenconner in August 1942 and Glenconner by Major General William Stawell at the end of 1943. At SOE London, the Balkan section was in the hands of Arthur Goodwill, soon to be replaced by James Pearson. By an arrangement reached in July 1940 between General Sir Archibald Wavell, Commander-in-Chief Middle East, and Dr Dalton, SOE would not carry out any sabotage operation unless sanctioned by the former. This would pretty much tie its hands, as Wavell was not inclined to favour clandestine operations.

The German lightning victories in Europe had revealed the weakness of Intelligence in countries allied to Britain. The object was not to spy on your ally but to make sure that an underground organization existed once the country was overrun. It was difficult to build an organization from the ground up as the experience had shown in Norway and France. SOE was to create underground organizations in countries where a German occupation could be anticipated. After the fall of France the nations earmarked for this work were Rumania, Yugoslavia and Greece; later Turkey would also be added.

In 1940 Greece was under the right-wing dictatorship of Metaxas with King George II in a nominal role. Its attitude towards Italy and Germany, in British eyes at least, was ambivalent. Metaxas had patterned his government on Fascist and Nazi methods but Greece had more to fear from Italy than Britain. In 1923 Mussolini had ordered the bombardment and occupation of Corfu only to be forced to evacuate by the League of Nations. From antiquity, Greeks have been known to be a seafaring people. At the start of the Second World War, the Greek merchant fleet was the ninth in the world and the fifth available to the democracies. With the dominance of the Royal Navy, the more than 500 Greek merchant ships were dependent on the goodwill of Great Britain and a large number were chartered in her service. By the time the war had erupted in the Mediterranean a number of Greek sailors had already lost their lives when their ships had been torpedoed by German U-boats or bombed by the Luftwaffe. At the same time, the British government feared that the Italians would occupy Crete and threaten their position in the eastern Mediterranean. Equally, the Italian government suspected the Greeks of collusion with Britain and that they might let the Royal Navy occupy the island of Crete to threaten their communications with the Dodecanese.

When Section D (sabotage) began operating in Greece in 1940, their only representative was J. R. Shotton. Little work had been done and when Arthur Goodwill of the London office toured the area in May 1940 he decided to replace him by four British businessmen and a secretary of the British Legion; they would be known as the APOSTLES. There was no immediate need to carry out sabotage in Greece and the main purpose of the section was to smuggle explosives to Yugoslavia, one objective being the blocking of the Danube waterway. It was only natural that Section D would try to recruit Venizelist republican officers who opposed the regime as they were found to be more reliable from a political point of view. Those who were not jailed or exiled by the Metaxas dictatorship were thus idle and available for recruitment. Later in the war, this reliance on republican elements would not sit well with the Greek government in exile who were determined to keep the king in power at all costs and would suspect SOE of plotting against it. Even the Foreign Office would accuse SOE agents of opposing British government policy.

In July 1940 SOE activities began in Athens; its first officer was Ian Pirie and the organization was run from his apartment at Platiya Lykavitou. Chris Harris, who used his cover as an agent of a British industrial firm, assisted him.

Harris was a Greek, born in Constantinople, and his real name was Christos Gogas. His service was invaluable and in time he would obtain a commission in the British Army. He would later recollect that they moved to Merlin Street, a short distance from the British embassy, and the organization was reinforced by the arrival of David Francis Pawson of the Athens Electricity Company, H. J. Sinclair of the Transport Company, Captain H. G. Watts, B. V. Priestley who worked as a cashier, Reginald G. Barwell and, finally, Miss Pamela Lovibond who acted as secretary. The staff would later be increased when Greece was attacked by Italy.

Sinclair would later relate that the blocking of the Corinth Canal had been discussed as early as June 1940 and he had looked for a suitable vessel for the operation. The Euxinos Shipping Company was set up as a front for SOE and was run by Barwell and the lawyer Michael Xilas. They purchased a few small caiques (schooners of the Greek type) with the help of Mr V. Giamalvia. Of their selection only *Eos*, a caique of seventy-five tons was in excellent condition, the remainder were found to be a poor lot.

Major Menzies, a Canadian who had been the Imperial War Graves Commissioner in Salonika, laid the foundation of the organization in this area, using, among others, Alexandros Zannas, head of the Greek Red Cross and Commander Ioannis Toumbas of the Royal Hellenic Navy who was a Venizelist. Both choices proved excellent and would do stellar work for SOE.

Organizing guerrillas was entrusted to Major William Barbrook from MI R (a branch of Military Intelligence) who operated in Athens under the cover of assistant Military Attaché while the renowned archaeologist John Pendlebury was sent to Crete as vice consul at Heraklion for the same purpose.

Beginnings were difficult; Wilkinson, one of the APOSTLES, attempted to smuggle explosives to Albania by using the Greek doctor Karvounis who owned some land there and could cross the border without raising too much suspicion. It failed when the weight of his suitcases aroused the curiosity of his taxi driver. This man opened one of them at a stop and, fearing he would also be held responsible, denounced the doctor to the Greek military authorities. The good doctor was arrested and exiled for a year.

In July 1940, the submarine HMS *Parthian* landed the Greek secret agent Spentidakis at Gromeno Bay (Crete); his mission was to contact General Georgios Mantakas. Mantakas, a well-known Venizelist, was to be enlisted to organize resistance should the Metaxas government make an alliance with Italy, allowing her to occupy Crete. Unfortunately, the mission failed within days, as Spentidakis proved too talkative. Pendlebury had not been informed of his arrival and the Greek was careless in his contacts. He was arrested and lucky to be only expelled, thanks to the intervention of the British government.

On 4 September, the Admiralty insisted that the blocking of the Corinth Canal be carried out at the first opportune moment. The Director of Naval

Intelligence ordered Section D (as it was still referred to in official correspondence) to look for a suitable vessel, which could be used for other purposes until the timing of the operation was ripe. It was proposed to use a secret Jewish organization, 'the Friends' (better known as the Haganah), for this purpose.

The Cyprian Shipping Company's old steamer *Danubian* was in Alexandria at the time. She was selected to be used as blockship for the Corinth Canal but no action was to take place before Greece would be involved in the war. This would come sooner than expected. Other vessels were also prepared for similar operations. In November 1940 the Greek *Aghios Nikolaos* was purchased by the Euxinos Shipping Company and was to be sent to Varna for a special mission (sabotage of Italian tankers in the Black Sea by using limpets). She had been used before the war as transport for Jewish 'illegal' refugees to Palestine, making four trips in all. The following month she went on a trip from Athens to Bourgas and brought back coal so as not to arouse suspicions. In January 1941 she was to return to Bourgas where an attack was to be carried out on ships of the Deutsche Levant Linie. She would later be earmarked for use as a blockship for the Corinth Canal. The Panamian *Sofia* was renamed *Darien* and scheduled to be armed with torpedo tubes to operate in the Aegean. Initially, she was to have been under the command of Lieutenant Commander Nicholl with a crew of five British officers and petty officers and twenty 'Friends'. Italian Naval Intelligence appears to have suspected the clandestine nature of this ship as Italian submarines were ordered to intercept *Darien* when it was learnt, on 2 September, that she had sailed from Candia (modern day Heraklion in Crete) for Alexandria. She managed to slip through the net and arrived four days later at her destination. On the way she was stopped by the destroyer HMS *Dainty* and an Italian subject was removed but the clandestine nature of the ship was not discovered.

Darien may not have proven suitable as the project fell through and command was then transferred to the 47-year old Lieutenant Commander Francis Grant Pool RNR, and would operate under cover in the Eastern Mediterranean. Pool would later gain distinction for his work in extricating stragglers from Crete. *Darien* was now earmarked for sabotage of Italian tankers at Constanza or Varna. The vessel does not appear to have been armed as it was feared that any armament might be reported when she crossed the Bosphorus and jeopardize her mission. She was used to bring Jewish refugees from Rumania as a cover but further employment hit a snag when an agreement could not be reached with Chaim Weizmann and Shertok (Moshe Sharett) and, by March 1941, the project was definitely shelved. Smaller vessels, such as the yachts *Dolphin II* and *Saad* (each of about 40 tons) and *Madalena* (35 tons), were taken over at Alexandria and consideration was given to sending them to the Red Sea to operate against Italian Eritrea. *Dolphin II* was used in November

1940 to smuggle through Piraeus explosives destined for Albania; this boat will later figure in our story. *Jadwiga* (112 tons) had also been requisitioned while she was at Split (Yugoslavia) in June 1940. In addition, the caique *Anna* was to be used for a reconnaissance of Leros in December.

At the instigation of Prime Minister Churchill, Jews were being trained in Palestine for sabotage. The reasoning behind this was not entirely altruistic; Jews could be trusted for their anti-Nazi sentiments and in case of capture on foreign soil the British government could deny involvement. They were willing pupils, eager to learn the techniques of sabotage and they could later use these for their own ends as they anticipated the coming struggle for Palestine. Not for the last time, the British Intelligence Service, reflecting the Foreign Office stance, was at odds with SOE and opposed any cooperation with the Haganah. According to Jewish sources, Major Taylor of SOE proved to be most encouraging and facilitated the training of Jewish recruits. The classical scholar Nicholas Hammond, who would later be sent to Greece, was one of their instructors. It was not long before one of the trainees would put in practice the lessons learnt with unforeseen consequences. The former French liner *Patria* was lying in Haifa harbour, carrying 1,800 Jews who had sought refuge in Palestine but, due to British restrictions on Jewish immigration in Palestine, the ship was now ordered to Mauritius. On 25 November 1940 a bomb was planted on the ship in the hope of disabling her and forcing the British government to accept these Jews on Palestinian soil. The plot misfired when the explosives proved to be more powerful than expected and the ship sank in only sixteen minutes. Many of the passengers were trapped inside the hull and 260 of them drowned. However, the surviving refugees were allowed to land on humanitarian grounds so the operation had not been in vain.

The Invasion of Greece
On 28 October 1940 Mussolini's divisions invaded Greece. Ill-prepared, they were soon driven back to Albanian territory. Earlier in the month Italian Military Intelligence (SIM or *Servizio Informazioni Militare*) had produced a study on Greece, and the Corinth Canal was duly described. Reflecting a purely military viewpoint, the bridges across the canal were given the most attention. The army viewed the canal as an obstacle to movements of troops across the isthmus while the navy viewed it as an essential link to their communications. The *Regia Aeronautica* bombed the canal twice on the first day of the war but caused no damage.

The Italian Navy was dealt a serious blow when Admiral Cunningham managed to take his Mediterranean Fleet to sea unnoticed and strike at the Italian main naval base of Taranto. During the night of 11/12 November, a handful of Swordfish torpedo-bombers took off from the brand new aircraft carrier HMS *Illustrious* and dropped their aerial torpedoes and bombs on the Italian battle squadron at anchor, sinking or badly damaging three battleships. Once again, the balance of power in central Mediterranean had shifted.

Prime Minister Churchill decided to offer assistance to the Greeks. The decision was more political than sound military strategy and he would later be heavily criticized for it. Helping Greece would now take precedence over the war in North Africa. The Western Desert Force had managed to occupy Cyrenaica but its extended lines of communications made it difficult to supply. It has been said that priority should have been given to the conquest of the whole of Libya. The expulsion of the Italians from North Africa might have saved Britain from two long years of constant battles in the desert. This may be true, but the prime minister could not ignore the Balkan situation so easily and it is not certain that expelling the Italians from Tripolitania would have been as easy as from Cyrenaica. To turn his back on Greece might induce Turkey to fall in the German camp and this could threaten the whole Middle East.

Already the Germans had begun operating in the Mediterranean theatre by transferring *X Fliegerkorps* to aerodromes in Sicily. This air wing had pilots particularly adept at anti-shipping operations. Their presence was keenly felt when they pummelled with bombs HMS *Illustrious* while she was giving air cover to a convoy to Malta (10 January 1941). The aircraft carrier nearly sank but, after brief repairs in Malta, managed to limp away to Alexandria. Eventually she would undergo extensive repairs in the United States. Furthermore, in February 1941, General Rommel arrived in Libya with the first units of the Afrikakorps and soon would begin in earnest the reconquest of Cyrenaica.

The Greek government of Metaxas was treading a thin line; ideologically, it was closer to Italy and Germany than to Britain. It was ready to accept British forces in Crete to check the Italian Navy but was reluctant to accept their presence on mainland Greece for fear that Germany–so far neutral in the dispute–would find itself bound to intervene. It had refused a proposal from General Wavell to land troops and air squadrons at Salonika as their presence might have appeared threatening to Germany, at least as far as oil supplies from the Soviet Union or Rumania were concerned. Greece was desperately in need of armaments, ammunition and aircraft. Convoys were now organized in Egypt to supply her with these.

Eventually RAF squadrons were moved to Greece, the German Foreign Office had agreed to raise no objections, provided they would not be based in Northern Greece. Metaxas was also anxious to secure the Dodecanese Islands for his country but could not get a British commitment. He was unaware that Churchill was ready to cede the Dodecanese to Turkey, to entice this country to enter the war on the side of Britain. The Greek government was careful not to antagonize Germany and British officers would complain that they were forced to dress in civilian clothes to stroll in the streets of Athens while their German counterparts had no such restraint.

To avoid conflicts between the different branches of British Intelligence, it was agreed in the early days of the campaign that SOE would restrict its actions to mainland Greece and the Aegean while MI R – Military Intelligence (Research) – would operate in Crete. SOE in Athens was now in the hands of Pawson and Pirie and they were busy training Greek agents in the use of explosives and distributing propaganda but were keeping a low profile to avoid friction with the Greek authorities. Ian Pirie, who was now head of Section D in Greece, would aptly remark in a letter dated 15 January 1941:

> The main difficulty here at the moment is that whereas the British are trying to make it clear that they are fighting Fascism and not the Italians, the regime here is trying to point out that they are fighting the Italians and not Fascism.[2]

Preoccupied by his preparations for Barbarossa, the invasion of Russia, Hitler found the intervention of his Italian ally ill timed. However, on 29 January 1941, Metaxas died suddenly and his successor, Alexandros Koryzis, proved more amenable to Churchill's demands. British troops were allowed on the mainland. On 13 March 1941 the caique *Irene* (Captain Georgios Vergos) brought 4,700lb of explosive and stores to Salonika. This SOE clandestine operation was carried out without the knowledge of the Greek government and the explosives were intended for Venizelist elements in the region that were considered more dependable than regular Greek forces. It also showed the ambiguity of the British attitude towards the current Greek government. The German threat was recognized as imminent and the explosives were destined to destroy the Salonika port facilities so that they should not fall into enemy hands. The outcome of this operation would provide SOE in the Middle East and Balkans with a badly needed success. There had been mounting criticism at home that it was not doing anything of value. To be fair, SOE had an agreement with General Wavell that it would not attempt an operation without his approval; so far this had not been forthcoming. By March 1941, over 58,000 British, New Zealand and Australian troops had landed in Greece but, as foreseen, Hitler did not let this move go unchallenged and on 6 April German divisions invaded Yugoslavia and Greece.

From the Italian perspective, the war in Greece had proven to be a sorry experience and a costly affair but its Dodecanese colony had been further isolated by the conflict and appeared very vulnerable to a Greco-British invasion. Not only was the use of the Corinth Canal denied but the passage north of Crete, which had been relatively safe from enemy intervention, was now rendered impossible by the British base at Suda. If foodstuffs could be purchased in neutral Turkey, fuel and ammunition would have to reach the bases of Leros and Rhodes by other means. The task of replenishing the Dodecanese would be a further cross to bear on the shoulders of the *Regia Marina*.

Chapter 4

The Corinth Canal and the Dodecanese Islands

In 1911, following a war with Turkey, the Dodecanese islands had been seized by Italy along with Libya. Although the population of about 120,000 was predominantly Greek, a number of Italian colonists now inhabited the islands. Fortifications had been built on Rhodes and Leros and a small force of destroyers and submarines were based there. Italian bombers could make an occasional raid on Haifa, or even the Suez Canal. For Italy, the Corinth canal was an essential link to the Dodecanese. And as long as Greece remained neutral, the canal could provide a safe passage to Italian tankers bringing much needed fuel from Rumania. Circumnavigation of the Peloponnese peninsula would have exposed them to interception by British forces.

The British and French high commands had held a pre-war conference with their Turkish counterparts to discuss the occupation of the Dodecanese. While the Allies were keen on occupying the smaller islands first, the Turks preferred making an initial strike at Rhodes. With the entrance of Italy into the war only a few days away, there was little time for planning, the collapse of France left little to encourage the Turkish government and the operation had to be abandoned, at least for the time being.

The geographical position of the islands made them especially vulnerable to the British Mediterranean Fleet based in Alexandria. Eight Italian merchant ships were stranded in the Dodecanese when the war had started and, from 20 June, all made a successful run across the Aegean to reach Brindisi.

At the same time, Italian naval and air forces based in the Dodecanese islands were in an ideal position to threaten British traffic with Turkey and Rumania. An attempt to reinforce the islands by sending two fast Italian cruisers *Bartolomeo Colleoni* and *Giovanni Dalle Bande Nere* met with disaster when they were engaged by the Australian cruiser *Sydney* and five destroyers of the 2nd Flotilla and *Colleoni* was sunk and *Bande Nere* put to flight in the Battle of Cape Spada on 19 July 1940. Because of the distance, the Italian air force was unable to provide effective air cover to ships supplying the Dodecanese.

Following the sinking of *Colleoni*, *Supermarina*, the Italian Naval High Command ordered the transfer of the fast transport *Sebastiano Venier* to Bari where she was to be loaded with 6,000 tons of stores for the Italian army and

air forces based in the Dodecanese. The size of the ship made it impossible to transit the Corinth canal with a full load. The use of the canal was not without its disadvantages; British Intelligence in Athens could easily monitor and report the passage of every ship trading with the Italians. There was much hesitation about sending this ship through the Aegean as it was conceded that British sea power dominated the passage between Cape Matapan and Crete and there was now a reluctance to rely on the *Regia Aeronautica* for protection. This was not without reasons: at the recent battle off Calabria (9 July 1940), the Italian air force had indiscriminately bombed its own ships as well as the enemy's. The despatch of *Sebastiano Venier* was finally suspended on 8 August and it was judged that small vessels might perhaps be better suited to run the blockade, but even this theory had already been challenged.

The *Ermioni* Incident

One such incident occurred when the small Greek tanker *Ermioni* (440grt, 1892) chartered by the Italians to supply the Dodecanese islands with petrol, was reported making the passage of the Corinth canal on 28 July 1940. The Mediterranean Fleet was at sea at the time and within striking distance. Quickly informed of the passage of this vessel, Admiral Cunningham detached the two light cruisers HMS *Neptune* (Captain R. O. O'Conor RN) and HMAS *Sydney* (Captain J. A. Collins, RAN) to intercept it. The warships raced at 27 knots and reached the Thermia channel at dusk. Almost immediately, Italian bombers were sighted and carried out an accurate attack, both cruisers escaping with very near misses. These were five SM.81 bombers of *92° Gruppo*, based in the Dodecanese. They reported attacking two cruisers between Thermia and Zea and encountering very heavy anti-aircraft fire. Though suffering some damage, they all returned safely. In Captain O'Conor's opinion, the presence of the aircraft in the Thermia channel confirmed that *Ermioni* was using this passage and in the evening the Greek tanker was sighted and ordered to stop. The crew abandoned the vessel, which was sunk by gunfire from HMS *Neptune*. Both cruisers would meet tragic ends during the war. In November 1941, *Sydney* was lost with all hands in an epic gun duel with the German armed merchant cruiser *Kormoran* off the west coast of Australia. A month later, *Neptune* strayed into an Italian minefield off Tripoli and blew up; only one survivor was found.

Following the sinking of *Ermioni*, the Greek government lodged a protest and remarked that this incident could only lead to an escalation, which could also be detrimental to British interests. In Italian circles the incident reinforced suspicions that there was collusion between Greek and British authorities.

Most incensed was the Italian governor of the Dodecanese Islands, De Vecchi di Val Cismon, one of the original founders of the Fascist party. He ordered the submarine *Delfino* (*Tenente di vascello* (Lieutenant) Giuseppe Aicardi), based in Leros, to carry out a retaliatory attack on Greek shipping.

This resulted in the sinking of the Greek light cruiser *Helle* anchored in Tinos during the Feast of the Dormition of the Theotokos (15 August 1940). This breach of neutrality was embarrassing to the Italian government as De Vecchi's action had not been sanctioned. References to this attack were excised from official documents and for many years involvement in this incident was denied. Relations were further strained when the Greek steamer *Attiki* was allowed to sail from Gibraltar after the Italians had promised safe passage but was intercepted and her cargo confiscated. Greek traffic was now forced to travel around Africa and via the Suez canal.

On 4 September, *Supermarina* planned Operation C.V. which consisted of supplying the Dodecanese by using the fast transports *Sebastiano Venier* and *Calitea* under heavy escort of no less than seven heavy cruisers, *Pola* (flagship of Admiral Riccardo Paladini, II Naval Squadron) with the First Cruiser Division (*Fiume, Zara* and *Gorizia*) and Third Cruiser Division (*Trieste, Trento* and *Bolzano*) and twelve destroyers of 9th, 11th and 12th Squadrons. They were to make the passage south of Cerigo and Stampalia and then to Leros and were to be covered by five submarines. The two transports finally sailed from Taranto on the evening of 5 October screened by the destroyers of the 12th Squadron, while *Pola*, the First Cruiser Division and the 9th Squadron followed the next morning. At the same time the Third Cruiser Division screened by the 11th Squadron sailed from Messina to join them. They were barely out when a report reached *Supermarina* that two enemy battleships, two cruisers and seven destroyers had been sighted between Alexandria and Kasos Strait. The information was fairly accurate; in fact Rear Admiral Layton (First Battle Squadron) had sailed from Alexandria on 3 October with two battleships (*Malaya* and *Ramillies*), one aircraft carrier (*Eagle*), two light cruisers (*Ajax* and *Coventry*) and eight destroyers.

In tacit recognition of British naval supremacy in the eastern Mediterranean, Operation C.V. was immediately cancelled and the ships returned to port.

The Blockade Runners
With any large-scale attempt to supply the Dodecanese now put aside, the task was entrusted to single ships. Two small vessels, *Tarquinia* and *Costante*, were used by the army and the air force to bring supplies to the Dodecanese Islands. The former passed through the Corinth Canal on 25 October arriving at Leros on the 28th, just in time for the declaration of war with Greece. The latter sailed from Brindisi on the 24th but bad weather forced her to take refuge at Porto Edda (Albania) and she arrived at Valona only on the 27th. The war with Greece prevented further movements through the Corinth Canal. British forces had now been authorized to take over the defence of the island of Crete and this made the supply of the Dodecanese even more difficult. Submarines were used to transport much needed material. Three large submarines had already carried out

supply missions earlier in the war: *Atropo* (22-26 June 1940), *Corridoni* (30 June-17 July 1940, via Tobruk) and *Foca* (27 September-1 October 1940). During the war with Greece, the smaller submarines *Ondina* (23-27 January 1941) and *Sirena* (25-30 January 1941) also made supply runs to Leros.

In addition, four fast transports slipped through the blockade by sailing from Italy via Libya to the Dodecanese in December 1940 and January 1941 until the fall of Cyrenaica temporarily prevented further reinforcements, except by the more direct but riskier route south of Crete.

Calino sailed from Naples on 1 December 1940 and reached Rhodes on 6 December. She sailed again from Gaeta on 20 January and arrived at Rhodes on 25 January 1941 and sailed back on 1 February. During her return trip, she was missed off Benghazi by two torpedoes fired from the submarine HMS *Truant*. She sailed again from Catania on 22 February and reached Rhodes on 27 February. *Calitea* sailed from Naples on 20 December 1940 and reached Rhodes seven days later. The armed merchant cruiser *Ramb III* sailed from Taranto on 26 December 1940 and reached Rhodes on the 29th. She sailed back on 1 January 1941. *Vettor Pisani* sailed from Naples on 23 January 1941 via Benghazi and arrived at Leros six days later. These ships made all the trips unescorted except for the last leg when they were met and escorted in by destroyers and torpedo boats from the Dodecanese squadron.

Italian vessels appear to have succeeded in supplying the Dodecanese with surprisingly little interference from the Royal Navy. British Naval Intelligence files show that they were aware of at least one such trip, the one by the motor sailing vessel *Nettuno I*. This vessel was reported to have sailed from Augusta on 23 March 1941 and was expected to pass east of Kasos Island at 0800 hours on the 28th before steering for Rhodes. It is likely that the Italian fleet sortie that resulted in the Battle of Matapan may have provided a much-needed diversion allowing *Nettuno I* to slip through the net; she actually reached her destination ahead of schedule on the 27th. The crew was rewarded with a bonus of 20,000 lire to share among them. Another sailing vessel *Nereus* sailed from Catania during the night of 24/25 March and was due to reach Rhodes at 0800 hours on 30 March. *Nereus* did not go very far and was reported to have sunk the next morning, the crew being suspected of having sabotaged their vessel. Both these sailing vessels could only make the passage at about 6 knots and only the darkness of the new moon period and their disguise could save them from interception. They had no hope of escape should their identity be recognized. Both *Nettuno I* and *Nereus* were carrying fuel for a unit of *X Fliegerkorps* which was to be based at the Dodecanese. On 5 March the hospital ship *Toscana* sailed from Rhodes for Taranto, passing between Cerigo and Cerigotto but her special status allowed her safe passage.

British Intelligence produced a study of the occupation of the Dodecanese as early as August 1939, but it relied heavily on the participation of the Turkish army and air force. While Turkey refrained from joining an alliance, the Italian invasion of Greece had isolated the Dodecanese islands. Italians could no longer use the Corinth Canal and the passage north of Crete was especially perilous. Yet the Greek government hesitated to threaten the islands, as it feared retaliation and the vulnerability of its own Aegean possessions. A sort of *modus vivendi* had been established, Italian forces based in the Dodecanese only carried out minor attacks on the Greek islands and the Greeks refrained from interfering. This did not suit British planning and a new plan had been drawn up to test Italian defences. During the night of 24/25 February 1941, a strong British commando landed on Kastelorizo with the intention of holding this small island (Operation ABSTENTION) until reinforcements from Alexandria could arrive via Cyprus. But the Italians reacted with vigour; a force was quickly assembled by Rear Admiral Luigi Biancheri, and landed in the harbour of Kastelorizo. After a brief fight, the island was retaken.

The failure of the British attempt at Kastelorizo marked the last attempt at occupying the Dodecanese while the war with Italy was on. A new attempt would be made after the Italian Armistice of September 1943, but this time with Italian Forces as co-belligerents. Prompt intervention by the Germans would doom it again.

Operation ABSTENTION had backfired as it gave Italian Forces a boost in morale and reinforced Turkey in its determination to remain neutral. The following month, the arrival of British forces on Greek soil would further isolate the islands, but by then the Dodecanese was relegated to the background, as the war in Greece was about to enter its final stage.

Chapter 5

The British Intervention
in Greece

With the Italian invasion of Greece, British forces lost no time in obtaining a foothold in Crete, the first elements landing at Suda Bay on 31 October 1940. However, a large commitment of land forces on mainland Greece would not occur before the following March. Proposals to send a few divisions to Salonika were being resisted by the Greek government, as they did not wish to provoke the Germans. The British government had emphasized that they could not promise quick reinforcements if the Greeks were going to wait for the Germans to come to the help of their ally.

In the meantime, the submarines HMS *Tetrarch* and HMS *Parthian*, returning from a patrol off the south coast of Italy, passed through the Corinth Canal on 12 and 13 January respectively. They stopped at Piraeus for three days before returning to Alexandria. This visit, which had been pre-arranged before their departure for patrol, was a success and gave their crew some time for relaxation.

The sudden death of Metaxas removed the last resistance to British involvement and Operation LUSTRE, the transport of British, Australian and New Zealander troops to Greece began in earnest on 4 March with the first elements landing at Piraeus three days later. By April, some 58,000 troops were transferred to Greece; this, however, fell short of the requirements of the Greek High Command who had requested nine divisions.

Blocking the Corinth Canal was considered once more by the British Admiralty but this could not be realized as long as Greece was an active ally. Greek warships, particularly submarines based at Piraeus were regularly using the canal to operate against Italian lines of communication in the Ionian Sea and the lower Adriatic. By this time SOE in Greece had become fairly well organized, recruiting former republican officers who were eager to join the fight but were denied from serving their country by the dictatorship.

In mid-February Rear Admiral Charles Edward Turle, the Naval Attaché in Athens, suggested that the captured Italian submarine *Galileo Galilei* might be made available to block the entrance of Durazzo harbour which was essential to supply the Italian army in Albania. This submarine had been captured in the Red Sea by HM Trawler *Moonstone* after a sharp gunfight. She entered British service and was renamed *X-2* but her poor condition prevented her use beyond training.

Turle had attended a Chiefs of Staff Committee meeting on 29 November 1940 where he discussed the assistance to Greece. He had rejected the suggestion that Rhodes be offered to Turkey and the remaining Dodecanese islands to Greece as he considered that the divided control of the islands would be doomed to failure. His opinion concerning the Corinth Canal would now be sought.

On 2 March the Admiralty, in a signal to Admiral Cunningham, Commander-in-Chief Mediterranean and to General Wavell, Commander-in-Chief Middle East, enquired if they had made provisions to carry out demolitions of Greek harbour installations and the Corinth Canal. At the same time, Axis aircraft were busy mining the Suez Canal. They succeeded in sinking or damaging a few ships and this canal was blocked but rarely for more than a few days.

The destruction of the Corinth Canal does not appear to have been the object of much discussion by the War Cabinet Committee and the Admiralty was the sole proponent of action directed against it. This was at a time when British troops had not yet arrived on Greek soil. It was emphasized that 'Greek authorities should not be consulted at this stage'. Although the British High Command had sought the participation of the Greeks in sabotaging their own harbour installations, it kept them in the dark about their intentions regarding the canal. It was feared the Greeks would oppose it. Six days later Cunningham sent a signal to the Naval Attaché in Athens enquiring if he had made preparations to block the canal. Turle, who had requested magnetic mines for the task on 1 March, was told that these were unavailable. On 15 March he replied that nothing had been arranged for the Corinth Canal and advised that 'nothing should be done at the present'. A more detailed letter dated 11 March was received by Admiral Cunningham on 23 March. In it the Naval Attaché wrote:

Nothing at all is prepared now for the Corinth Canal and I would deprecate any attempt to make detailed arrangements at present. Apart from the danger of leakage of information, there is the local political situation at the time of demolition which must be considered and which has so many different possibilities. The most that is suitable to do at present is to keep locally a good store of explosive, and this perhaps can be arranged when the more urgent military commitments have been met.[3]

This discouraging remark does not appear to have disturbed Cunningham, as he did not reply. Understandably, the Commander-in-Chief of the Mediterranean Fleet was very busy with the task of covering troop convoys to Greece. On 27 March 1941 he sailed to intercept the Italian Fleet; this resulted in the Battle of Matapan. The modern battleship *Vittorio Veneto* was torpedoed by an Albacore from the aircraft carrier *Formidable* but managed enough speed to slip away. The three heavy cruisers, *Pola*, *Zara* and *Fiume*, and two destroyers were not so fortunate and were sunk during a one-sided night action that underlined the advantage of radar. Some 2,400 Italian sailors lost their lives. It was a staggering defeat that discouraged the *Regia Marina* from using its battle fleet to interfere with Greek convoys. Destroyers of the Royal Hellenic Navy were rushed from Piraeus across the Corinth Canal but arrived too late to take part in the action, they could only rescue a number of Italian survivors.

On 6 April German forces invaded Greece and Yugoslavia and the military situation took a dramatic turn. The same night German bombers raided the harbour of Piraeus and hit the ammunition ship *Clan Fraser*; the ensuing explosion destroyed or damaged a large number of ships and devastated the port facilities. On 10 April Turle informed Cunningham that the only suitable vessel he could find to block the canal was the old Greek battleship *Kilkis*, but she could not steam and the Greeks wanted to use her as an accommodation ship should Salamis be evacuated.

The next day Turle reiterated his objections to the operation, stating that blocking the canal could only be temporary and would likely antagonize the Greeks. This time Cunningham replied immediately that it was very important to block the canal since it would provide an easy access for Italian traffic to eastern Greece and Turkey. If the canal were blocked, traffic would be forced to sail around the Peloponnese, and could then easily be attacked by British forces based on Crete.

By Easter Sunday, 13 April, it was becoming evident that the situation in Greece had reached a critical stage. The hope that British and Greek forces could hold the Aliakmon line and prevent a German advance crumbled. Turle had cabled Cunningham, who was in Alexandria at the time, that an evacuation had to be envisaged within six weeks. This turned out to be optimistic. The German *Blitzkrieg* overwhelmed Greek defences and Imperial troops were forced into a fighting retreat. Without permission, General Georgios Tsolakoglou surrendered his troops to the Germans and Prime Minister Koryzis committed suicide. He was a native of Poros, an area that was to play a key role in our story.

On 14 April Admiral Turle, his reticence for the operation now overcome, replied that Sutton was leaving the next day with five 'cucumbers' (magnetic mines) and asked if he could be allowed to retain one to block the canal.

Lieutenant A. W. F. Sutton RN, was Senior Officer and Fleet Air Arm Liaison Greece. The five mines had been brought by the light cruiser HMAS *Perth* on 11 April. They were offloaded the same day to the destroyer HMS *Hero* and disembarked at Skaramanga Bay. Two days later, six Swordfish bombers of 815 Squadron, based in Paramythia, flew off to lay the five mines at Brindisi (one aircraft was armed with a torpedo). This was the only time when Swordfish used mines during the Greek campaign; on most of their sorties they were armed with torpedoes or bombs. They had registered some successes. On 13 March five torpedo bombers attacked the harbour of Valona and sank the Italian freighter *Santa Maria*. At Valona the following day, three torpedo bombers sank the Italian hospital ship *Po* with two hits and on 17 March they torpedoed and sank the torpedo-boat *Andromeda*. By 16 April surviving Swordfish of 815 Squadron were being withdrawn and used to transport mines and torpedoes to Maleme in Crete.

To Turle's request Cunningham replied immediately that 'cucumbers' were required for operations and were not to be used for demolitions. He added that depth charges were more suited for the job. In retrospect, had Turle been allowed to retain one or more mines it would have made his task much easier. The following day, the Naval Attaché, in a prophetic reply to the Commander-in-Chief, expressed his doubts that Crete could be held without adequate fighter protection and that a mere fifty fighters could have made a difference in the situation in Greece. Nevertheless, he would carry on preparations although he thought that a mine exploding under a ship in the canal would have been the best option. Turle could speak of experience, having been Mine Clearance Officer for the Aegean and Black Sea in 1919.

Chapter 6

First Attempt

Michael Cumberlege

On 5 February 1941 Donald Perkins from the SOE Greek section at London headquarters drew up a list of fourteen targets that the organization should deal with in the event of a German invasion and a Greek collapse. By order of importance, the Corinth Canal was only ninth on the list after the power stations of St George's Bay, New Phaleron, Salonika and Patras, State and SPAP railways, and finally the ports of Piraeus and Salonika. With a German invasion appearing imminent, Major Taylor was reminded of the list at the end of March and was asked if any steps had been taken to deal with them.

SOE London had wired Ian Pirie, head of its Greece station, to enquire if any plan by the Greek or British authorities to block the Corinth Canal existed. London also wanted to know if SOE had been assigned any part in it. The exact date is not recorded in the SOE war diaries but it was probably about 10 April. Pirie was more at ease with propaganda work and was already very busy handling SOE operations in Albania and Yugoslavia and he appears to have delegated the work to a colleague. On 21 April Admiral Turle sent another signal stating that he had put the operation in the hands of Lieutenant Cumberlege who had eight depth charges and had managed to scrounge one mine as [Sutton?] (the message was garbled) was unable to use them. He added that Cumberlege would require an old or disabled ship to carry out the operation.

Lieutenant Claude Michael Bulstrode Cumberlege RD RNR, the eldest son of Rear Admiral Claude Lionel Cumberlege, was born in London on 26 October 1905. For a future sailor of the Royal Navy, this was a good omen, the country having just celebrated the centenary of the Battle of Trafalgar. His father was loaned to the Australian Navy and at the start of the Great War was in command of the destroyer HMAS *Farrago*. Shortly after, he would take over the First Destroyer Flotilla and by the end of the war, had commanded cruisers of the Royal Navy. After the war, he became captain of the battle cruiser HMAS *Australia*. Three years later, he was promoted to rear admiral and retired.

His son, Claude Michael, 'Mike' to his friends, would follow his example. He attended the Nautical College, Pangbourne in Berkshire (1919-1922) and joined the Royal Naval Reserve as a midshipman on 1 May 1922. After three years in the Merchant Navy, he obtained a Second's Mate Certificate. Promoted to lieutenant in the RNR on 22 July 1933, the same year he sailed on *Lady*

Beatrice, an 8-ton cutter built at Looe in 1912. He loved the sea, wrote articles in nautical magazines such as *Yachting World* and his penchant for small boats would show even in the war to come. He also wrote poetry, a trait certainly inherited by his son Marcus, a well-known poet living in Bruges at the time of this writing. In 1934 Mike took charge of *Jolie Brise*, a 45-ton sailing vessel and former le Havre pilot cutter. From 27 May 1934 to 1 September 1935 he sailed with *Jolie Brise* from England to the Mediterranean on an 11,500-mile cruise, stopping at Malaga, Barcelona, Marseille, Naples, Palermo, Taormina, Dubrovnik, Zara, Venice, Argostoli among others. He crossed the Corinth Canal, which would become forever linked with his destiny, before proceeding to Santorini, Delos and Rhodes.

A modern day buccaneer, Mike Cumberlege would later be known by a distinctive golden earring he wore on his right ear. In 1936 he married Toronto-born 21-year-old Nancy Pemberton and retired from active service on 24 September 1937. They settled at Cap d'Antibes on the French Riviera, and their son Marcus was born on 23 December 1938.

Mike was a friend of Henry Denham, also an avid yachtsman and future naval attaché in Sweden. This was the same Denham who would be inadvertently linked to the sabotage of the Kiel Canal (see Appendix J) and alert the British Admiralty of the departure of the battleship *Bismarck* on 20 May 1941. While visiting the young couple just before the war, Denham met another friend of the family, Admiral John Henry Godfrey, Director of Naval Intelligence. Godfrey would always be supportive of Mike and closely follow his career. According to Denham, it was at Godfrey's instigation that Cumberlege had used the yacht *Landfall* to reconnoitre Italian-held coastlines in the Mediterranean before the war erupted. Since Godfrey became DNI on 24 January 1939, we have to assume that Mike was approached shortly after. The *History of Naval Intelligence in the Second World War* makes no mention of Mike's role and it is quite possible that he was not formally employed but voluntarily supplied the information. The yacht belonged to the American millionaire R. C. Payne and Mike Cumberlege, who had a well-deserved reputation in yachting circles, was hired as skipper. The two men had already sailed together in 1938. Mike had just supervised some changes made to *Landfall* in Bremen and sailed the yacht to Patras with his cat, Prince Bira, listed as the ship's mascot. On 28 April 1939 Payne and his guests joined the yacht. They sailed round Cape Matapan for a cruise in the Aegean, visiting on the way Delphi, Navarino, Santorin, Khios, Mytilene, Istanbul and Skiathos and ending the cruise at Phaleron (Athens) on 29 May.

Landfall carried out an Adriatic cruise on the eve of the Second World War, from 29 July to 22 August. Also listed as part of the crew and acting as steward was the Bohemian Jean [Jan] Kotrba. In the cruise book, Payne described Kotrba as follows:

Jean's friendly smile and brisk perpetual motion at the table or cleaning up about the cabins remind me of the best type of highly-trained wagon-lit attendant. He is young, good looking, slim, ambitious, and at present is waiting for War and a chance to enlist in the Czech foreign legion for a crack at the boches.

Mike was equally appreciative of the qualities of Kotrba and would later ask him to volunteer for his second attempt at blocking the Corinth Canal.

The cruise books of this yacht do not reveal any undercover activity and it is doubtful that Mr Payne was aware that his captain may have taken notes of every suitable landing spot for future clandestine operations. This was a good cover, an American yacht was perceived as neutral as the clouds of war gathered over Europe. The yacht sailed from Naples where 'DUCE DUCE DUCE' and other fascist slogans were painted in huge letters on warehouses. After a stop at Capri, they made their way to Corfu, then to Ulcinj (Yugoslavia), Budva, Kotor, Dubrovnik, Zara, Brioni and finally to Venice where Nancy Cumberlege and infant Marcus were reunited with Mike. The cruise was cut short as war appeared to be imminent.

The 34-year-old Cumberlege was called up for war service on 15 January 1940 and was appointed as head of Contraband (Control Duties) at Marseille from 25 January 1940 to 15 July 1940; this was followed by a brief stint at the Liaison Office to General de Gaulle (16 July 1940 to 2 August 1940) before an assignment as Consular Special Adviser at St Vincent (Cape Verde Islands) from 3 August 1940 to 14 February 1941. This had been arranged by Admiral Godfrey, Mike being chosen to replace a paymaster lieutenant who had just met with an accident. There are indications that he helped prepare Operation SHRAPNEL, the occupation of these islands. Following the failure of Operation MENACE (the attempt to occupy Vichy-controlled Dakar), 102 Royal Marine Brigade, under Brigadier R. H. Campbell, had been assembled at Freetown for this purpose, but the British government was dragging its feet and hesitated to give the go-ahead. The operation was finally postponed indefinitely.

On 25 January 1941 Major Searight of the SOE Middle East section was informed by London that Lieutenant Cumberlege, who had been strongly recommended, was on his way to Egypt to take command of one of the para-naval vessels. He replied that *Dolphin II*, apparently the only available vessel, had sailed from Alexandria for Crete the next day. This boat had already been used on an SOE mission in the Aegean in the autumn of 1940, but the cruise had been a complete fiasco and Major Searight had fired the whole crew, save an officer. On 6 February 1941 Admiral Godfrey appointed Cumberlege to HMS *President* for special duties with MO4 (as SOE was known in the Middle East) and five days later he left England for Cairo. HMS *President* was a vessel moored in the Thames and all naval personnel at the Admiralty or working elsewhere in London were assigned to her books.

It is not known which route he took but this was probably roundabout via Takoradi. Flying across the Mediterranean had become excessively dangerous; the German air force had established its mastery of air space in the Central Mediterranean from its newly established bases in Sicily.

Lieutenant Commander Pool flew from Cairo to Athens to inspect the four caiques that were to constitute a Dodecanese patrol. Barwell had purchased these boats and they had not proven very satisfactory. A telegram dated 18 February from Major Taylor confirmed that Lieutenant Michael Cumberlege RNR had been appointed to control para-naval work in the Middle East. The Admiralty rejected a request that he receive a promotion in view of the task expected. It was then suggested that perhaps Admiral Cunningham, Commander-in-Chief of the Mediterranean Fleet, might be induced to approve this recommendation but this was also ignored.

The SOE war diaries report from a despatch of 20 March that a conference on para-naval work was held (probably in Cairo) between Colonel Pollock, Major Searight, Cumberlege and Bousfield. They had decided to restrict para-naval activities in the Dodecanese as this could hinder major naval operations. The failure of Operation ABSTENTION was still fresh in their minds. The yachts used in special operations, *Dolphin II* and *Saad*, were to remain under naval control (i.e. under NID) and only used to transport stores. At the end of March consideration was given to using the SOE vessel *Aghios Nikolaos* to block the Corinth Canal. She had just been used to evacuate personnel from the British legation in Rumania but, when ordered to Greece, her crew had practically mutinied and forced her master to turn back to Istanbul and events were to move too quickly to bring this about.

In Alexandria Mike had been joined by his cousin Major Cleland 'Cle' Alexander Cumberlege of the Royal Regiment of Artillery and the latter introduced him to three Jewish members of the Haganah who had been trained by SOE and given Royal Artillery uniforms. Cle was born on 14 September 1906, only son of Captain Cleland Bulstrode Cumberlege DSO. They all boarded the troop transport *Pennland* and sailed in convoy for Piraeus where they arrived two days later. The three Jews were Yitzchak Spector, Shlomo Kostika and Yoel Golomb; the last named has written an account of his participation in the events that followed. They had taken a naval course given by the Haganah with the intention of training sailors to help in 'illegal immigration'. At this time Great Britain had severely curtailed Jewish immigration to Palestine for fear of antagonizing the Arab states who were firmly opposed to it. The three Haganah members were sent to man the SOE caique *Aghia Varvara*. Mike immediately took over command of *Dolphin II* and consideration was given that he should take her back to Egypt. His crew consisted of his cousin Cle, in charge of *Dolphin II*'s 'gunnery' (a pompous term for a vessel armed with only a 2-pounder gun and a few machine-guns), Able Seaman Ernest Frank Saunders and another trio of Palestinian Jews who had preceded Golomb and his friends. They were Yaakov Ageiev, Mordechai Lishchinski and Shmuel Ben Shaprut, already selected to operate with SOE caiques. Cumberlege had arrived just in time as, within days, Hitler would unleash his armies on Yugoslavia and Greece.

Dolphin II was a ketch of about 40 tons built in Haifa. On 4 November 1940 she was being considered to smuggle explosives in the Salonika area but had to undergo repairs in Alexandria. Major Searight appears to have been misinformed when he reported *Dolphin II* sailing from Alexandria on 26 January 1941. The war diaries of Suda Bay (Crete) list her as arriving there on 20 January 1941 and sailing for Heraklion on 4 February. According to an account by Nicholas Hammond, she was armed with two Lewis guns, two Brens and a 2-pounder gun. Golomb made a similar description: a gun at the bow and two Lewis machine-guns, one on each side of the bridge.

Cumberlege caught up with her in Piraeus and took over command on 3 April. The SOE war diaries imply that Mike had taken *Dolphin II* to sea and escaped from the air raid that devastated Piraeus on 6 April. This is contradicted by Golomb who recollects that his three Jewish colleagues were on board the yacht when the air raid occurred and anchored close to the ammunition ship *Clan Fraser* when she blew up, destroying most of the harbour facilities and sinking a number of ships. According to Golomb, his three friends escaped certain death as the debris from the explosion flew over their heads. The war diaries record that their caiques *Taxiarchis* and *Aghia Varvara* were damaged while *Eos*, though unscathed, was laid up for repairs. The only operational SOE vessel left was *Dolphin II*, now on her way to reconnoitre the Dodecanese islands and she is reported to have brought back valuable information. Golomb relates that there was a change in crew with Yaakov Ageiev and Mordechai Lishchinski being posted to *Aghia Varvara*, while Yitzchak Spector, Shlomo Kostika and himself were sent to *Dolphin II* where they joined Shmuel Ben Shaprut who had been retained as mechanic. After about a week in Athens, they sailed for an operation; it lasted two weeks and took them to Crete but was uneventful. Although Golomb recalled meeting Major Camberledge (sic) and Captain Camberlede (sic) in Alexandria, he only mentions two nameless British officers on board *Dolphin II* who were 'aristocratic' and did not treat them well. Again according to Golomb, they were just back at Piraeus when an air raid occurred. This does not match the timetable as the SOE war diaries, which are not always accurate, report that *Dolphin II* was sent to reconnoitre the Dodecanese and that the attack occurred on 15 April. Golomb writes that the Captain (Mike) ran to the bridge, knocking him down on the way while Yitzchak 'Chakko' Spector manned the Lewis gun on the starboard side and fired at the lead plane which was hit and trailed smoke and kept on firing at the second plane which was also hit. The testimony is confirmed by the SOE war diaries, which claimed that during the action a twin-engine bomber was shot down, and perhaps a second one. We have to assume that Major Cleland Cumberlege, in charge of the 'artillery', must have taken a prominent part in the action. After this action, Golomb and Spector were sent to *Aghia Varvara*; and of the Jewish crew only Shmuel Ben Shaprut and Shlomo Kostika remained on board *Dolphin II*.

The First Operation

Admiral Turle had approached SOE with a request to block the Corinth Canal. Two schemes had been proposed while the Navy was also reported to have devised a third scheme with explosives provided by SOE. At about the same time SOE was smuggling explosives into Yugoslavia through Salonika to block the Danube waterway.

Mike had already studied the possibility of blocking the Sulina Channel of the Danube for the D section (sabotage section, which also used the notorious Kim Philby as an agent) and he now switched his attention to the problem of blocking the Corinth Canal. The operation had to occur at the last possible moment to enable the canal to be used by Allied troop movements until the evacuation of the Peloponnese was completed; it had to be carried out in such a manner that British involvement would not be suspected.

To Admiral Turle's request for a blockship to block the Corinth Canal, Cunningham replied that he concurred and suggested they use *Quiloa*.

The British cargo ship *Quiloa* had run aground at Skaramanga on 14 April. On the morning of 20 April, the corvettes HMS *Salvia* and *Hyacinth* with the help of Greek tugs had attempted to free her, but to no avail. *Salvia* went on to examine the Danish tanker *Marie Maersk* damaged by dive-bombers on 21 March while travelling with the AN 21 convoy. She had suffered further damage on 12 April and could not be moved.

The plan to use a caique for the operation originated from Lieutenant David Pawson, who worked for SOE in Athens and would later take charge of the Smyrna branch. He suggested that the vessel might be sent on a pretext to evacuate British personnel from Patras and could mine the canal during the return trip. The operation had to be kept secret from the Greeks, as it was feared they would oppose it. At no time was consideration given to the destruction of the dredgers that kept the canal free from obstructions caused by landslides and the natural deposit of sediments. Disposal of the dredgers would have seriously impaired Axis efforts to clear the waterway.

The Admiralty was also pressing the naval attaché in Athens for action. HMS *Salvia* provided eight depth charges to be used by Cumberlege; Admiral Turle had hoped to get a Greek vessel to use as a blockship but this did not work out.

Piraeus harbour had still not recovered from the disaster of 6 April and facilities were in shambles.

Cumberlege was offered the caique *Taxiarchis* for the operation but it did not prove suitable and he preferred to use *Dolphin II* instead. He also had the assistance of David Pawson and Ian Pirie. The vessel was taken for a dummy run along the canal to the west end, engine defects were simulated to delay the return and enable the team to reconnoitre the area.

During an air raid over Athens, a magnetic mine from the Fleet Air Arm was brought to *Dolphin II* on a truck driven by the classical scholar Captain Nicholas Geoffrey Hammond (in May, Hammond would join the crew of *Dolphin II* in Crete and would later take an active part in the resistance in Greece). He was assisted by Able Seaman Saunders who is reported to have sat on the mine. Despite their cultural differences, the 34-year old Hammond befriended the cheerful sailor who had that quiet assurance of seventeen years' experience in the lower deck and he described him as having rabbit teeth, sandy hair and an engaging grin. The mine weighed 1,500lb and was put on a special platform on the port side of the yacht.

The origin of this mine is uncertain. HMAS *Perth* had brought five mines on 11 April and, according to Admiral Turle, they were the only mines left there. The diary of 815 Squadron Fleet Air Arm records that, on the same day, five Swordfish bombers had taken off from Paramythia and flown to Eleusis to pick up the mines. They returned the next day. At first, the mines were to have been laid at Durazzo but it was not certain if the harbour had already fallen into Italian hands. Eventually, all five mines were reported to have been laid at Brindisi on 13 April. Where did the sixth mine come from? Was the mine a defective leftover from a previous shipment? Are the operational records of the Fleet Air Arm squadron in error? Admiral Turle may have been mistaken or misinformed; the same diary mentions that, on 16 April, six aircraft evacuated torpedoes *and mines* to Crete.

After stopping on 19 April at Nea Epidavros in the Saronic Gulf, *Dolphin II* sailed through the canal towards Patras. To avoid suspicions, mechanical defects were invoked for the delay. A large oar boat was purchased in Corinth and christened *Corinthus*. The Greeks were not to be informed of the operation lest they should object to it.

The difficulties faced by SOE were caused by the refusal of the King of Greece to agree to wholesale demolitions which would antagonize his people. Opposition came even from British Army quarters. When SOE proposed to use men in plain clothes to blow up the main power station, General Wilson informed them that his men would shoot on any saboteur, Greek or British, in uniform or in mufti.

The Greeks would be told that *Dolphin II* was to bring supplies to Itea. On 23 April *Corinthus* was loaded with the eight depth charges supplied by HMS

Salvia. The same day they reconnoitred the area again and were alarmed to see British troops retreating across the canal. Cumberlege travelled to Athens on the same day and secured permission from Admirals Baillie-Grohman and Turle to proceed with the operation; he returned to Corinth at dawn the next day.

At 0630 hours on 24 April the canal was opened to traffic and four boats were also waiting for passage. Mike let them go first and *Dolphin II* followed with *Corinthus* in tow. Fortunately, the boat was not searched and they proceeded towards their objective, a spot about 350 yards east of the rail bridge near the eastern bank. The location had been selected because, at the very spot, a large fall had occurred in 1938 leaving a large crack and there was no retaining wall. It was hoped that the explosion of the mine combined with that of the depth charges might bring down the bank.

Everything proceeded without a hitch. Using an axe, Major Cumberlege scuttled *Corinthus* before jumping on board *Dolphin II*. The boat settled slowly and disappeared from view. Luckily, the sentry on the bridge had just strolled off and the action was unobserved. Seconds later and about sixty yards farther east, the magnetic mine was dropped over the port side; it had not been set for electric firing but two limpets were attached. The mine was covered with a piece of old canvas hanging over the side and this muffled the noise of the splash. The depth charges and the mine had been set to detonate by limpets with a seven-day fuse (i.e. on 1 May) even if a vessel did not detonate the magnetic mine. The narrowness of the passageway made it vulnerable to a landslide. Mike Cumberlege now attached the dinghy to the yacht as a precaution in case she had been reported as towing a boat. If he had hoped to achieve complete secrecy, he was mistaken. This was Greece, and secrets were hard to keep.

Admiral Turle visited the west end of the canal on 25 April and was surprised to be told by the Greek watchman that *Dolphin II* had made the passage with a load of mines. Embarrassed, the naval attaché gave the excuse that they were destined for Phleva Island.

The operation had been carried out just in time as within forty-eight hours German paratroopers would seize the waterway. Having reached the east end of the canal where he paid the canal dues, Mike reported to the authorities that he had been recalled and turned back without raising any suspicion. His cautiousness was unwarranted: British, Australian and New Zealand troops had already occupied positions on both sides of the canal. He now informed Rear Admiral Baillie-Grohman that the operation had been successful.

Later Nicholas Hammond would write a slightly different story; according to him Saunders was sitting on the mine covered with a tarpaulin which was installed on the dinghy and Mike Cumberlege had joined him to activate the mine, which was then dumped overboard after observing faults in the rock (i.e. where the cliffs might collapse in the canal). Cumberlege's report does not mention the presence of Hammond and only describes the part played by his cousin Cle. Turle's report of 8 July 1941 is equally silent, recording only that Cumberlege received assistance from Lieutenant Pawson and Mr Ian Pirie. Curiously, Hammond's recollections do not include Cle Cumberlege and the fact that the mine was actually carried out onboard *Dolphin II* and not on the dinghy (actually *Corinthus*), which held only the depth charges when it was scuttled.

His account is further contradicted by Ian Pirie's report of SOE operations in Greece.[4] According to Pirie, Pawson, Hammond and four sappers under Major West left for Lake Copats on the evening of 23 April, after having secured permission to destroy the stocks of cotton seed near Livadavia from General Wilson. Hammond is reported to have left the site the following evening after setting up the explosives. If this is correct then Hammond could not have taken passage on *Dolphin II* on the same day. It is, however, possible that Pirie's chronology is at fault as he erroneously mentions the mining operation as occurring on the 26th instead of the 24th while Captain Harris' account states that the cotton stocks were destroyed on 20 April. It is equally surprising that Hammond's book *Venture into Greece* makes no mention at all of his participation in the canal operation.

SOE in Athens is reported to have supplied the Navy with half of the explosives at their disposal to sink a blockship in the canal. Apparently the German air force sank the ship before it could be placed in position. The identity of this ship has not been found in the SOE papers, but perhaps it refers to the wooden barge which was found sunk at the western entrance of the canal.

At about the same time the mine was dropped, the New Zealand Division was ordered to ensure that the Corinth Canal installations were prepared for demolition but the orders do not appear to have specified that the canal should be blocked. A section led by Lieutenant C. M. Wheeler of 6 NZ Field Company Engineers assisted by Lieutenant J. T. Tyson of the Royal Engineers had prepared the bridge for destruction. By this time, travelling during daylight hours in the Corinth area had become hazardous as enemy aircraft were strafing the roads. It had been the intention of the British Expeditionary Force to withdraw southwards across the canal to embarkation points in the Morea but events were about to prove this most difficult.

Chapter 7

The Canal is Seized

The Airborne Assault

The capture of the canal had been a strategic objective of the *Regia Marina* and a newly constituted unit of forty paratroopers from P Battalion (for *Paracadusti*) of the San Marco Division (Italian Marines) had been trained especially for this mission.

On 16 March 1941 the Deputy Chief of Staff of the Italian Army, General Mario Rotta, issued a memorandum (Project 2 P), proposing the capture of the Corinth Canal and preventing the destruction of the bridge by using two battalions of paratroopers dropped from twenty-six German-built Junker 52 (with four more held in reserve) or thirteen Savoia SM.82 aircraft (with two more held in reserve). He suggested that the action needed to be followed up by a naval landing to consolidate the gain, perhaps with some assistance from MAS (motor torpedo-boats) boats. Ten days later, the *Regia Aeronautica* threw cold water on the proposal by stating that it had no aircraft available for the transport of airborne troops. The Savoia 82 aircraft at its disposal could only be lent at the detriment of traffic with Italian East Africa which was in imminent danger of falling to the British invading forces.

But the Italian Army was not easily dissuaded and, on 5 April, a new memorandum gave more precise details: two battalions (740 men, including the San Marco unit) would be landed with 108 light machine guns, six heavy machine guns and twelve flame-throwers. Opposition was expected to come from about 500 Greek troops in the immediate vicinity and a battalion from Corinth which could come at short notice. MAS boats would provide fire support from the west side and eventually penetrate the canal and operate also on the east side.

On 20 April, without authorization from his commander-in-chief, General Tsolakoglou surrendered the Greek Army to the Germans. Ten days later, Tsolakoglou became the head of a collaborationist government in Greece. After the war he was condemned to death (later commuted to life imprisonment). He died in prison in 1948.

It became very clear to the British High Command that there was no longer a possibility of containing the German invasion. Imperial troops were now in full retreat towards evacuation points in the Peloponnese. The choke point was the lone bridge over the Corinth Canal.

In a letter dated 4 March, the German Military Attaché had promised to provide aircraft for the Italian airborne contingent, but the German invasion of Greece forced a review of the operation and it was now entrusted to the Wehrmacht.

On 22 April 1941 General Franz Halder, Chief of Staff of the German Army, recorded in his diary the discussion of a preventive airborne operation on the canal with General von Brautschitsch, Commander-in-Chief, German Army. The order would come directly from Hitler. This raised the fear that the Führer, whose mood was often erratic, might miss the critical moment. Three days later, the order finally was issued for the operation to take place the following day.

The task had been assigned to the 2nd *Fallschirmjäger* Regiment from the 7th *Fallschirmjäger* Division which was assembled near Plovdiv in Bulgaria. Already German airborne troops were being transferred to the aerodrome of Larissa, some 120 miles (200 kilometres) north of the canal.

ULTRA had revealed the content of the relevant messages and, in the late afternoon of 25 April, the First Sea Lord, Admiral of the Fleet Dudley Pound, sent the following signal to Admiral Cunningham:

INFORMATION RECEIVED SHOWS GERMANS WISH TO AVOID DAMAGING CORINTH CANAL. REPORTS ALSO INDICATE THAT IT MAY BE THE INTENTION TO SEIZE CANAL BY USE OF PARACHUTISTS TO ENSURE ITS SECURITY (A.1). IMMEDIATE ACTION SHOULD THEREFORE BE TAKEN BLOCK CANAL BY EXPLOSIVES FOLLOWED BY BLOCKSHIPS AS SOON AS POSSIBLE.[5]

In the early hours of 26 April, in a foretaste of the Crete operation, some 800 German paratroopers, two battalions of the 2nd Regiment, known as *Detachement Süssmann* (from the name of its commander, *Generalleutnant* Wilhelm Süssmann), and other elements under the direct orders of *Oberst* (Colonel) Alfred Sturm, were dropped on both sides of the Corinth Canal (Operation HANNIBAL).

Following the devastating air raid on Piraeus, the Greeks had despatched the T.40/39 anti-aircraft unit under engineer D. Nikolaoy (RHN) to protect the Corinth Canal. It consisted of three 88mm Krupp guns, two 37mm and two 20mm guns, but they were old and the morale of the gun crews was low; some of the men had already deserted. By the time of the air assault, Nikolaoy had only four men left but they were now reinforced by a British force, although the Greeks had little contact with them and only heard rumours that the bridge across the canal was to be destroyed.

This was the Isthmus Force which had been hastily created and put under Major R. K. Gordon of the New Zealand 19th (Wellington) Battalion. Most of the force had arrived only the previous day. It included 16 Heavy Anti-Aircraft and 122 Light Anti-Aircraft Batteries, the New Zealand Wellington West Coast Company of 19th Battalion, a squadron of 4th Hussars and part of an Australian brigade, which was to be relieved by a New Zealand brigade. They now came under fire first by nine Messerschmitt Bf110 fighters and these were followed by many more fighters of the Messerschmitt Bf110 and Messerschmitt Bf109 types which continuously strafed the British positions while Junker 87 Stuka dive-bombers dropped a number of bombs. It was estimated that eighty to one hundred fighters and twenty to thirty dive-bombers had taken part in the softening of the defensive positions. One of the lessons learned was that it was necessary for defensive troops not to reveal themselves until the actual parachute drop occurred. There were no RAF fighters to interfere with the German effort and this was to prove decisive. The main opposition came from four 3.7-inch guns of 16 Heavy Anti-Aircraft Battery, situated some 1,500 yards south of the bridge over the canal. It was somewhat too far to defend it effectively and the buzzing Stukas diving and flying very low proved too fast for the guns to be trained on them. The anti-aircraft positions closer to the bridge were silenced one by one by the German bombers.

About half an hour later, six DFS-320 gliders carrying fifty-four men of the German *6./Fallschirmjäger Regiment 2* landed near the bridge. Three gliders landed on the north side and three on the south side, no farther than 600 feet from their objective and the nearest only a few yards from it. One glider was struck by a direct hit and fell heavily on the ground. The two platoons were under Leutnant Hans Teusen and Leutnant Häffner, the latter leading a team of engineers purposely sent to disarm explosives which the British might have installed. They quickly overwhelmed the British defences in the immediate vicinity. Shortly after, some 300 Junkers 52 troop carriers appeared and flying very slowly at an altitude of only 300 feet (90 metres) began disgorging paratroopers. Several were killed as their parachutes failed to open in time or were drowned in the canal. The Germans soon occupied the high grounds to the south of the canal; a few units were also dropped on the north side. This was a textbook attack, eliciting admiration from Imperial troops on the receiving end. To Fred Woollams, who belonged to B Company of the 19th Battalion, the attack appeared surrealistic and brought to mind something from *Things to Come* by H. G. Wells. Major Gordon had established his headquarters at a small fir-covered hill some 800 yards north-east of the bridge with 11 and 12 Platoons of Wellington West Coast Company. After a sharp fight that earned it the name of 'Blood Hill', the position had to be abandoned and the wounded left behind. Woollams was himself hit in the leg but managed to limp away with a small group of soldiers. Like many of his fellow soldiers, he would be unable to reach an evacuation point in time. After being hidden by friendly Greek families for several months, he would eventually be captured as he tried to reach Athens on foot.

On the other side of the canal, the Australians were quickly overwhelmed and the tanks of 4th Hussars were obliged to withdraw.

The suddenness of the German attack had prevented Lieutenant Tyson from destroying the bridge with the explosives he had planted the previous day. One of the German gliders had landed very close to the fuse and it was now impossible to get close to it. Tyson had shared a foxhole with Captain J. F. Philipps of the Devonshire Regiment and they managed to slip away to a safe distance. Tyson suggested that since gelignite had been used a rifle shot might be enough to set it off. Philipps climbed up a bank and took a shot but missed. He came immediately under fire and had to crawl to a new firing position from where his second shot is credited with hitting the charges; the bridge blew up and collapsed, killing a dozen Germans. Leutnant Teusen, who had landed on the south side of the canal, had seen his engineers remove the explosives from the steel structure and pile them on the bridge. The photographer from the Propaganda Company, Ernst von der Heyden, had just joined them to take pictures for posterity when the explosion occurred. Aerial photographs timed it at exactly 0701 hours. To his horror, Teusen watched helplessly as the bridge fell in the canal, killing von der Heyden and several of his men. The Germans would later believe that the explosion was caused by a lucky British anti-tank shell. The collapsed bridge would become the most serious obstacle to navigation in the canal. The cost had been heavy: seventy-nine paratroopers were killed or missing and 174 wounded, but the German sappers quickly built a temporary bridge. The capture of the bridge cut the retreat of British troops caught on the wrong side of the canal and many would have to surrender to the Germans. The paratroopers linked up with German Waffen SS reconnaissance units led by the hard-driving *SS-Sturmbannführer* Kurt Meyer.

The following day, German troops entered Athens. The temporary bridge allowed the 5th Panzer Division and SS *Leibstandarte Adolf Hitler* Division to cross into the Peloponnese and rush south. Their quick intervention would lead to the capture of 8,000 Imperial troops stranded at Kalamata as their re-embarkation could not be organized in time.

The Clearing of the Canal
On 29 April, 5,000 Italian troops had been landed in Corfu; the next day a reconnaissance had reached the west end of the canal and reported it obstructed by a vessel. This was apparently the work of Section 3 NID but details have not been found in the archives.

The Italians wasted no time in examining the canal. Initial reports had indicated that a ship blocked the western entrance. Italian engineer Colonel Enrico Zoppi was assigned to the task and driven first to Bari, then to Taranto whence he flew to Corinth on 2 May. Upon examination of the canal, he concluded that the main obstacle was the collapsed bridge; no other obstacle was encountered except for an 80-ton wooden lighter sunk in the harbour of Corinth at the western end. Zoppi made contact with the German battalion of sappers to establish their respective tasks to remove the obstacles in the canal. To help with the clearing operation, the Italian tug *Boeo* (equipped with German echo-sounding equipment) and the magnetic minesweeper *Ichnusa* sailed from Saseno and arrived at Patras in the afternoon of 4 May. Two days later, three minesweepers of the 21^ *Squadriglia* based at Argostoli were exploring and clearing the approaches to Patras and Cape Papas, followed shortly after by the minelayer *Azio*. The Germans had sent *Korvettenkapitän* (Lieutenant Commander) Jung to coordinate operations with the Italians. Italian army units now occupied Patras where the local population met them with hostility. They were now ready to move on and occupy the Corinth Canal but initial contacts with the Germans were decidedly cool, with the latter reluctant to relinquish their authority.

The Germans had not been idle either. A two-masted vessel of about 80 tons (the lighter mentioned above) reported sunk at the western end was dynamited by sappers of the 70th Pioneer Battalion led by *Oberleutnant* Resseguier. They opened a passage about 30 metres wide with a depth of about 6 to 8 metres. The same unit would later tackle the obstruction caused by the fallen bridge. For traffic across the canal, two temporary wooden bridges were built at the eastern end.

On 10 May it was reported that the canal would be ready for use as of 15 May by vessels of a width up to 14 metres with a draught of 7.3 metres or with vessels of up to a width of 16.5 metres and a draught of 6.2 metres.

Passage was urgently needed for the supply ships *Padenna* and *Avionia* escorted by the torpedo boats *Sirio* and *Sagittario*. They sailed from Gallipoli, Italy, and arrived at Patras on 10 May bringing ammunition and fuel for Operation MERKUR, the invasion of Crete. The tanker *Rondine* had sailed from Messina on the 10th to bring 8,000 barrels (1.6 million litres) of fuel required by the Luftwaffe for the airborne assault. Some 500 Junkers 52 transport aircraft were to take part in the operation and each required some 2,000 litres of fuel per trip (700-kilometre round trip) or about one million litres for each sortie. The invasion was expected to require up to ten sorties per aircraft. Some of the fuel shortage was made up by the capture of RAF stocks. Escorted by the torpedo boat *Alcione, Rondine* finally arrived at Patras on the 12th but damaged her propeller while attempting to reach the mooring quay. Two days later, she tried to sail again, her escort reinforced by the torpedo boats *Sagittario* and *Sirio* but had to turn back. The canal was still not open and they were forced to disembark their cargoes at Patras; these had to be brought overland, a lengthy process.

On 11 May the light cruiser *Bari*, flagship of Admiral Vittorio Tur, the torpedo boats *Antares* and *Aretusa* and the large freighter *Viminale* arrived at

Patras and disembarked elements of the San Marco Regiment who were to occupy Patras and Cape Papas. The hospital ship *Gradisca* also arrived the same day to help evacuate a number of former Italian prisoners of war who had been held in poor sanitary conditions in the Patras area. The following day the minesweeper *Boeo* began the process of clearing the canal. Work to remove the debris of the fallen bridge had already been begun by Greek divers, but by 13 May it had not progressed sufficiently. Quarter-Master Lieutenant-Colonel Seibt of the German XI Air Corps had divers flown from Kiel expressly to clear the canal. The most serious obstacle now was the fallen bridge that blocked the passage for a width of 18 metres and at a depth of 4 metres but, despite being hampered by bad weather, the German sappers managed to clear it.

Admiral Tur met with his German counterpart, Admiral von Stosch (*Befehlshaber Griechenland*), in Athens on 13 May and an agreement was reached that Italian jurisdiction would extend on the coast of Morea with the exclusion of the Gulf of Athens, which would remain under German control. The Corinth Canal defence was temporarily assigned to the Germans as they already had an anti-aircraft defence in place. This would be ceded to the Italians as soon as they were able to provide an adequate air defence. Because it was believed that only low-flying aircraft could effectively bomb the canal, it was suggested that this defence would be better served by a number of quick-firing 37mm and 20mm guns.

In Axis documents there are no indications that the mine and depth charges planted by Cumberlege had detonated and caused damage. The last obstacle was the bridge destroyed on 26 April. A 45-ton crane was brought on 15 May but when the time came to lift the largest remaining part it broke down and complete clearing would not be achieved for another month. With the imminent invasion of Crete, time was of the essence and the passage of supply ships could no longer be delayed. The next day at 1300 hours, the canal was reported ready for passage by ships drawing up to 6.2 metres. *Kapitän zur See* Herwarth Schmitt was put in overall command of the Canal Zone and took charge of controlling traffic at the western end, while *Kapitänleutnant* Kavallar did the same at the eastern end.

Led by the auxiliary *Ichnusa*, on the afternoon of 16 May the Italian torpedo boat *Sirio* followed by her sister-ship *Sagittario* were the first vessels to enter the canal, exiting at about 1740 hours. About an hour later, they were moored in Piraeus.[6] The next day a convoy consisting of the steamers *Alicante, Procida, Castellon, Maritza* and *Santa Fé*, escorted by the torpedo boats *Curtatone* and *Monzambano* arrived at Corinth. They were reported to have a draught of less than five metres and could make the crossing. A third torpedo boat *Calatafimi* was delayed by boiler problems.

The invasion of Crete had originally been set for 18 May but the late arrival of fuel had forced a postponement of two days. The barrels of fuel were unloaded at the eastern end of the canal and by the evening of 19 May they were delivered to the airfields. The invasion of Crete would start the next morning.

It had been anticipated that the Royal Navy might strike at the shipping being assembled in the Gulf of Patras. Following a report that a submarine had been sighted in the area, the *Regia Marina* ordered the submarine *Menotti* (*Capitano di Corvetta* [Lieutenant Commander] Ugo Gelli) to sail from Taranto on 18 May and take up a position to the south of Zante. Before midnight on 20 May, *Menotti* observed a dark shape travelling eastward at about 15 knots. This was probably the minelayer HMS *Abdiel* which successfully laid a field east of Cape Dukato shortly after. Within hours the gunboat *Matteucci* proceeding independently to Patras had blown up on a mine and shortly after it was the turn of the torpedo boat *Mirabello* escorting an Italian convoy. The German transports *Kybfels* and *Marburg* had arrived at Patras to pick up the 3rd Panzer Regiment (2nd Panzer Division) being repatriated for the upcoming invasion of Russia. They were not alerted to the danger and sailed early on 21 May without escort. It should be observed that relations at that time between the German and Italian authorities at Patras were strained to say the least. They ran into the minefield and both were sunk. The armed merchant cruiser *Brindisi*, which had lingered in the area to pick up the survivors of the two Italian warships, had just sighted them but had not managed to warn them of the danger in time. The loss was a serious setback: sixty-six guns, ninety-three tractors, fifteen armoured cars, 136 motor vehicles and 680 other vehicles were lost. In all, they carried some 1,330 troops and 120 crew members but rescue was quickly organized and some 1,155 survivors and fifty-six bodies were recovered.

The Italian sailing vessel *Albatros* sailed from Catania for Tripoli, Syria, with a cargo of aircraft bombs and twenty mines of a special model to supply German aircraft on their way to Iraq. This country had been in turmoil since 1 April, when a coup engineered by Rashid Ali had deposed the pro-British Regent Abdallah. The new government was pro-Axis but, from the German point of view, this revolt was premature as Greece was not yet in their hands and only limited assistance could be given. The Iraqi Army laid siege to the RAF air base at Habbaniya but the German air force could only provide a handful of Messerschmitt Bf110 fighters and Heinkel 111 bombers, supplemented by a few aircraft from the *Regia Aeronautica*, and they had to use Vichy airfields in Syria to refuel. By late April Iraq was being invaded from the west by the Arab Legion from Transjordan while Indian troops were being landed at Basra in the east. The RAF quickly neutralized the Iraqi Air Force and the few Axis aircraft. On 29 May Rashid Ali fled to Persia and the Regent was restored at the head of the Iraqi government.

Albatros reached Patras on 26 May and crossed the Corinth Canal but had the misfortune to be at Piraeus on 30 May when the German-chartered Bulgarian transport *Knyaguinya Maria Louisa* caught fire. The ship was being towed away when she blew up. The Rumanian *Jiul* was near her and sank immediately, *Albatros* was set afire and detonated, the steamer *Alicante,* devastated by numerous explosions, capsized and sank. Later, the courier ODYSSEUS would claim that this had been the work of his 'Piraeus gang', a communist group in Piraeus. This is doubtful as communists were lying low and would only spring into action when Russia was invaded the following month. At the same time Wellington bombers had raided the harbour and claimed to have sunk the ship but this is not confirmed by German accounts. According to the American air attaché in Athens, the Bulgarian ship had been sabotaged by Greek Air Force officers because they had disclosed their intentions to him twelve hours before the ship blew up. It is quite possible that the explosives were provided by SOE.

With Axis forces now occupying Crete and Vichy France having authorized the passage of their aircraft through Syria during the Iraqi Revolt, Great Britain could no longer tolerate the increasing threat to its position in the Middle East. On 8 June 1941 Lebanon and Syria were invaded by British forces and elements of the Free French.

By 10 June canal traffic appeared to be back to normal, but the next day the Italian freighter *Vesta*, on passage to Rhodes, hit the pier on the Isthmia side (eastern entrance) and navigation was interrupted for the whole day. This was not the last time *Vesta* would block the canal; in 1944 she would be used for this very purpose. It was reported that ships drawing up to 8 metres could make the transit but this proved to be premature, a week later this was revised down to 6.8 metres.

The Italian authorities had expected to occupy the Canal Zone without further ado but were frustrated by their German counterparts who were reluctant to cede the area to their allies. The Germans had already organized an anti-aircraft defence of the canal with twelve 88mm and twelve 37mm guns. Negotiations ensued with the Italians successfully playing the *Regia Marina* card as the Germans were almost entirely dependent on Italian shipping for their movements. On 12 June *Kapitän zur See* Schmitt finally relinquished the command which was now to be handed over to the Italians. *Supermarina* had intended that *Capitano di Fregata* Giacomo Monroy, commanding officer of the gunboat *Azio,* would assume command. In the last days, he had worked tirelessly to iron out differences with his German colleagues but he was tragically killed when, on 3 June, his CANT Z.501 seaplane had an engine breakdown and crashed. He was replaced by *Capitano di Fregata* Mastrangelo. Some 450 men of the San Marco Regiment were now moved in to take over the defence. General of Artillery Lama had just paid a visit and promised the army would supply more anti-aircraft guns which would raise the total to twenty-six 76mm and twenty-two 20mm guns. Later some of the guns were transferred elsewhere and the air defences would prove to be inadequate when the canal was raided by the RAF in August 1941.

By mid-June the auxiliary *Panigaglia* brought anti-torpedo nets to be laid at both ends of the canal and at the entrance of Patras. These were especially needed to protect the tankers from submarine attack while they loaded or unloaded their cargo.

The Tanker War

For the *Regia Marina* traffic with the Black Sea was now resumed after coming to a virtual stop during the war with Greece. On 1 June, the Italian tankers *Annarella*, *Dora C.* and *Strombo*, escorted by the torpedo boats *Calatafimi* and *Castelfidardo*, made the eastward passage through the canal towards the Dardanelles. However, Italian tankers were too large to make the westward passage fully loaded. Even before the occupation of Greece, *Supermarina* had decided that an oil pipeline should be built along the bank and tankers could be discharged at the east end, the oil pumped to the west end where other tankers could be loaded. This pipeline would also be useful if canal navigation was interrupted through bombing. The work was started on 19 May with material and personnel brought by the transports *Città di Savona*, *Casaregis* and *Rina Corrado*. In the meantime, tankers would make the crossing but not before disembarking part of their cargo which was transferred overland across the isthmus to be reloaded at the other end. When the pipeline was later completed it was not put into use and would be dismantled in April 1943. Instead small to medium-sized tankers were especially sought as they could make the Corinth Canal crossing. The biggest drawback was that any Axis tanker crossing the Bosphorus was bound to be reported by British observers in Turkey and they could alert lurking submarines now operating in the northern Aegean. Axis anti-submarine measures appear to have fallen short of providing effective protection. The situation was not one-sided; when the Soviet tanker *Varlaam Avanesov* made the Dardanelles crossing on 19 December 1941 she was promptly sunk by the German submarine *U-652*.

On 31 May, in London, the Ministry of Economic Warfare had issued a memorandum on the Axis shipping situation in the Mediterranean and had concluded that for the moment it was sufficient to meet its needs. However if the 4 per cent of losses of the previous months could be sustained the enemy would be forced to use only safe routes. The fall of Crete had virtually assured that the Aegean would become an Axis lake, immune from air threat save for night attacks and these could do little damage to enemy shipping. Only British submarines of the First Flotilla based at Alexandria could now penetrate it and threaten the oil traffic. They were now reinforced by five Hellenic submarines which had just escaped to Egypt but were all now undergoing refits and repairs.

On 3 June, the submarine HMS *Parthian* drew first blood when she torpedoed the Italian tanker *Strombo* in a convoy proceeding from Piraeus for the Dardanelles, but the latter was only damaged and managed to run aground;

she reached Istanbul two days later. On 6 June it was the turn of HMS *Torbay* to torpedo the French tanker *Alberta* on a trip from Marseille to Constanza. She was beached on Rabbit Island and abandoned. Four days later the same submarine sank the Italian *Giuseppina Ghirardi* in another convoy from Piraeus to the Dardanelles. On 10 July *Torbay*, in a second patrol, again torpedoed *Strombo* as she was returning to Piraeus. She managed to limp to Skaramanga where she was beached. The following month an explosion completed her destruction. Initially believed to have been caused by a mine this may have been due to sabotage.

On 18 July London ordered Pollock and Pirie of SOE in Cairo that interrupting the traffic from the Black Sea to the Adriatic or France (i.e. via the Corinth Canal) was of the highest priority. No action could be taken in Turkish waters to avoid any provocation but British submarines were already operating along this route and some of them might be used to land agents in Greece.

The next victim was the tanker *Maya* that was sunk south-west of Tenedos by HMS *Perseus* while on passage from Piraeus to Dardanelles on 5 September 1941. For the Axis high command, the only consolation was that the tankers had been sunk or damaged while in ballast and no oil had been lost but the situation was about to change. On 22 June 1941 Germany invaded Russia and from now on she would be entirely dependent on Rumanian oil as the oil exports from the Caucasus were now denied to her. About two weeks later, the British Admiralty requested the Naval Attaché in Moscow, Rear Admiral Miles, to press the new Allies to attack oil tankers in the Black Sea as these tried to enter the Bosphorus. They concurred and, on 21 September, the Soviet submarines *M-34* and *D-5* attacked without success the tankers *Tampico* and *Superga* in convoy. Eight days later, *Superga*, loaded with oil and proceeding with *Tampico* towards the Bosphorus, was torpedoed and sunk by the submarine *Shch-211*. *Tampico* herself was disposed of by HMS *Proteus* in the Doro Channel; she was carrying 4,000 tons of oil to Piraeus. The tanker *Torcello* was sent to the bottom on 5 November by the Soviet submarine *Shch-214*. HMS *Thorn* would conclude the year by sinking the German tanker *Campina* on passage from Patras to Taranto on 30 December.

The Italian fuel situation, never satisfactory, would be exacerbated by the exactions from Allied submarines and air forces and within a year would become critical, forcing the operations of the surface fleet to be curtailed. Oil traffic from the Black Sea via the Aegean and through the Corinth Canal would have to be redirected almost exclusively through the Danube waterway. By 1943 most of the fuel for the Aegean would not be shipped directly from the Black Sea but from Trieste in the Adriatic through the Corinth Canal.

Use of the Corinth Canal by the Axis Navies
The opening of the canal had now enabled the Italian Navy to re-establish links

with the Dodecanese which the war with Greece had made extremely difficult. Admiral Tur and the newly-appointed commander of Marimorea (Italian Naval Command of the Peloponnese), Admiral Alberto Morenco di Moriondo, visited the anti-aircraft defences on 20 June. The submarines *Micca* and *Beilul*, based at Leros, made the westward passage on 15 and 20 June respectively. *Micca* went on to Taranto while *Beilul* continued all the way to La Spezia; both were badly in need of a refit. On 24 June they were followed by *Onice,* also to refit at La Spezia. The submarine *Jantina* was not so fortunate. She had sailed from Leros for Italy with the intention of using the Corinth Canal but was intercepted at dusk by the British submarine *Torbay* south of Mykonos and sent to the bottom with a salvo of torpedoes on 5 July 1941. Only six men survived from a crew of forty-eight.

Italian submarines would not use the canal for the remainder of the war. The reason may have been to preserve the secrecy of their movements. There were relatively few movements between Leros and Italy: most of them occurred when the Leros-based submarines were in need of a refit which local facilities could not provide. Others followed patrols south of Crete or in the Cerigotto Channel making the use of the canal impractical. It must be noted that this restriction did not apply to Italian surface warships. Destroyers and torpedo boats made frequent use of the waterway and the largest Axis warship to use it, the light cruiser *Luigi Cadorna,* made the passage on 18 December 1941 on her way to Crete. She brought 10,000 cans of gasoline to Suda but the recent sinkings of the light cruisers *Da Barbiano* and *Di Giussano* while on a similar mission to Libya caused the experience not to be repeated.

By the end of the summer of 1941 German submarines began arriving in the Mediterranean and some were based at Salamis. The first U-boat to make use of the canal was *U-77* which made the crossing on 7 April 1942 while transferring from Salamis to La Spezia for a refit. On 1 July 1942 it was the turn of *U-371* on passage from Salamis to Pola. More would follow (see Appendix E for a complete list).

Before the Italian Armistice, the only major German surface warship in the Mediterranean was the destroyer *Hermes (ZG-3),* the British-built former Hellenic destroyer *Vasilefs Georgios* which had been scuttled in April 1941 but was later repaired. She would use the Corinth Canal on her way to Tunisia where she would be lost during the days preceding the capitulation of Axis forces in North Africa.

But we must return to our story.

Chapter 8

Retreat and Recriminations

On 21 April 1941 the British Legation at Athens cabled the Foreign Office in London, informing them of the extensive sabotage carried out in Salonika. They also pointed out that no blockship was available for the Corinth Canal. Two days later the Admiralty had sent a signal to Admiral Turle requiring confirmation that the Corinth Canal would be blocked. On 25 April the Admiralty repeated its command to the naval attaché and alerted him that they had information that the Germans wanted the Corinth Canal intact and would be using paratroopers to seize it; immediate action was now required to block it. We know that by this time the operation had been completed and Allied troops were rushing to embarking points to evacuate Greece. SOE personnel were already making arrangements to leave the Greek capital. Ian Pirie and Christos Gogas escaped from Athens on 24 April by embarking at Turkolimano, near New Phaleron, on the caique *Irene*. They made their way to the island of Hydra where they joined David Pawson and Nicholas Hammond who had fled on the small caique *Fotini* under the command of the smuggler and SOE recruit ODYSSEUS (Gedeón Angelopoulos, aka Gerasimos Alexatos). The following day, the two caiques made another stop at Kremydi Bay, a little to the north of Monemvasia, but the arrival of a number of British barges forced them out as it was feared that they would attract the attention of the Luftwaffe. They moved to Yeraka, another bay a little farther to the north, but *Irene* was hit by two bombs and sunk on 27 April. Fortunately, all the passengers and crew had already landed but all the gold and currency from the organization went down with the vessel. Joined at Yeraka by Captain Nicholas Hammond, they finally all sailed on *Fotini* and, after picking up twenty-three survivors from the destroyer HMS *Wryneck*, they reached Suda Bay on 29 April.

The Corinth Canal operation was not the only operation to involve SOE on Greek soil. The YAK Mission led by Peter Fleming, brother of Ian Fleming, future creator of James Bond, had attempted unsuccessfully to slow down the German advance in Northern Greece. In addition, Commander John E. P. Brass (Assistant Naval Attaché in Athens) used the yacht *Calanthe* (370 tons) to bring explosives to destroy the Salonika installations before the evacuation. On 8 April the Royal Engineers (a detachment led by Major West of the Canadian Corps Troops, three officers and twenty-five other ranks), assisted by Commander Toumbas of the Royal Hellenic Navy, carried out some of the destruction. The action helped legitimize the role of SOE in the Middle East. The organization badly needed to prove its worth as it had little to show so far. *Calanthe* sailed on 23 April from Piraeus taking members of the Legation to Heraklion. During a stop at Pyracos, near Milos, she was sunk on 24 April by air attack but fortunately only after the personnel of the Legation had been landed. They later managed to reach Crete.

Following the operation in the Corinth Canal, Mike Cumberlege returned to Athens where, according to his report, he received 'a hostile reception from the natives' (he did not elaborate).[7] He took *Dolphin II* to Navplion where he arrived the same evening and helped out with the ferrying of troops. Operation DEMON, the evacuation from Greece, was now in full swing. Once again the Royal Navy had been called upon to rescue a British Expeditionary Force.

During the night of 24/25 April, 5,500 troops were evacuated on board the transport HMS *Glenearn*, the light cruiser *Phoebe* and the destroyers HMASs *Voyager* and *Stuart*. Two nights later *Dolphin II* and other small vessels were active again on the same beach as 2,600 troops were ferried to the Dutch steamer *Slamat*, the anti-aircraft cruiser *Calcutta,* and the destroyers *Isis* and *Hotspur*. However, this time the events took a tragic turn as *Slamat* was bombed and sunk and over 600 lives were lost.

Embarking from Navplion had become difficult; there were still 1,700 troops ashore and through the lack of transport they were ordered to another beach. Cumberlege took Lieutenant Commander J. E. Clark RN, beachmaster at Navplion, on board and they proceeded to Monemvasia where they helped out with the evacuation. However, more than 8,000 troops were left stranded at Kalamata in the southern Peloponnese; this was due to lack of defensive positions which enabled German troops to enter the town before an evacuation could take place. In all *Dolphin II* ferried some 1,250 troops to various ships from 25 to 27 April. Eventually, she sailed for Crete. Once again, the Royal Navy had come through. After Norway and Dunkirk, over 50,000 troops had been extricated from Greece.

In the meantime, on the morning of 26 April, Admiral Cunningham informed the Naval Officer in Charge, Suda Bay that the Naval Attaché Athens had been instructed to block the Corinth Canal and that he should verify if this had been carried out. If he failed to reach Admiral Turle, he would have to use one of his ships as a blockship. A ship that was ear-marked for this purpose was sunk by air attack on 27 April but it was still hoped that Cumberlege's mission would succeed.

On 29 April Rear Admiral Baillie-Grohman arrived on board Cunningham's flagship and told him that a message from Lieutenant Cumberlege was received stating the operation had been completed, but this had yet to be confirmed.

On 11 May Admiral Cunningham was informed by the Admiralty, citing the newspaper *Giornale d'Italia* as the source, that the canal was now open to traffic. A week later he reported his findings to the Admiralty and mentioned that Rear Admiral Turle and Lieutenant Cumberlege were still in Crete and that the latter was under the impression that the operation had been successful. Cunningham could not explain why a blockship had not been used despite his instructions. Asked if the Royal Air Force could bomb the waterway, the answer was that bombs presently available could not cause serious damage. The best bet was to use Swordfish bombers equipped with 'cucumbers' and these would have to be based at Maleme in Crete or launched from an aircraft carrier. However, events in Crete would soon overshadow the Corinth operation.

Dolphin II had arrived at Canae, Crete, where Captain Nicholas Hammond (SOE agent D/H52) joined the crew and they sailed to Heraklion. There the two Palestinian Jews Shmuel Ben Shaprut and Shlomo Kostika, nicknamed 'Sam' and 'Johnny', left the vessel. They were replaced by a Rhodesian private of the Black Watch, James 'Jumbo' Steele, who would also take part in Cumberlege's second attempt at the canal in 1943 and a Greek sponge diver, Kyriakos Kiriakides, from the Dodecanese. Hammond laconically mentions, 'Before we sailed, we rid ourselves of the two Palestinians ...' without giving any reason for their dismissal.[8] On 1 May the caique was sent to reconnoitre Messara Bay, in Southern Crete, to see if it was suitable for unloading stores. The spot had not escaped the attention of the Italians; on 26 May, *Marina Rodi* (Rhodes Naval Command) ordered the submarine *Topazio* to investigate it but nothing was found.

In the war diaries of the NOIC (Naval Officer in Charge) Suda Bay, *Dolphin II* is also listed as having sailed again from this port four days later. At Heraklion Cumberlege met renowned archaeologist John Pendlebury, the British vice-consul, who used this cover for clandestine activities. Pendlebury had carried out extensive digs in Tell Amarna in Egypt before going to Crete and doing excavation work in Knossos. He was recruited by Military Intelligence in June 1940 and sent back to Crete. His popularity on the island was such that he was described as the 'uncrowned King of Crete'. The one-eyed archaeologist found in Mike Cumberlege a kindred spirit. The two men shared a common taste for adventure and quickly became good friends; Pendlebury was made honorary crew member of *Dolphin II*.

According to the SOE war diaries, on the evening of 11 May Cumberlege had been ordered to sail *Dolphin II* for Haifa where he was to meet Colonel Pollock, the head of SOE in the Middle East. With the imminent threat of an invasion of Crete, SOE had already anticipated that Palestine and Vichy-controlled Syria might follow. The Vichy French were known to have provided facilities to Axis aircraft on their way to Iraq to assist the revolt of Rashid Ali. It was not unreasonable to believe that a German invasion of Syria would not be resisted. In Palestine Haifa was an important oil terminal and the Army had reported that they could be counted upon to demolish it should a German invasion occur, but SOE was required to take care of the oil refineries at Tripoli in Syria. Major Sir Anthony Palmer took the launch *Sea Lion* and sailed from Haifa for this mission on 18 May with a commando of twenty-three Palestinian Jews of the Haganah under Tsvi Spector but they disappeared without a trace. This was Operation BOATSWAIN. Their disappearance has never been solved. When British and Free French forces occupied Syria, all the prisons were searched but without result. For a time it was believed that they may have been shipped to France but subsequent research proved negative. There were rumours that bodies had washed ashore near Tripoli, Syria, but, if so, none appeared to have been positively identified.

Cumberlege either ignored or never received the order, as communications with Crete were poor. With Pendlebury, he instead planned to raid the Italian-held islands of the Dodecanese. On 15 May they selected as their first objective the island of Kasos on the eastern side of the strait which bears the same name. This small island, about ten miles long and less than 100 nautical miles from Heraklion, was believed to be poorly defended. Cumberlege would later write to John Pendlebury's father 'it was going to be a terrific party and stood considerable chances of success'.[9] The same night Cumberlege took *Dolphin II* to reconnoitre the area while Pendlebury was given a week to gather a raiding party. The war diaries of Captain M. H. S. MacDonald DSO OBE RN (Retired), the NOIC Heraklion, records that *Dolphin II* took pilot and chart and sailed at 2300 hours on 15 May. As she left harbour, the caique met the light cruisers HMSs *Gloucester* and *Fiji* entering Heraklion; there were no mishaps but within a week both cruisers would be lost to German dive-bombers with heavy loss of life.

A new signal dated 20 May, addressed to Ian Pirie, repeated the order that Cumberlege should bring *Dolphin II* to Haifa where he was to report to Captain Lydekerr. Cairo reiterated the request for *Dolphin II* to leave Crete even if it was engaged by the Navy for duties there and this time asked Mike to report to Cyprus. To get his new instructions he was to meet Captain Cadogan through Commander Spencer Wilkinson. Pirie could not reach Cumberlege as *Dolphin II* was not equipped with radio and he would have to wait for his return.

On the morning of 21 May *Dolphin II* was in the Kasos Strait when intense air activity was observed. Mike decided to hurry back and alert Pendlebury that the operation would have to be postponed. He decided to stop at Sitia, about fifty nautical miles from Heraklion, and tried to inform Pendlebury of his impending arrival the same evening, but the telephone line appeared to have been cut. Cumberlege and his crew were unaware that the invasion of Crete had just begun.

The Invasion of Crete
With mainland Greece and all the Aegean islands occupied by German and

Italian forces, the island of Crete was the only free Greek territory. ULTRA signals had warned that the Germans were preparing an airborne assault. By now New Zealand and other Imperial units, numbering 30,000 troops under the command of Major General Bernard Cyril Freyberg VC, had reinforced the garrison and they were confident that the attack could be repulsed.

The Royal Navy was patrolling the waters north of Crete and Freyberg was persuaded that the main assault would come from the sea, but the RAF was conspicuously absent; the German air force quickly overwhelmed the few fighters left. Again, the lack of air cover would prove to be decisive. Luftwaffe General Kurt Student had 10,000 paratroopers at his disposal for the assault but he was short of air transport and only half of these could be landed at one time. Unfortunately for Freyberg, a shortage of radio sets prevented the defence from making co-ordinated counter-attacks. Lack of communications allowed the Germans to capture the Maleme airfield when their situation was desperate and, mistakenly, Imperial troops were ordered to withdraw at a critical time. The seizure of Maleme was decisive, allowing German reinforcements to pour in despite dreadful losses.

At sea the situation appeared well in hand. The Italian torpedo boat *Lupo* had sailed from Piraeus leading a ragtag invasion fleet consisting of twenty-two sailing vessels. A British naval squadron intercepted them in the evening of 21 May some five miles north of Cape Spada. The British squadron was led by the light cruisers *Dido* (flagship of Admiral Glennie), *Ajax* and *Orion*, escorted by the destroyers *Hereward*, *Hasty*, *Janus* and *Kimberley*. To defend her flock, the Italian warship bravely moved to the attack firing two torpedoes at HMS *Janus*. She then closed at a range of 700 metres and fired her two remaining torpedoes at HMS *Dido*. All torpedoes missed and the torpedo boat was now smothered by gunfire from the British squadron. Hit no less than eighteen times, *Lupo* was lucky that only three shells actually exploded as the others apparently failed to arm or were armour-piercing shells, which just went through her. She had only two killed and eighteen wounded and made good her escape despite the belief in Glennie's squadron that she had been 'pulverized'. The British squadron now savaged the invasion flotilla but the manoeuvre of *Lupo* had allowed it to scatter and only ten vessels were sunk; 800 German soldiers were drowned. Unfortunately this success was short-lived and in the end German paratroopers would prevail and conquer the island, despite suffering heavy losses that would curtail their future employment. Nevertheless they would play a pivotal role in the reconquest of Leros in 1943.

Led by the torpedo boat *Sagittario*, another convoy of small vessels was sailed to bring German troops to Canae. In the early hours of 22 May, they sighted an enemy squadron of four cruisers and two destroyers. The torpedo boat laid a smokescreen to cover the retreat of his flotilla, at a distance of 12,500 metres and came under fire but closed at 31 knots, firing two torpedoes from

7,200 metres at an enemy cruiser. Although a column of water was observed on the target, this was not confirmed by British documents. *Sagittario* now came under air attack. The Italian ship avoided six attacks by Stuka dive-bombers, which shook her but caused no damage before the Germans realized their error and shifted their attacks to the British warships. When it was learnt that the *Lupo* flotilla had been decimated, the convoy was diverted to Milo. *Sagittario* continued alone to search for survivors from these unfortunates.

The destroyers *Sella* and *Crispi* and the torpedo boats *Monzambano*, *Libra* and *Lince* sailed from Piraeus to bring German Alpine troops to Candia in Crete. These ships were also mistaken for enemy by the Luftwaffe and indiscriminately attacked by Stukas. *Sella* suffered some damage and had five killed and thirty wounded, half of them German troops; she was forced to turn back. The remainder reached their destination without further interference.

The full wrath of the German air force would now be directed at the ships of the Royal Navy.

Having failed to contact Pendlebury by telephone, Cumberlege and his crew brought *Dolphin II* to Heraklion at dusk on the 21st. He would later describe how they had seen a large fire and clouds of smoke as they neared the harbour and were surprised to see the harbour wall deserted. Cle Cumberlege and Nicholas Hammond were sent ashore to ask for permission to enter but hurried back as they had seen bodies of British soldiers lying in the street and the Nazi flag flying from one of the buildings. *Dolphin II* immediately made for the open sea amidst a fierce fusillade. They had not been able to contact John Pendlebury who had been wounded the same afternoon. He was brought to the house of Aristea Drossoulakis and treated by a German doctor but his luck ran out two days later when a party of German paratroopers found him. They had suffered terrible losses and were not inclined to show mercy. Pendlebury was not in uniform and was treated as a *franc tireur*. He was made to stand against the wall and executed. SOE in Cairo had decided that Hammond would be put at the disposal of Pendlebury to carry out sabotage in Crete, not knowing that the latter was now dead.

The Escape from Crete

Unaware of the fate that had befallen his friend, Cumberlege brought *Dolphin II* to Suda Bay but her engines had finally given out and she was abandoned. Nicholas Hammond wrote that he himself laid demolition charges in her engine room, hull and guns to prevent the vessel from falling into enemy hands. Cumberlege was forced to commandeer the 15-ton red wooden-hulled caique *Athanassios Miaoulis*, built in 1931. To John Pendlebury's father, he would later describe her as 'a stolen caique' although this does not appear to be quite true. The owner 'Old Johnny' agreed to come along with his first mate, 21-year old Efstratios 'Strati' Bournakis, and two other Greeks. Bournakis was from

Kinouria, near Loutraki, and had crossed the Corinth Canal on 28 April. He told Mike that he had seen the collapsed bridge, but this obviously referred to the army engineers' action. The plucky Bournakis had brought to Crete a party of British personnel with his own caique, the *Constantinos*, but it was sunk by air attack at Castelli Bay and he had now joined *Athanassios Miaoulis*. In 1942 Cumberlege was impressed enough to request him to join his team for his second attempt at blocking the Canal. The caique was armed with one anti-tank rifle and three machine guns, but without mountings.

In the early hours of 28 May *Athanassios Miaoulis* sailed from Suda as the town was being evacuated and, in the process, narrowly missed being rammed by the destroyer HMS *Imperial* that had jammed her steering. Hammond remembered that the whole crew was annoyed as Mike Cumberlege insisted on carrying out a reconnaissance of Dia Island, about seven miles northeast of Heraklion, in case they would one day return to Crete. They counted seventy-nine unescorted troop carriers (Junkers 52) flying towards Crete but were not disturbed. They hid in a bay and rested ashore before sailing again after dusk to cross the Kasos Strait, east of Crete. The bad state of its engine prevented *Athanassios Miaoulis* from crawling at more than 2 knots and this only for a few hours at a time. They reached the Yanisades Islands early next morning and stopped there for a few hours, observing what appears to be an E-boat (or Enemy boat, a term used to describe Axis fast motor boats, in this case probably an Italian *MAS* boat) which had arrived on the other side of their island. They were unaware that the Italians had just carried out an amphibious operation and 2,500 men of the *Regina* Division had landed unopposed on the eastern part of Crete, fifteen miles from Cape Sidero. In fact the force had sailed from Rhodes on the evening of 27 May, in a ragtag assortment of fifteen small vessels barely capable of 5 knots, escorted by the destroyer *Francesco Crispi*, the torpedo boats *Libra*, *Lince* and *Aldebaran* and two *MAS* boats. They were led by *Capitano di vascello* Aldo Cocchia, former commander of the submarine *Luigi Torelli* and former Chief of Staff at BETASOM, the Italian submarine base at Bordeaux. The little armada had barely missed Admiral Rawlings' squadron which had crossed Kasos Strait a few hours earlier on their way to evacuate troops from Crete. During the night of 28/29 May, the destroyer *Crispi*, the torpedo boat *Aldebaran* and six *MAS* boats carried a sweep of the area but *Athanassios Miaoulis* eluded them. The destroyer HMS *Hereward* was not so fortunate; attacked by bombers the following day, she was sunk. *Crispi* rescued 229 survivors.

On 29 May *Athanassios Miaoulis* crossed the Kasos Strait on the way to the south coast of Crete where Mike wanted to get in touch with one of Pendlebury's contacts, a Cretan named Solacksis. Unaware of his friend's death, Cumberlege was hoping to renew contact and assist him in setting up resistance cells. They laid anchor opposite the deserted islet of Koufonisso and made contacts with the local monks. Mike was thinking of returning to Sphakia and assisting in the evacuation and argued with Cle who thought it was too late. Hammond was asked to cast the deciding vote and opted to sail for the Egyptian coast. They sailed at dusk on the 30th of the month.

As long as their caique had stayed on the north coast of Crete, they had been relatively safe as Axis aircraft hesitated to attack a vessel that might carry their own troops. No doubt German pilots had been chastized for attacking their own convoys earlier in the campaign. *Athanassios Miaoulis* was now vulnerable as a southbound caique could only be taken for an enemy vessel. At about 0900 hours on 31 May it was set upon by a Messerschmitt 110 fighter-bomber, which swooped down to the attack. The aircraft strafed the caique which was helpless as her slow speed prevented her from taking avoiding action. Major Cleland Cumberlege was killed outright; Able Seaman Saunders was mortally wounded and Mike Cumberlege was hit by a fragment in the elbow joint. Despite the pain, he remained in command. A Greek crew member and Private Steele were slightly wounded; the latter had his skull grazed by a bullet. The Rhodesian private did not lose his composure and fired away with a machine gun. He managed to hit the aircraft as it was coming in for a second run. The bomber pulled away and disappeared in the distance with one engine smoking. Saunders was given morphine but died soon afterwards.

The sudden death of their two comrades-in-arms had shaken the small crew. According to Hammond's recollections 'Mike was sobbing, and we were all near tears'. Cle and Saunders were wrapped in a Union Jack and buried at sea. Luckily none of the bullets, which had peppered the boat, hit the cargo of explosives. There was no other choice but to escape to Egypt and, on 3 June, the caique limped to Mersa Matruh where she was left in the care of her owner. This small harbour would play a crucial role when Rommel would attempt his drive at Alexandria in 1942.

The following day, in company of Hammond and Steele, Mike took passage on a three-masted brig which brought the trio to Alexandria. Cumberlege and Hammond went on to Cairo where they reported to Major Searight on 7 June.

This was not the end of the story for *Athanassios Miaoulis*. In September 1941 it was taken over by the Economic Advisory Committee in Alexandria. The caique would later be used for special operations; notably for transporting the SOE courier ODYSSEUS from Greece to Turkey (11-13 November 1941).

For Imperial forces the invasion of Crete was a disheartening experience. Despite outnumbering the German paratroopers, they were defeated by the lack of air cover and adequate communications. The Royal Navy managed to evacuate over half of the troops but was badly mauled in the process. The light cruisers *Fiji* and *Orion*, the destroyers *Kelly, Kashmir, Juno, Greyhound, Hereward* and *Imperial* were sunk by air attacks. The battleships *Warspite* and *Valiant,* the aircraft carrier *Formidable* and other vessels were damaged. Nearly

2,000 British sailors were lost. Some 12,000 Imperial troops and 5,000 Greek soldiers were left behind but the Germans had trouble rounding them up and a number of them managed to elude capture. They would later be the objects of several attempts to extricate them by MI9, the department of Military Intelligence in charge of arranging the escape of British prisoners of war.

Rear Admiral Turle was also evacuated from Crete and reached Alexandria where he reported to Cunningham about the Corinth operation on 16 June. He disclosed that Lieutenant Cumberlege had used *Dolphin II* for the operation and had laid the mine in the western section of the canal and that an Italian engineer was reported to have arrived on 3 May to clear a sunken ship.

Having interviewed Lieutenant Cumberlege, Major Searight from the SOE Cairo headquarters reported to London on 22 June 1941, giving an outline of *Dolphin II* and *Athanassios Miaoulis'* operations in Greece and Crete. He mentioned Mike's praises for the courage and coolness of Private Steele.

Cumberlege wrote an expanded report of the operation, *Memorandum on Corinth Canal*, dated 8 July 1941. The Mediterranean Fleet Commander-in-Chief, Admiral Andrew B. Cunningham had squarely blamed Admiral Turle for the failure to block the canal, although the latter had only limited means at his disposal. His initial opposition to the operation had done little to enhance his defence. Turle wrote a letter to the Secretary of the Admiralty in which he tried to explain his motives. Writing to the First Sea Lord, Admiral Godfrey was equally critical of Turle, blaming him for his reticence and lack of preparation. Turle's wartime career as naval attaché was terminated and, in October 1941, he was appointed to the post of Commodore of Ocean Convoys based in Liverpool. In October 1944, in recognition of his past services, he would join the British Fleet returning to Greece.

Turle had been in a difficult situation; he lacked suitable explosives and adequate blockships. Certainly Cunningham had his share of the blame as he had opposed the lending of mines from the Fleet Air Arm. Also he had left to Turle the task of finding a ship at a time when every vessel in a sailing condition was being requisitioned to evacuate British and Greek troops.

In retrospect, Admiral Cunningham expressed his reservations that he had not assigned a Naval Officer in Charge for the port of Piraeus who could have relieved Admiral Turle from some of his tasks. The Director of Naval Intelligence, Admiral Godfrey, praised Lieutenant Cumberlege whom he described as 'an officer exceptionally well qualified for work of this nature'.[10] On 24 July he had proposed his promotion to lieutenant commander but this would not be accepted for another two years.

Chapter 9

The Royal Air Force Attempts

In mid-June 1941, Military Intelligence had received information that the canal was being extensively used by the enemy and suggested that the RAF bomb it or use a large mine to block it. On 16 June, at a meeting of the War Cabinet Defence Committee (Operations), Lord Hankey had raised the possibility that the Germans might move half a million tons of oil from Rumania through the Mediterranean and this would ease the Axis' chronic shortage of oil. Speaking for the RAF, Air Chief Marshal Sir Charles Portal had admitted that bombing the Rumanian oilfields was very difficult and it was best to attack the German transportation system and this meant striking at the German and Italian tankers crossing the Aegean. A week later, the Germans invaded the Soviet Union and thus removed another source of oil supply, at least for the immediate future. Admiral Cunningham requested the RAF to bomb the Corinth Canal to force the enemy to go round the Peloponnese where they would become exposed to his submarines and the RAF bombers from Egypt and from Malta. The Corinth and Piraeus areas were reconnoitred on 15 July 1941 by a Maryland of 39 Squadron. No traffic was observed in the canal, which was photographed.

During the night of 8/9 August, thirty-six Wellington bombers from 257 Wing based in Egypt raided the Piraeus area. Ten Wellington bombers from 37 Squadron from Shalufa air base, near the Suez Canal, took part in the attack, nine carrying two 1,000lb bombs and one with three 500lb bombs. The bombs were dropped from about 7,000 to 8,000 feet, aimed at a point 3,000 yards from the east end of the canal. They reported only light and medium anti-aircraft opposition and no searchlights. Weather conditions had been excellent. On its return trip, one bomber had to ditch near El Daba, on the Egyptian coast, but the crew was saved. Four Wellingtons from 38 Squadron also participated in the raid, carrying two 1,000lb bombs each, but a fifth failed to find the target. No. 70 Squadron contributed eleven Wellingtons, one of which was to bomb Crete, and 140 Squadron another eleven aircraft, some of them carrying mines.

The aerodrome of Eleusis was successfully bombed as a diversion by two Wellingtons. The war diaries of Admiral Aegean (German Naval Command) confirmed that two Heinkel 111 bombers were destroyed; two Heinkel 111 and two Messerschmitt Bf108s were damaged. Between 0100 and 0300 hours, fourteen aircraft bombed the central part of the Corinth Canal while others laid six magnetic mines, four at the entrance of the canal and two more in Corinth harbour. Three Wellington bombers armed with mines had been severely damaged by anti-aircraft fire and the wing commander raised objections as to the suitability of this type of aircraft for minelaying.

A total of twenty-one tons of bombs was dropped on or near the Canal, which incurred damage due to earth slides. Italian sources confirmed that three landslides had occurred respectively at 200, 400 and 700 metres west of the bridge. The first two were not serious enough to impede navigation but the third had also caused the rupture of the metal pillars holding the pipeline causing a distortion on a length of about sixty metres, and this needed to be repaired. Traffic was immediately suspended until the magnetic minesweeper *Ispmi* cleared the area. Initially it was estimated that the canal would be open for small vessels within two days but large vessels might require ten to thirty days before the debris was cleared.

The main opposition to the raid had come from the three Italian anti-aircraft batteries of 76mm (four guns each) and twelve 20mm guns, but they did not provide a sufficient deterrent. In September they would be augmented by a fourth battery and eight 20mm Scotti guns. German authorities were also asked to contribute two batteries of 88mm and three or four batteries of 20mm.

On the following morning a Maryland from 39 Squadron was flown to assess the damage incurred but cloud banks from 8,000 to 26,000 feet prevented a proper reconnaissance of the canal area. Another attempt on 11 August was more successful but the best information would come from ULTRA decrypts.

On the night of 13/14 August another raid achieved more damage. Again ten Wellingtons of 37 Squadron participated in the raid but only two carried 1,000lb bombs, the remainder having a mixture of 500 and 250lb bombs, and they were dropped from about 7,000 to 10,900 feet. A total of thirty-one tons of bombs was delivered and anti-aircraft opposition was only slightly heavier than in the previous attack. Six Wellingtons from 38 Squadron, eight from 70 Squadron and ten from 140 Squadron also took part in the raid. Italian reports mention that eighty bombs were dropped and more work had to be done to clear the canal. The raid had lasted nearly three hours and anti-aircraft ammunition was getting desperately short. *Marimorea* issued an urgent plea to have their stocks replenished. Had a raid occurred the following night, anti-aircraft opposition would have been negligible but there was no follow up. An ULTRA intercept from a German air force signal had revealed that the raids had been a success with damage to the bank of the canal, some 450 yards east of the bridge, which had caused a land slide some 200 feet wide at its base. The canal would be closed to navigation for a period of two weeks to a month.

In fact, the canal would be opened earlier but to limited traffic. On 21 August the steamer *Castellon* made the trip through.

During the night of 27 August the RAF bombed the Corinth Canal again. German authorities reported eleven bombs falling near the bridge without hitting it; however, some damage was caused to the embankments, but not serious enough to disrupt traffic.

A fourth raid during 8/9 September, with 37 Squadron contributing seven aircraft, achieved little results. Ideally the best outcome would have been to sink a large ship in the middle of the canal but this was easier said than done. With usually only one or two ships making the transit daily and since this took less than an hour, it would have been sheer luck to have an air raid catching a sizeable target in the canal. Since, at this time, only high-level bombers could carry out these strikes, the likelihood of a direct hit on a vessel was remote.

At *Supermarina*, the naval headquarters in Rome, the raids had raised the concern that the canal might be blocked and it was decided to put two fast freighters of the Dormio-, Neghelli- or Ezilda Croce-class at the disposal of *Marimorea* so they could be employed to go around the Peloponnese should the need arise. The Italians had only twelve tankers that could go through the Corinth Canal and these would be needed to supply the Axis forces in North Africa.[11]

In London, the Vice Chief of Air Staff and the Air Ministry questioned the policy of bombing the Corinth Canal at a time when it was felt that most of the efforts ought to be directed at Benghazi and other targets in Libya. On 2 October Air Marshal Tedder replied that much of the supplies for North Africa were being routed through the Corinth Canal and the raids could have a serious impact on Axis supplies in Libya.

At RAF headquarters the raids had barely been carried out when a proposal was made to convert six Wellington Mark II bombers to carry the new 4,000lb bombs, also known as 'Cookies', and it was hoped to use them to block the canal. Group Captain Foster and Group Captain A. G. R. Pelly, Air Staff Plans, discussed the plan and came to the conclusion that Wellingtons of No.3 Bomber Group should be sent to Malta with twelve 4,000lb bombs, six of these to be used on the canal and the remainder on targets in Tripoli. They believed that the 4,000lb bombs would be enough to block the canal. This would not be the first time these bombs were used; the first had been dropped on Berlin during the night of 17/18 April 1941.

However, the problem was how to transfer the bombs and bombers to Malta. A study showed that, with a picked crew, they could be flown by 19 September while the twelve 4,000lb bombs could be sent by submarine. The submarines *Proteus* and *Porpoise* were prepared for the job and brought the bombs in special casings. Once in Malta, the focus of the RAF changed and the bombs were used on land objectives in Naples, Benghazi and Tripoli, among others.

Intelligence had shown that the raids had not created a serious disruption of traffic. In the meantime the harbour at Piraeus was bombed twice on the night of 6/7 and 12/13 October, causing some damage. The following month considerations were given to drop aerial mines in the canal but the project appears to have been put on the back burner.

The focus of the war had now shifted to the Libyan Desert where Operation CRUSADER was being planned to drive Rommel out of Africa, and in the Eastern Front, where the German offensive was finally checked in front of Moscow. On 7 December 1941, the Japanese attacked Pearl Harbor and, four days later, the United States were at war with Germany and Italy. Greece had been forgotten; plundered by the Axis forces, blockaded by the Allies, with a fragile economy already devastated by the war, Athens was now afflicted by what would become known as 'the Great Famine'. An estimated 300,000 would perish from starvation during the terrible winter of 1941-42. Even Turkey, the enemy of yesterday, sent several ships to Greece to bring foodstuffs. It was only thanks to the intervention of the Red Cross that an arrangement was made for the blockade to be relaxed and Canadian wheat was allowed to reach Greece in Swedish ships. By the summer of 1942 the situation was finally corrected.

It was only on 26 August 1942 that the Royal Air Force would carry out a new attempt to block the canal; this time four RAF Liberators and eleven USAAF Liberators took part. They claimed two near-misses on a ship transiting the waterway. German records show that eleven bombs fell in the vicinity of the bridge but left it unscathed, although some damage was caused to the banks and the Italian authorities briefly closed the canal to traffic until it was confirmed that no magnetic mines had been laid.

Other means to impede navigation in the canal would have to be sought.

Chapter 10

Clandestine Work for MI9

Cretan Interlude

The evacuation from Greece had forced SOE to re-organize and move to Istanbul, and later to Smyrna (Izmir); they had been preceded there by their ISLD (another name for MI6) colleagues but relations between the two services were cool at best and sometimes almost hostile. The Secret Service preferred working in the shadows while SOE sought spectacular operations; it was not surprising that the two services were frequently at odds. In January 1942 SOE in the Middle East moved its headquarters to Cairo with responsibilities ranging from Hungary to Persia; Smyrna became a sub-division.

Ian Pirie, David Pawson, Chris Harris and the others were busy setting up a small fleet of caiques, which could be used to smuggle agents and weapons into occupied Greece. When Crete was evacuated, the courier ODYSSEUS was left behind. A smuggler by profession, he was left to his own devices to return to mainland Greece and make contact with PROMETHEUS I and PROMETHEUS II. Lieutenant Richard O'Brien McNabb had been sent from Crete to contact Petros K. Mavromichaelis, aka 'Black Michael', and organize a Greek resistance group in the southern Peloponnese. Following the terrible famine of the winter of 1940/41, Mavromichaelis was to take a leading part in the transactions that would allow the Red Cross to bring foodstuffs to Greece. McNabb was captured by the Italians in June 1942.

At the end of June 1941 Lieutenant Commander Pool and Lieutenant Cumberlege were based in Alexandria and put in charge of para-naval activities (D/HV section in SOE parlance); they were allotted up to three caiques and crews for clandestine work. This was a joint G (R) and SO2 activity on behalf of MI9. Mike had been 'lent' from G (R). MI9 was a relatively new organization, set up with the object of securing information from British prisoners of war and assisting them to escape.

The invasion of Crete had left a large number of Imperial troops stranded on the island; some of them were captured but had managed to escape as the Germans had set up only rudimentary camps for prisoners of war. Others had just evaded capture and found refuge with local inhabitants. The Cretan population had taken considerable risks in hiding them as punishment consisted often of a summary execution.

The first successful attempt to collect stragglers was made by the submarine

HMS *Thrasher* (Lieutenant P. J. Cowell RN), using Lieutenant Commander Pool of MO4, as SOE in the Middle East was now known, who was borrowed by MI9 for this mission (Operation DORSET, part one). During the night of 27/28 July, they managed to extricate sixty-two British soldiers, five naval ratings and eleven Greeks from the south shore of Crete. The submarine HMS *Torbay* (Lieutenant Commander Anthony C. C. Miers) would take another 125 escapers (Operation DORSET, part two, night of 19/20 August). This operation was again organized by Pool.

On his previous patrol Miers had been accused by the Germans of having murdered the survivors of the caique *L V* of the Werther Flotilla, an incident that was kept secret for over thirty years. This did not deter the aggressive commander of *Torbay* from becoming one of the most successful British submarine commanding officers of the Second World War. His submarine and HMS *Talisman* were used for landing the commandos of Operation FLIPPER, the attempt to attack Rommel's headquarters at Beda Littoria in Cyrenaica on 14/15 November 1941. He would return to Crete in January 1942 to land a sabotage party, led by Captains Turral and Xan Fielding, assigned to complete the destruction of HMS *York*. This heavy cruiser had been sunk in the shallow waters of Suda Bay following a daring attack by Italian explosive boats in March 1941 and it was feared that she would be raised by the Italians and repaired. The attempt was abandoned as the limpets were found to be defective. Tony Miers would wreak havoc and destruction on Axis shipping. He was later decorated with the Victoria Cross for his audacious attack inside the Corfu roads on 5 March 1942.

At the same time a small number of Greek caiques managed to make their escape from Greece, some making their way to Turkey, others to Egypt. Cumberlege would interview their crews and passengers and collect information that could be useful for future operations. One such vessel was a small 20-foot sailing vessel that was renamed *Escampador*. Mike would mail a picture of her to his wife Nancy and write on the back her brief story. Her 'owner' was a young Greek who sold his car for 450,000 drachmas and hired the boat for a month for 150,000 drachmas. With his remaining 300,000 drachmas he purchased fuel but, as he was ready to leave Athens, the Greek police requisitioned it. However, when they learned the true purpose of the trip, they returned the fuel with some to spare and, in August 1941, the boat sailed from Piraeus. She was manned by fourteen men including four British officers who had managed to elude capture. One of the men was Roy Farran who would later write an account of his trip. The vessel was christened *Elpice* (Hope) by them. The original name is not known but her owner was Catina Boslanopoulos. She was 30 feet in length, with a beam of 8 feet and a draught of 2 feet 6 inches, with a cruising speed of 6 knots. She could normally carry half a ton of cargo and two passengers along with her crew of three. In the Kasos Straits, the boat broke down in bad weather but managed to escape the attention of Italian E-boats (fast patrol-boats). She was repaired only to run out of fuel when sixty miles from Alexandria. By burning her hatch boards and building a still with a 4-gallon kerosene tin, they managed to carry on another twenty miles until the destroyer HMS *Jackal* was met and towed them in. Mike personally interrogated the fourteen men and was so impressed by the Greeks that he kept them in his employ. He liked the qualities of the boat and decided to take it over and converted it for his own use.

But Cumberlege was not satisfied with just interrogating escapees from Greece and Crete. He prepared a paper for SO2 outlining his plan to strike back at the Germans.[12] His six main points were:

1. Sabotage of enemy vessels at Suda and Heraklion by using limpets.
2. To give information and advice to the Cretans to build up a sound resistance organization.
3. Establish communications by radio and other means.
4. Organize arms and ammunition dumps.
5. To try to establish communications with Greece proper by using Cretan caiques trading with the mainland.
6. To keep Cretan morale pitched high but avoid overt acts until the day they could carry extensive sabotage of communications, attack airport personnel and act as guides to the main bodies of [liberating] troops.

He proposed the following personnel:

Organization and Signals: Lieutenant Michael Cumberlege RNR
Sabotage and Toys [limpets]: Captain Nicholas Hammond
Cretan Liaison and Information: Lieutenant Jack Smith-Hughes
Cretan Liaison: E. Demetracakis
Alternative personnel: Captain Ogilvie-Grant

Mike noted that two methods, flying boats and submarines, had been used but should be avoided as they were likely compromised. He suggested that a destroyer be used as her speed might enable her to be far from the coast by daylight. An alternative was to use a small slow auxiliary vessel, which would not arouse German suspicion.

His plan was not immediately adopted but MI9 was keen on enlisting Mike to try his last method as there were still many escapees at large in Crete.

Caiques such as *Hedgehog* and *Porcupine* were being used to evacuate soldiers who had been left behind during the Crete evacuation. Derna and Mersa

Matruh were occasionally used as advanced bases. On 27 October Cumberlege took Lieutenant John Campbell with *Hedgehog* (ex-*Peled*, a motor caique of about 60 tons) and the little *Escampador* to Crete. The two men had sailed together before the war. Xan Fielding, who met both men at that time, described Mike and John as very dissimilar in character. While John spoke in monosyllables, Mike's conversation was 'robust'. Fielding wrote that Mike knew the coastline of Crete more intimately than any man alive. He would also add that he had a corsair's flair for discovering unknown beaches and hidden coves, a pirate's passion for taking individual action at sea, and had shown an almost Barbarossian skill and spirit of defiance when roving off German-held shores in his diminutive *Escampador*. He even looked like a pirate—short and square and stubborn, with one ear pierced by a small gold ring, which made an anachronism of his modern naval uniform.[13]

At 1018 hours on 28 October the submarine HMS *Talisman* (Lieutenant Commander M. Willmott), returning to Alexandria from a patrol off the Libyan coast, recorded meeting a one-masted motor lighter, (*Hedgehog*), armed with a stern quick-firing gun and a motor lifeboat in company on course 330° at 7 knots in position 32°18' N, 27°55' E. After a challenge which was correctly answered, the motor lighter skipper announced their destination as Crete. The submarine captain ordered his crew to secrecy as obviously this was a clandestine mission. The 'lifeboat' was most certainly *Escampador* and Willmott described one of his two occupants as 'a most suspicious looking character of appearance similar to 'Electric Whiskers' (Bergonzoli), a reference to the famous whiskers of Italian General Annibale Bergonzoli, nicknamed '*barba elettrica*', captured at Beda Fomm in 1941. This was most likely a Cretan guide; the other man was Mike Cumberlege.

Once *Hedgehog* and *Escampador* reached the coast of Crete contact was made with the STILETTO party. The STILETTO party was formed by Second Lieutenant Jack Smith-Hughes (SOE), wireless operator Sergeant Ralph H. Stockbridge, Royal Signals (ISLD) and Cretan chieftain Satanas. They had been landed by the submarine HMS *Thunderbolt* on 9 October to establish a link with the Cretan resistance.

Mike made contact with Jack Smith-Hughes and brought back an important report. He picked up seventeen refugees (nine Britons and eight Greeks) and arrived in Alexandria on 2 November.

On the next trip he again took Campbell with *Hedgehog* with *Escampador* in tow and they arrived in Crete on 25 November. A group of escapees had been gathered at Tris Ekklesies by Smith-Hughes with the assistance of Lieutenant Jim Carstairs. Campbell left the next day with *Hedgehog* carrying eighty-six British and four Greek refugees and reached Alexandria on 28 November without mishaps. Cumberlege, with Sergeant James Steele, Petroka Georgios, Kyriakou Viagtes (a sponge diver) and two Cretan guards, elected to remain behind with *Escampador* and explore the coast between Cape Lithinon and Tsoutsouros Bay, searching for suitable landing spots. They carried two tons of stores to be delivered to the Cretan resistance. Mike eluded German patrols by taking his boat in remote bays or hiding in caves such as the one of the 'Remarkable Cascades'. They visited villages, hoping to locate British soldiers who had escaped capture.

This was not the only rescue operation under way. The Royal Hellenic submarine *Nereus*, Lieutenant Alexandros Rallis, had sailed from Alexandria on a similar mission. The operation was not without some difficulty; the submarine ran aground as it arrived near its destination, Kerato Bay, about ten miles east of Tris Ekklesies. During the night of 11/12 December an emissary of Admiral Sakellariou, Antonios Fakaros, made contact with the Greek resistance and twenty-six refugees were picked up, including three Britons, and brought back to Alexandria. Fakaros would become a personal friend of Mike Cumberlege and the latter would request that he join his team for his second attempt at blocking the Corinth Canal in 1943.

On 13 December Mike met with Captain Harris, Second Lieutenant Smith-Hughes, the Abbot of Preveli and the monks of Tris Ekklesies; they had helped hide a number of Australian soldiers evacuated earlier by HMS *Torbay*. Later the Germans found out and retaliated by destroying the lower monastery of Preveli. Cumberlege finally picked up fourteen refugees; only one was a soldier, the remainder were agents or Greeks and they left Crete on 15 December. His exploits earned him the DSO and it was awarded in February 1942. A Bar was added in 1946 and he was also awarded the Greek War Cross Third Class.

During his absence, the Mediterranean Fleet had suffered a heavy blow when the battleship HMS *Barham* had blown up north of Sollum, in a spectacular explosion after being hit by three torpedoes from the German submarine *U-331*. There had been heavy loss of life. The Japanese had attacked Pearl Harbor and the United States was now at war with the Axis powers. The European war had become a world war.

Mike had barely reached Alexandria when disaster again struck the Mediterranean Fleet. During the night of 19/20 December three Italian human torpedoes, launched by the submarine *Scirè*, managed to enter the harbour. They selected for their targets the last two battleships of Admiral Cunningham, *Queen Elizabeth* and *Valiant*, and the Norwegian tanker *Sagona*. All three ships were sunk or badly damaged, effectively altering the balance of power in the Mediterranean. It is not known what Mike Cumberlege thought of this attack but his love of clandestine operations must have elicited a grudging admiration.

Life in cosmopolitan Alexandria was no hardship at all. One was far from the London Blitz, and Axis aircraft seldom hit populated areas, as they did not want to alienate the local population although collateral damage was sometime unavoidable. Food was plentiful and nightclubs were doing brisk business. But the Egyptian government was known to have Axis sympathies and King Farouk had many Italian friends. Although Egypt was on paper a sovereign state and technically not at war, the Suez Canal was under the protection of the British but the majority of the Egyptian population resented what was perceived as a de facto military occupation.

The winter months appear to have curtailed the activities of *Escampador* but Mike prepared future activities as he had made several contacts with the Cretan resistance. Several postcards he received from Greeks praising his help and courage in assisting them attest to this. He would mail these cards to Nancy, adding a few words of explanation. He was full of admiration for the Greek people and their determination to fight on.

In one such card, he would write on the back:

Captain Boreas who sailed a 25-foot open boat which had been on an open beach for four years to Egypt. He cut down a telephone pole to make his mast and brought 11 people with him. Two people baled all the time, and the old man stayed at the tiller practically continuously for four days. These my darling are the men I am fighting for – their courage and faith in the British is beyond belief – I hope we don't let them down.

Your loving husband,
Michael

In December 1941 Mike contracted typhoid upon his return from Crete and appears to have been inactive until the following May when he returned to London. *Hedgehog* attempted another trip to Crete about Christmas 1941 with Campbell in command and seconded by Lieutenant Stanley Beckinsale, a veteran of SOE Red Sea operations; Captain Woodhouse had gathered about 100 escapees but the operation failed when *Hedgehog* was damaged in bad weather and had to turn back. The little *Escampador* would not survive the war. On 7 February 1943, after leaving Alexandria the previous day to carry out Operation BASILIC, she was lost in bad weather while being towed by *Hedgehog*. There were no casualties.

Corinth Canal traffic appeared to have returned to normal in the autumn of 1941. The following winter, the Operational Intelligence Centre in London estimated that excluding local traffic, the following figures were recorded:

	January	February	March
Eastbound	27,052 tons	51,064 tons	42,867 tons
	8 ships	13 ships	13 ships
Westbound	30,181 tons	34,779 tons	72,743 tons
	10 ships	11 ships	20 ships

These figures may appear small but one must remember that traffic in the Aegean consisted mostly of a few small to medium-sized vessels. The bombing of the canal during the previous summer had hardly affected traffic and the Royal Air Force now had more pressing objectives as the war in the Western Desert was about to enter its climax. Operation CRUSADER had managed to relieve the siege of Tobruk and removed the Axis threat to the Suez Canal. The front had stabilized on the Gazala line and both sides were now regrouping in anticipation of future operations. The task of blocking the Corinth Canal had become secondary and was now to be entrusted to the Greek resistance.

Chapter 11

The Greek Resistance

The first manifestation of Greek resistance to Axis occupation occurred as early as 31 May 1941 when two students, Manolis Glezos and Apostolos Santas, removed the Nazi flag flying over the Acropolis. This was a symbolic gesture but the news spread as wildfire and for a brief moment at least warmed the hearts of those who had not accepted the defeat. Yet the Greek Resistance had a slow start. There were a few acts of minor sabotage but initially resistance was passive and mostly expressed by the act of sheltering British and Imperial troops who had evaded capture. SOE had left some explosives with Naval Commander Koutsoyannopoulos (codename PROMETHEUS II) but he had found it very difficult to rally men around him. He had tried to contact elements of the communist party but they were reluctant to commit themselves.

The Greek Communist party (KKE) had been decimated by the Metaxas dictatorship; some 2,000 members had been jailed or exiled to remote islands. At the start of the war with Italy, Zachariadis, the General Secretary of the Party, had advocated that its members should support the government for national unity, only to be rejected by his own central Committee. The Communist Party had even denounced any collaboration with Britain as 'imperialistic'. It must be remembered that, at the time, the Soviet Union had signed a non-aggression pact with Germany and relations between the two countries were still good, at least on the surface. When Greece was occupied several of the key communist members were released from jail by the Germans. The communist resistance would crystallize with the invasion of Russia in June 1941.

The Communist Party would create the Greek National Liberation Front (EAM) and its military branch the Greek People's Liberation Army (ELAS). Although initially few in numbers—at the last democratic-held election the communists had won only 6 per cent of the popular vote—they brought their experience of clandestine work and a discipline and organization that the other Greek resistance groups lacked. By initially claiming to be apolitical, they would manage to recruit a number of Greeks who did not necessarily share their political views. Several resistance groups would mushroom, usually due to local initiatives. Outside the communists, the most prominent group was the National Republican Greek Army (EDES) led by Colonel Napoleon Zervas and he professed to owe allegiance to General Plastiras who was living in exile in the south of France.

There was hardly any royalist resistance movement in Greece; the officers and men who were faithful to the king had followed him to Egypt and provided a nucleus of an army in exile. Those who had remained behind preferred to stay aloof of politics or embraced the New Order. Britain saw in King George II a valuable ally who had stood by her side in her hour of need. The majority of the Greek people thought otherwise; they associated the king with the Metaxas dictatorship and rejected his eventual return to Greece without a plebiscite.

We saw earlier that while Crete was still unconquered, SOE had despatched Lieutenant (temporary Captain) McNabb with a Greek interpreter, the 19-year-old Leo Limberopoulo, to organize resistance in the Peloponnese. It was believed that some 800 Imperial troops had evaded capture in this area and were still in possession of their weapons. They could be transformed into a guerilla force and possibly become a thorn in the flesh of the occupying forces. McNabb had made contacts with some of them and retreated to the snow-covered Taygetus massif, west of Sparta. Most of these evaders proved to be reluctant to engage in covert operations and MI9 had already made contacts to facilitate their escape. On 18 September 1941 Captain Mark Ogilvie-Grant from MI9 and Captain Alfred W. Lawrence from SOE were landed by the submarine *Tetrarch*, Lieutenant Commander G. H. Greenway RN, in the Gython area of the southern Peloponnese in an attempt to make contact with McNabb. A Greek agent, Nikolaos Ktzikambouris, who was to contact PROMETHEUS II, was also landed with them.

Five days later the submarine was back at the rendezvous and made contact with Lawrence who reported that forty stragglers could be rounded up in forty-eight hours but *Tetrarch* had now been ordered to resume her patrol and the task of picking up the men would be entrusted to another submarine, HMS *Osiris*, Lieutenant R. S. Brookes RN. At the appointed time, *Osiris* arrived in the area of Cape Matapan and cruised in vain; the two British officers and the stragglers had been arrested by the Italians.

The McNabb group had no wireless set and could only maintain contact with Cairo via an occasional courier. In June 1941 Limberopoulo was caught by the Italians with his mother who was bringing funds from Athens. The young man's uncle, Theodoros Asimakapoulos, was later arrested but then released; he managed to reach Cairo in December and brought news from the organization.

Stricken by dysentery and malaria, McNabb was now hunted by the Italian police. Joined by two British soldiers, he was forced to flee from the mountains of the Peloponnese. In January 1942 they made their way to the Poros area on the north-east shore of the Peloponnese. Although Poros is an island, the area facing it on the Peloponnese coast also bears the same name. There they met Dimitrios Sambanis who owned lemon groves on the coast and were provided shelter. The Greek would later assist Mike Cumberlege in his second attempt at the Corinth Canal. McNabb also met his brother-in-law, Kleanthis Porfyropoulos; this man had previously helped Captain Frank Macaskie escape from Greece.[14]

The two soldiers left by caique despite the opposition of McNabb who judged it too dangerous. Porfyropoulos offered the British captain assistance to reach Athens and after about a month they left. Sambanis had made contact with Captain Constantinos Arvanitis of the Royal Hellenic Navy, who agreed to hide McNabb in Athens for a short time before finding him a safer lodging at the house of his cousin Ioannis Karamanos.

Once in the capital, McNabb met with Emmanuel Vernikos who was working with MI9 and helped with the evacuation of escapees and evaders. Vernikos had barely avoided being captured by the Italians at Antiparos (see below). The British officer's movements in Athens were always made after dark and he remained in uniform throughout his stay, but his days were numbered. In May 1942 McNabb, Vernikos and Porfyropoulos were arrested by the Italian police. Porfyropoulos was fortunate that he obtained his release after ten months of prison. During his stay in the Averoff prison he had met several members of the Greek resistance who had been incarcerated after the Antiparos fiasco and from them he had gathered a few facts about the case. Porfyropoulos decided to keep some distance from Athens and the Italian police; he returned to Poros in the winter of 1943. As we shall see in Chapter 14, he would renew his contact with Dimitrios Sambanis and through him meet Mike Cumberlege.

Disaster at Antiparos
While Cumberlege was now in charge of para-naval work from Alexandria and busy with MI9 operations in Crete, the Corinth Canal was never far from Admiralty and SOE planning. On 5 October 1941 the submarine HMS *Thunderbolt*, Lieutenant Commander C. B. Crouch DSO, sailed from Alexandria to carry out two special operations. The first was a landing of two British agents in Crete and the second was the landing of four Greek agents at Marathon Bay (Operation FLESHPOTS) on 13 October. These were Lieutenant Commander Ioannis Abatzis of the Royal Hellenic Navy, Ioannis Lekkas, telegraphist Nikos Karabasas and the Polish-born Jerzy Szajnowicz Iwanow; the latter would become one of the great heroes of the Greek resistance. Their task was to contact the Kanellopoulos organization and organize sabotage and the disruption of traffic in the Corinth Canal. They were also to contact Captain Lawrence who was assisting McNabb and Captain Savage who was organizing the escape of British stragglers in Greece. In all, some 2,500 British and Imperial troops had managed to evade capture with the help of the local population but contact with these two men could not be established as they were both captured by the Germans. There is no indication in SOE files that any new attempt on the canal was actually tried. Mixing SOE and MI9 missions may have been sound from an economic point of view, but in practice this would lead to frictions between the two services and failures would lead to mutual accusations and recriminations.

Operation ISINGLASS was to replace Operation FLESHPOTS. It was planned by Major Anthony Simonds who had already carried out special operations against the Italians in Abyssinia with Major Orde Charles Wingate. In July 1941 Simonds was put in charge of a special school for SOE agents in Palestine. Among its training instructors were Captains Christopher Montague Woodhouse and Patrick Leigh-Fermor, both destined to play major roles for SOE in mainland Greece and Crete respectively. Simonds had now joined MI9 in Cairo as GSO2 (General Staff Officer) A Force, which included MI9 in the Middle East. The head of A Force, Colonel Dudley Clarke, was away in London and involved in deception work.

When Simonds arrived in Alexandria, he met with Mike Cumberlege who was glad to help should he need a caique for his plans. Cumberlege introduced him to Commander S. M. Raw of the First Submarine Flotilla, to the Chief of Intelligence Staff (COIS) Alexandria and to the personnel in the Ministry of War Transport.

According to Cumberlege, Simonds had promised he would consult him should he embark on a naval career but did nothing of the sort. He enlisted the help of Lieutenant Morris RNVR, from the Fleet Air Arm, to see Commander Raw and request a submarine for his operation, bypassing both Commander Pool and Lieutenant Cumberlege who were usually present for these interviews. Morris would later confide to Cumberlege that he was uneasy at the statements made by Major Simonds but did not wish to 'butt in'.

During this interview Simonds personally vouched for a Greek caique owner Ioannis 'Harry' Grammatikakis. He also claimed that no Axis troops were found on Antiparos where the landing was to take place. His confidence would prove to have been misplaced. Grammatikakis was a Cretan born in 1911; like many soldiers of the 5th (Cretan) Infantry Division, he had found himself stranded on mainland Greece when the armistice was signed. There was no way to return to their island as island traffic was now tightly controlled and there was an acute shortage of food in Athens. The Cretans, most of them without relatives in Athens, depended for sustenance on the Greek Red Cross, organized by Alexandros Zannas, but the latter had very limited means at his disposal. Zannas was recruited by SOE and used his profession as a cover for his clandestine activities. Grammatikakis was a resourceful man and had managed to acquire the caique *Venetia* with the necessary papers to bring a load of wine to Antiparos. He picked up a number of his fellow Cretans at Piraeus and Anavyssos, near Cape Sunion, with the intention of using Antiparos as a stepping stone for their eventual repatriation to Crete.

Antiparos is a small island in the Aegean separated by a half-mile-wide channel from the larger Paros Island. At Paros there was an Italian garrison under Commander Giovanni Rustichelli. The Italian officer was well liked by the locals as he was just and cared for their well-being. Grammatikakis had secured his assistance in getting papers for several caiques to bring foodstuff for the local population. He used this cover to smuggle a number of Cretan soldiers to Antiparos and from there to Crete. Zannas, who was well aware of Grammatikakis' activities, asked him if he could also help six Britons to escape. One of them was Second Lieutenant John George Patterson Atkinson, a Scot of the Royal Army Service Corps. The 30-year-old Atkinson had been wounded and captured at the end of the Greek campaign. He had managed to escape from his hospital with the help of Lela Karayianni and eluded capture for several months by hiding in different Greek homes in Athens. He was also aided by Alexandra (Sofia) Poubouras, a close collaborator of Zannas who now requested Grammatikakis to arrange for his escape to the Middle East.

Grammatikakis was offered payment for his services but refused. He brought the caique *Koimisis tis Theotokou* to Loubarda Bay, Attica, and embarked the British escapees, some Cretan stragglers and a few Greek officers who wished to escape to the Middle East. The caique belonged to the Fournarakis brothers who were not aware of the mission. They sailed on 29 September 1941 and landed the Cretans at Mirabello Bay, Plaka, in Crete. When his crew became aware of his intention to go on to Egypt they refused to leave. This did not deter Grammatikakis who very quickly managed to get a replacement crew and left on 2 October. They came under fire from the garrison at Spinalonga Island but reached the open sea without sustaining damage. They braved a storm, which caused serious flooding, and five days later the caique finally reached Alexandria at night, nearly colliding with the battleship *Valiant*. They were received as heroes and MI9 immediately recruited Atkinson and Grammatikakis to arrange further escapes.

On 10 November 1941 the submarine HMS *Thorn*, Lieutenant Commander R. G. Norfolk, sailed from Alexandria for Antiparos with Lieutenant Atkinson, Grammatikakis, Sergeants John Alexander Redpath of 19 Army Troops, 2 NZEF (2nd New Zealand Expeditionary Force), and Alan Howard Empson of 18th Battalion NZEF, and three tons of stores. They were disembarked at Despotiko Bay without incident during the night of 14/15 November. The lawyer Spyros Tzavellas offered his house, the 'Casa Rosa', to shelter them. A rendezvous had been arranged with the submarine during the night of 23/24 November. Atkinson and Grammatikakis travelled with the caique *Despoina* to Piraeus and reached their destination on 20 November. They met with Zannas and collected twenty-two Britons and six Greeks, including Doctor Kostantoulis, an emissary from Zannas for SOE in Cairo. They brought the refugees to Antiparos but only twenty-one of them sailed back with Atkinson and Empson on HMS *Thorn*. Grammatikakis and Redpath were left behind to organize a base for further operations.

Major Simonds had requested from Commander Raw of the First Submarine Flotilla the loan of a submarine for a second rescue attempt at Antiparos. When

Raw asked him on what grounds he based his report that there was no enemy garrison on the island, Simonds replied confidently that the information was received three days earlier. This was true, but the garrison at Paros was not far away.

Atkinson was again put in charge of the operation. For reasons unclear, he approached SOE and volunteered his services on condition that this would not be disclosed to MI9. The New Zealander Second Lieutenant James William Charles Craig, who would sail with him for this operation, later disclosed that Atkinson had deliberately lied to Simonds. When Simonds confronted him, Atkinson denied vehemently that SOE had asked him to work for them.

At MO4, as SOE was known in the Middle East, headquarters the offer was accepted as they were anxious to make contact with the Kanellopoulos organization and submarines were used parsimoniously in landing agents. Panayiotis Kanellopoulos was a former professor at Athens University and was widely respected for his political views. He had been offered a cabinet post in the Greek government in exile and urged to join them in Egypt. Atkinson proposed the Cypriot-born, ISLD-trained, Diamantís Arvanitopoulos, codename DIAMOND, who also used the alias of Kostas Kipriadis, who was a very good radio operator and would contact leaders of the resistance in Athens, Captain Kondouriotis, RHN, and Major Tselos. This would be known as the ISINGLASS operation.

HMS *Triumph*, Lieutenant J. S. Huddart RN, embarked the ISINGLASS party in Alexandria on 26 December 1941 and sailed for Antiparos. They were landed on 30 December, along with two tons of stores and three tons of fuel for caiques. The submarine then sailed away to patrol between 36°00' N and 39°00' N and 23°00' E and 23°50' E and mark time while the evacuees were being rounded up by Atkinson. The submarine was due back at Antiparos during the night of 9/10 January but failed to show up.

The disappearance of HMS *Triumph* is a mystery which has never been solved, but it is believed that she was probably mined around 9 January. Her exact whereabouts after landing the ISINGLASS party are unknown. At 1450 hours on 4 January the motor cutter *Sofia* belonging to the Panigaglia *Netzsperrverband* (net-layer squadron) reported being attacked by a submarine in 36°07' N, 24°14' E. Two days later an observation post south-east of Milos sighted a surfaced submarine, on course 250° at 4 knots. On 9 January the tug *Taxiarchis*, towing the large lighter *Rea*, claimed to have been missed by a torpedo near Cape Sunion. If these attacks were genuine, and there is no absolute certainty that they were (a significant proportion of attacks reported were actually bogus), *Triumph* would have moved to the south-west, perhaps operating on the Piraeus-Suda route before turning north. She may then have been mined in the area of Cape Sunion, off Aghios Georgios or Poros, where the Italian minelayer *Barletta* had laid four minefields on 4 and 6 December

1941. The possibility of an accidental loss cannot be discounted; the weather was particularly severe on 7 January and submarines were not immune to it.

The ISINGLASS party was now stranded on Antiparos and hiding at the 'Casa Rosa' but believed they were betrayed.

According to the recollections of Lieutenant Craig and Sergeant Redpath who survived the Antiparos fiasco and escaped from Italy in 1943, Grammatikakis was very talkative and more involved with love affairs than with his undercover work. He had impregnated a young girl and then left her for another. The mother of the first girl was upset and had already threatened to denounce him to the Italian authorities if he did not marry her. Grammatikakis had taken Redpath's revolver and threatened to shoot her in return. She was the person most likely to have betrayed the party. During the night of 5/6 January the Italian police suddenly surrounded the house where they were hiding.

Actually no betrayal appears to have taken place. Earlier in the day, Lieutenant Gianluigi Galli of the Paros garrison had arrived at Antiparos by the caique *Despoina*, the same that had been used by Grammatikakis, with a party of four or five unarmed soldiers to cut wood. When this was finished, Galli asked Tzavellas if he could get a drink of ouzo at his house. The lawyer panicked and claimed that he had lost the keys but Galli had observed smoke coming out of the chimney. Furthermore, several wrappings that the British had left were seen near the house. The Italian officer said nothing but reported the incident upon his return. The popular Sub Lieutenant Carlo Ribolzi volunteered to lead a small party and returned to Antiparos with Second Lieutenant Munarini and eight men. They boarded *Despoina* and arrived in front of the Tzavellas house at 0100 hours on 6 January.

Tzavellas answered the door and was taken away, along with the radio operator 'Diamond' Kipriadis who was with him at the time. In an adjoining room, Atkinson, Craig and Redpath had hurriedly dressed in the dark and armed themselves. Four or five Italians had been left around, and shortly after they began searching the house. As they were about to enter their room, Craig and Redpath held their sub-machine guns ready to fire while Atkinson had drawn his Colt 45. As Ribolzi stepped into the room, Atkinson immediately shot him in the chest. Redpath did not understand why his leader had not disarmed the Italian instead and used him as a hostage to facilitate their escape. At the sound of the shot the remaining Italian *carabinieri* stumbled out of the house, Redpath firing a burst from his Sten gun to help them out. The Italian officer was now lying on the ground, agonizing and making motions to reach a hand grenade. It would have been easy for Atkinson to have just pushed the grenade out of his reach but he chose instead to finish him off with a second round. This gratuitous act would seal his fate.

Shortly after, the Italians outside threw a couple of hand grenades in the room. Atkinson was wounded in the left eye and Redpath in the leg but all three men managed to flee from another window. A third grenade exploded between them and they became separated in the darkness. Eventually Craig located Redpath and they were joined by Kipriadis who had managed to give the slip to the Italians and carry away the two suitcases belonging to Atkinson. Unknowingly, one of the suitcase contained secret documents which the Scottish officer had failed to destroy. There was no sign of Atkinson who had broken a leg and tried to crawl away in the bushes.

A few hours later, Ribolzi would be brought to Paros but would expire shortly after. His body was transported to Syros where he was buried with full military honours on 8 January.

The ISINGLASS party and the escapees waited in vain for the return of HMS *Triumph*. The Italians were very upset at the death of their officer and a large-scale search was carried out. Atkinson was captured within three days. He was now accused of murder. MO4 had given him a list of important contacts in Greece to memorize and destroy it before leaving the submarine. In an unforgivable lapse of security Atkinson apparently had forgotten to get rid of the document and the Italians found it. After a few days all the others were rounded up and brought to Syros; Craig and Redpath were incarcerated in the same cell as Captain Macaskie, Roy Natusch and other escapers.

Shortly afterwards Major Parish of MI9 and Commander Vernikos arrived at Antiparos by caique and narrowly missed being captured by the Italians. On 30 January Parish reached Smyrna and brought news of the capture of Atkinson and his group.

In the meantime Grammatikakis was busy in Piraeus in early December securing two caiques. The operation had hit a snag when Alexandra Poubouras had been arrested with four or five British escapees after being given away by the traitor Bekes. Fortunately, Grammatikakis had avoided being trapped, thanks to Alexandra's sister Evgenia Zannas, who had informed the Athens Chief of Police, Colonel Evert. Evert was secretly helping the Allies and he sent warning to the Cretan to leave as soon as possible. Grammatikakis sailed from Anavyssos for Antiparos and reached his destination without trouble. He again left for Piraeus on 30 December, the day before *Triumph* arrived. He later criticized the British for their lax security as they lavishly distributed English cigarettes and biscuits, and fished with hand grenades.

Grammatikakis returned to Despotiko on 10 January, the same day that Atkinson had fallen into enemy hands. He barely escaped capture and, after numerous adventures, fled to Turkey and made his way to Egypt. He joined the Royal Hellenic Navy and was dismissed in 1945. He died in 1977, a forgotten man.

As we shall see further on, attempts would be made by MI9 and SOE to free Atkinson. Ultimately they would all fail. Atkinson, Arvanitopoulos, referred to as Kipriadis in Italian documents, Tzavellas, Isandanis and Pandelis, were tried and executed on 23 February 1943. Craig and Redpath ended up in a prisoner of war camp in Italy. At the Italian armistice, the Germans took over and moved the prisoners northward, but both men escaped and reached allied lines.

PROMETHEUS II

Commander Charalambos Koutsoyannopoulos (PROMETHEUS II) was the most dependable agent SOE had in Greece. On 3 February he warned Cairo of the situation. At MO4 Headquarters there was considerable doubt that Atkinson could have been captured with the list on him; he was believed unlikely to have committed such a basic mistake. The document had been provided by DSO (Directorate of Special Operations). It was less security conscious and was given without DPA's (Director of Policy and Agents, who was usually in charge of the briefing of agents) knowledge. The fiasco was partly blamed on the re-organization done by Maxwell in Cairo.

The situation was catastrophic and this forced Kanellopoulos to leave hurriedly for the Middle East but others, such as Captain Kondouriotis, Major Aristides Pallis and Alexandros Zannas, were not so fortunate and were arrested and imprisoned.

This would have disastrous consequences for the future of Greece. The Atkinson list contained the names of resistance leaders representing the centre parties and moderate republicans. Their elimination would leave a vacuum that the communist leadership would be quick to fill and the seeds were sown for the civil war that would soon follow. The collapse of the ISINGLASS mission removed any hope SOE might have entertained of blocking the Corinth Canal. Luckily, Koutsoyannopoulos had managed to escape the net and was able to keep contact with Cairo.

Before the evacuation from Greece SOE had made contact, through Miss Elli Papadimitriou, a fierce opponent of Metaxas, with an underground group of republican officers led by the 'Red Colonel', Evripidis Bakirtzis, code name PROMETHEUS. Bakirtzis was born in 1897 in Seres, Macedonia; he was awarded the DSO for his service during the Great War. In the 1920s he had been Chief of Staff to General Plastiras. He was believed to be a social democrat and not a communist. During the war with Italy Bakirtzis wished to rejoin the army and appointed Lieutenant Commander Charalambos Koutsoyannopoulos of the Royal Hellenic Navy as his successor (PROMETHEUS II). As the war went on, the two PROMETHEUS would diverge in their way; the former was veering increasingly to the left and was found timid and untrustworthy by PROMETHEUS II who remained a staunch nationalist and republican.

It was Ian Pirie's intention to supply the organization with radios and explosives that could be used to carry out sabotage when Greece was occupied. After the fall of Greece a link was established with the SOE section in Turkey by using Gerasimos Alexatos, codename ODYSSEUS, a tobacco smuggler by profession, as a courier with caiques as mode of transportation. ODYSSEUS was regarded by SOE as a very reliable man. Later he was to suffer from bouts of insanity and had to be treated in an asylum in Cairo. He was reported to have recovered. Spotted by Major Michael Ward of SOE in a street in Athens just after the war, he disappeared very quickly in the crowd, leaving Ward under the impression that ODYSSEUS had probably reverted to his former profession.

On 12 November 1941 ODYSSEUS left Smyrna on the caique *Athanassios Miaoulis*, Captain Helias, the very same caique that Cumberlege had used to escape from Crete in May. The Greek courier landed at Tselevinia on the Peloponnese coast, facing the island of Hydra. In 1943 Cumberlege himself would choose the same area for his second attempt at the canal. From there, ODYSSEUS walked for three hours and reached the village of Galatas and then crossed over to the island of Poros. After a brief stay, he took the ferry to Athens where he established contact first with PROMETHEUS I and then with PROMETHEUS II.

PROMETHEUS II and his organization were highly regarded by British Intelligence and were for a time the only link they had with Greece. Naval sabotage was carried out by using limpets that could be affixed to the hulls of ships. They claimed to have sunk with explosives a 5,000-ton transport en route for Libya in November 1941 and damaged the Greek destroyer *Vasilefs Georgios* that had been scuttled in April 1941 but was now being raised and repaired by the Germans (later renamed *Hermes, ZG 3*).

Commander Koutsoyannopoulos was known to have a sound mind and provide reliable information. Though his sympathies lay with the republicans, he was equally distrustful of Colonel Zervas, whom he suspected of personal ambitions, and of the communists who professed to be the only valid resistance movement and were bent on eliminating all competition. Grudgingly, he would come to admit that EAM/ELAS was the most effective resistance organization. Yet he made efforts to unite all factions of the resistance. He had now made wireless contact with Cairo and SOE mounted three air-drop operations to supply him with weapons. These were operations CRACKLING I, near Kyme on the island of Euboa on 2/3 March 1942, CRACKLING II, near Diaselon in the Ghiona mountains, on 28/29 May 1942, and CRACKLING III, on a plain near Zamia on 12/13 June 1942. These had not been very successful as the aircraft involved had trouble locating the drop zones and in some cases missed them by thirty kilometres! Most of the weapons of the first shipment ended up in Italian hands, but two limpets were recovered and they provided the first opportunity for naval sabotage. More would follow, but in three attempts the detonators failed to work. PROMETHEUS II was keen on sabotaging the Corinth Canal but had found the limpets unreliable and the detonators he was supplied with had delays of only one hour (they were later provided with limpets with three-hour and nine-hour delays). To make them more reliable they had to be shortened to half an hour, but this was insufficient time for a ship to blow up in the middle of the canal; ships were often delayed for an hour or two before entering the waterway.

Cumberlege's Views on the Atkinson Affair
Cumberlege contracted typhoid and, on 17 May 1942, had to return to the United Kingdom on sick leave. While in London he was asked to give his opinion on the 'Atkinson affair' which had caused some bad blood between SOE and MI9. Since he had been working for both organizations in the Middle East, he was in a unique position to clear up some of the confusion that had arisen from this affair. At the crux of the matter was the loss of the submarine HMS *Triumph*, believed to have resulted from the lax security surrounding the mission. The Admiralty was expressing second thoughts on the use of submarines in clandestine operations.

At first Cumberlege preferred to give his opinion verbally and was reluctant to put it down on paper. However, when pressed by Major Boxshall, he produced a report which was highly critical of Major Simonds and Atkinson. He had taken a great risk in attacking the ambitious Simonds who was shortly to succeed Dudley Clarke at the head of MI9 in the Middle East. He also implied that a Greek named Vernikos, who was a caique owner, may have played a role in the loss of *Triumph*.

Emmanuel Vernikos was the owner of the large tug *Irene Vernikos* and had been employed by Captain MacDonald, NOIC Suda Bay, in an attempt to salvage the heavy cruiser HMS *York* in May 1941. His tug was left behind and, by a curious turn of fate, would be sunk by HMS *Triumph* on 24 November in Candia (although raised shortly after). Captain Parish and Captain Hildyard had been held in a prisoner of war camp at Galatas in Crete and had escaped on 7 June 1941. Vernikos who, like most Cretans, was of Venizelist sympathies and strongly pro-British (his wife was from Harbour Grace, Newfoundland), offered his services to help them reach the Middle East. They met with more stragglers including the Australian Captain Fred J. Embrey and, after a series of adventures which brought them to the southern Peloponnese and the island of Milos, they finally reached Turkey on 4 September 1941. Vernikos and Parish were both recruited by MI9 and returned to Greece to arrange for more evacuations.

Cumberlege expressed the greatest reservation, describing Vernikos as a man 'willing to sell himself to the greatest bidder'. His connection to operation ISINGLASS is not clear but he was suspected of having informed the Axis authorities. Before leaving for London, Mike met with Colonel Dudley Clarke, head of MI9 in Cairo, on 15 May and warned him about Vernikos. Clarke made a note of it and at the end of the day told him that the man had 'disappeared'.

Cumberlege's judgement may have been harsh. In fact, Vernikos, who had been sent to Athens by Captain Parish, was reportedly betrayed by an agent of

SOE and ended up in an Italian jail in Bari. He was liberated at the Italian armistice. Parish had the highest regard for Vernikos whom he described as 'possibly one of the least rewarded Allied officers operating in the Middle East with the British'. Pending further information, the matter was put to rest.

By May 1942 events were unfolding at a rapid pace. On the Russian front the German Army was renewing its offensive which would be carried out as far as Stalingrad. In the Pacific, the Imperial Japanese Navy was preparing an amphibious assault on the island of Midway. In the Libyan Desert, Rommel was poised to attack the Gazala positions and the importance of the Corinth Canal would again be emphasized.

Chapter 12

The Corinth Canal and the Battle of El Alamein

In the spring of 1942 the Corinth Canal was in focus again as the latest round of the battle for Libya was developing. The island of Crete and the Peloponnese were providing the Axis air forces with suitable bases to harass the flank of the Eighth Army and to threaten any attempt to re-supply Malta from the east. At the same time, Colonel William J. 'Wild Bill' Donovan of the newly born OSS (Office of Strategic Services, forerunner of the CIA) was vying for increased American participation in clandestine operations in the eastern Mediterranean. This was met with mixed feelings at ISLD and at SOE headquarters, but American material support was becoming essential to win the battle for North Africa. Long-range American-built Liberator aircraft were sought to parachute supplies to the different missions in the field and the trade-off had to be accepted.

During the winter of 1940-1941 Donovan had travelled to the Balkans and Middle East on a scouting expedition on behalf of President Roosevelt. He had returned with the conviction that the area deserved the full attention of the United States with oil not its least feature. American and British policies were not in complete accord; the British government preferred its reliance on established monarchies while the Americans were sympathetic to the nationalist movements. In April 1942 Lieutenant (later Lieutenant Commander) Turner H. McBaine USNR, was the first OSS representative to be sent to Cairo. He was shortly joined by Lieutenant Commander Joseph Leete, a former professor at the American University in Cairo, who was fluent in Arabic. It can be said that the organization was born in Cairo and it was there that its first steps were taken. McBaine would prove a most successful liaison officer with British Intelligence and he reached an agreement with ISLD that they would share intelligence with the budding organization. The Americans were new at the game but would learn fast.

Since 1941 another American officer from the Cairo Embassy had had an unforeseen impact on the war in North Africa. Colonel Bonner Fellers, the American Military Attaché, had been kept informed regularly by the British authorities of the various operations and military plans. He duly relayed the information in detail to Washington but the State Department was unaware that its embassy in Rome had been burgled by the Italian Intelligence Service and the codebooks photographed. Rommel had made good use of this intelligence of strategic value, as well as operational intelligence gathered from mobile radio intercept units until one fell into the hands of an Australian infantry unit after imprudently operating close to the front line. Whether decrypts had revealed this leak is not certain, but it would have been awkward to alert the persons involved without breaching the ULTRA secret.

It is certain that decrypts were revealing increased enemy traffic in the Corinth Canal and SOE London received a project to block it from their Istanbul station. They advised Cairo that they would send them the information available to them and that a plan ought to be made. Station 333, operated by PROMETHEUS II, had received some limpets and it was suggested that they be affixed to a ship at Kalamaki just before she entered the canal. On 25 May London had told them to put the operation on hold until the 'other plan' (this may have referred to Operation THURGOLAND) was ready and to synchronize both operations for maximum effect. The next day Cairo cabled David Pawson in Istanbul requesting him to make discreet enquiries on the Papadia bridge and the Corinth Canal (see questionnaire in Appendix F).

At the time Pawson was absent and on his way to Cairo; Captain Harris, his assistant, forwarded the demand to PROMETHEUS II. On 30 May he again cabled PROMETHEUS II enquiring if the latter had made any plan to block the canal. Republican agents had reconnoitred the canal and reported that only government-controlled vessels were allowed through, and only during daylight hours. Limpets had recently been delivered to Kymi, Euboa Island, and it was hoped that these could be used.

According to Koutsoyannopoulos, in a report of his activities compiled in mid-1943, an attempt was made on the Corinth Canal by using two saboteurs and a small fishing vessel. The plan was communicated to Cairo on 6 June 1942 and revealed the intention to use a caique to go to the forbidden zone of Kalamaki, at the eastern entrance of the canal. Once there, saboteurs could swim to plant a limpet on one of the ships awaiting passage. If this was not possible, then they might stage a collision with a ship before it entered the waterway and take advantage of the commotion to stick the limpet to the hull. In both cases it was impossible to time the explosion to occur when the vessel was inside the waterway. However, the attempt came to naught when the Italians stopped the caique and the two men were arrested. Apparently, one of them was named Maryelis (first name unknown) and was sentenced to a thirty-year prison term. Perhaps to escape a death sentence, he betrayed several PROMETHEUS II collaborators.

The limpets provided at this time were found unreliable. An Italian ship was limpeted in Piraeus on 26 May with a nine-hour delay fuse and, two days later, a German tanker was sabotaged with a three-day delay fuse. Neither was reported to have exploded. It was decided that no more attempt should be made on the Corinth Canal until the fuse problem was corrected.

In the meantime Mike Cumberlege had left Cairo for London. One source implied that he was returning on medical leave to recover from his bout of typhoid. This may have been partly true, but SOE war diaries clearly show that he left Cairo on 11 May for London, and perhaps even for Washington, to look for suitable vessels for his para-naval activities. SOE London had been surprised at the visit and wanted to be sure that he would consult them before undertaking such a mission.

Cumberlege had just left Cairo when the military situation in the Middle East took a turn for the worse. In the preceding months unrelenting air attacks had reduced fortress Malta to impotence. Surviving submarines from the Tenth Flotilla had been forced to evacuate to Alexandria and then to Haifa and Beirut. Efforts to maintain a minimum fighter air defence were barely succeeding. Rommel had taken the advantage afforded by the lull in the attacks against his lines of communications to reinforce his forces in Libya. In the last week of May 1942, he launched his attack on the British Gazala Line. Within days, he had achieved a breakthrough and the British Eighth Army was being destroyed, with surviving elements beating a hasty withdrawal towards Egypt. At Bir Hakeim, a Free French brigade held its position for thirteen days, buying precious time for the retreat of the Eighth Army. On 21 June, fortress Tobruk which had been held by the Australians for eight months in 1941, succumbed in one day. Axis forces had taken some 33,000 prisoners and large stocks of fuel, weapons and ammunitions.

Rather than consolidating his positions, Rommel elected to pursue the British forces despite his communication lines being stretched to the limit. On 28 June, Mersa Matruh fell into Axis hands. *Panzerarmee Afrika* appeared to be unstoppable but General Auchinleck had anticipated such an event and prepared his stand by heavily fortifying the El Alamein defences. Protected by the Alam El Halfa ridge and the Qatarra Depression, the position could not be turned easily. On 1 July the German tanks reached El Alamein, about 100 kilometres short of Alexandria, but they lacked fuel and ammunition and their advance was finally checked. The front had now stabilized on the El Alamein line with both sides strengthening their positions by digging trenches and planting huge defensive minefields.

The problem of severing Rommel's supply lines was foremost in British planning. In June, an attempt to supply Malta, Operation VIGOROUS, had failed. It was only in August 1942 that the PEDESTAL convoy, despite terrible losses, managed to get through with enough fuel to resurrect the island as an operational base. Submarines returned to the base, as well as Swordfish torpedo-bombers and Wellington long-range bombers.

The growing threat to Axis lines of communications with Libya emphasized the importance of the Corinth Canal route. The route was not without danger but it was the safest. It was outside the range of the Swordfish torpedo-bombers based in Malta but within reach of the Wellington heavy bombers. However, an attack would have to be timed perfectly as they would have only a short time above their targets. It was also at the maximum range of the small U-class submarines operating from Malta and the larger T-class submarines, which had now relocated to Beirut.

Up to the beginning of July Axis supplies to the front were sent from Italy or Tripoli to Benghazi and some of it redirected from there to Tobruk. An important convoy sailed from Taranto for Benghazi; it consisted of three fast transports, the German *Ankara* and the Italians *Nino Bixio* and *Monviso*. This convoy had a strong escort and was covered by two Italian light cruisers and four destroyers. Despite its existence being known through ULTRA decrypts, there was little interference from Malta or Egypt and it arrived safely.

But Benghazi was now too far from the front line and the next convoy, consisting of six transports, was sent via the Corinth Canal and, after stops at Piraeus and Suda, arrived at Tobruk on 10 July. The convoy was formed by the tanker *Alberto Fassio*, the German transports *Delos* and *Santa Fé* and the Italian *Città di Alessandria*, *Città di Agrigento* and *Città di Savona*, escorted by the German destroyer *ZG 3* (*Hermes*), the Italians *Mitragliere* and *Turbine* and the torpedo-boats *Sirio* and *Cassiopea*. Once Tobruk was reached, troops, fuel and stores would be unloaded to lighters that would ferry them to Mersa Matruh. From this time on, almost all supplies to the El Alamein front would use this route. At one time or another the *Regia Marina* would commit to the escort of these convoys some sixty destroyers and torpedo-boats and a number of gunboats and patrol vessels.

Mersa Matruh had a small harbour with limited unloading capacities, but the Germans had developed a type of motorized lighter which could address this problem. These were the F-lighters armed with a 75mm gun and some light anti-aircraft guns; they could carry about seventy tons of cargo. Their shallow draught allowed them to disembark supplies directly onto the beach and they were a difficult target for torpedoes, which usually ran under them. The Italians copied the design and referred to them as Mz-boats (for *Motozattere*). Larger ships would be directed to Tobruk or Derna. Benghazi had the largest harbour in Cyrenaica but it was strewn with wrecks and was now over 1,000 kilometres from the front. Other ships would use the coastal route, but the main hub was Tobruk. From Naples, Taranto or Brindisi, the vessels would cut across the Ionian Sea, follow a coastal route from Corfu to Patras, then cross the Corinth Canal. They usually stopped at Piraeus and at Suda before continuing to Tobruk. The poor sea-keeping qualities of the F-lighters forced them to use the Corinth Canal route, which afforded them more protection from bad weather.

About 100 F-lighters, two-thirds Italian and one-third German, were committed to this task. A third of them would be lost, most of them to air attacks from Beaufighters of No. 201 Group RAF assisted by ASV (Air to Surface Vessel radar) Hudsons and Bisleys from 15 Squadron South African Air Force (SAAF), as well as Swordfish and Albacore bombers from the Fleet Air Arm.

The Germans lost no time. On the evening of 29 June, within hours of the capture of Mersa Matruh, the first F-lighters arrived from Sidi Barrani and Tobruk. Sailing vessels would also be used and most of them were impounded Greek caiques.

Larger transports had been sent to Mersa Matruh but there was only one quay to unload and only vessels of about 2,000 tons could enter the small harbour. In the afternoon of 11 July the German transport *Brook* was hit and set afire in the harbour by Beaufort bombers. Another German transport, *Sturla*, had escaped the bombing; she managed to unload her cargo but was sunk by the destroyer HMS *Beaufort* as she was leaving the harbour the same night.

In the early hours of 20 July the main quay was rendered useless when a bombardment carried out by the light cruisers HMSs *Dido* and *Euryalus* and escorting destroyers sank the Italian transport *Città di Agrigento* while she was alongside. Thereafter, traffic could only be unloaded at a fishing vessel quay and only by the F-lighters or sailing vessels. Travelling singly, F-lighters or Mz-boats were vulnerable to air attack but in convoys of four or five their combined firepower could prove a significant deterrent, even to a determined airman. Although some F-lighters had reached Tripoli via Sicily and then followed the coastal route to Cyrenaica, their seaworthiness and range were limited and they could not make the trip to Tobruk directly from Italy. They were now exclusively routed through the Corinth Canal.

With Axis forces now close to Alexandria, SOE was multiplying its operations behind enemy lines. For Axis forces the supply situation had become desperate. Rommel's supply lines were now extended and very vulnerable. His main port where stores could be unloaded was now Tobruk, over 500 kilometres to the west. He was within range of all British airfields in the Egyptian Delta. His closest airfields were small airstrips at Mersa Matruh, about 100 miles to the west of the El Alamein position, but the Luftwaffe and the Regia Aeronautica had few forces to spare for them.

In Alexandria preparations were being made for the demolition of the port. The Mediterranean Fleet was being relocated to Haifa and Beirut. This period of febrile preparations for evacuation was to be known as 'the Flap'. Wednesday 1 July would become known as 'Ash Wednesday' for the columns of smoke that were seen in Cairo as the British burned their documents, including many SOE files. SOE headquarters were temporarily moved to Jerusalem but returned to Cairo the following month when the front appeared to hold.

Vice Admiral Sir Henry Harwood had been appointed as the head of the

Mediterranean Fleet in the Levant while Cunningham remained in overall command in the Mediterranean theatre. Harwood's appointment was viewed favourably at SOE headquarters as he appeared to have a positive view of their service. SOE had been promised fast motor launches which could be used for their communications with Crete and mainland Greece. Four such vessels belonging to the 27th Motor Launch Flotilla had arrived at Gibraltar but they could not make the direct passage through the Mediterranean as Malta had just been neutralized by the Axis air forces. They might be sent around Africa but then this would probably wear out their motors and these would have to be replaced. Until then submarines and caiques remained the only viable option to deliver delicate cargoes such as mines.

On 22 July 1942 the Admiralty requested Cumberlege, who was still in London, to produce a new plan for the blocking of the Corinth Canal. This would become known as Operation LOCKSMITH. Mike diligently put himself to work and within ten days had produced a preliminary study.

The demands to block the canal were now becoming urgent. MO4 in Cairo had received a similar demand from Admiral Harwood. They now requested that SOE London follow the procedure and transmit any request from the Admiralty or the Air Ministry through proper channels, i.e. to the Commander-in-Chief Mediterranean who could then pass it on to MO4.

On the afternoon of 17 August, with Operation PEDESTAL barely concluded, the matter of the Corinth Canal was raised once again by Vice Admiral Sir Henry Moore, Vice Chief of Naval Staff, at a meeting of the Chiefs of Staff. He recalled that the canal had been bombed the previous year and enquired if it could be attacked again with heavy bombs. Air Chief Marshal Sir Wilfrid Freeman, Vice Chief of Air Staff, who chaired the committee, was asked what type of bombs were envisaged and stated that at least 4,000lb bombs would be required. The Royal Air Force was then asked to bomb the waterway and damage as many dredgers as possible to slow down any attempt at clearing the canal. But all available bombers were now busy meeting more pressing demands to stop Axis forces at El Alamein, as this was the most immediate threat. It was especially important to prevent German reinforcements from being sent to North Africa via the canal and Crete to assist Rommel in his drive towards Alexandria. The following day the news that the Maikop oilfields in the Caucasus had fallen into German hands reached the Chiefs of Staff. This raised the possibility that Axis tankers would be transferred from the Mediterannean to the Black Sea. Renewed efforts had to be made to stop this traffic and would underline the necessity to block the Corinth Canal.

July and August were turbulent months for MO4. With Egypt on the brink of being lost, and perhaps even the whole Middle East, the organization was busy setting up cells to operate after occupation and even locating beaches on the Red Sea coast that were suitable for evacuation. At the same time, MO4 itself was being re-organized. On 13 August Lord Glenconner arrived in Cairo to replace Maxwell at the head of the organization. The unpopular but very efficient Brigadier C. M. Keble was to become his chief of staff and Colonel Guy Tamplin the Head of Country's Sections. In charge of operations in Greece was Ian Pirie, head of B6 section (Greece Country Section). In royalist quarters, Pirie was distrusted and suspected of leftist sympathies and Major John M. Stevens would replace him before the end of the year. In the coming months Pirie's considerable experience in Greek affairs would be sorely missed.

In September 1942 the British would carry out a bold raid on Tobruk, Operation AGREEMENT, in an attempt to sever the Axis lines of communication, but seldom was an operation so ill-served by poor weather intelligence. The submarine *Taku* failed to land a commando party due to the rough seas and, worse, its periscope was seen by the Italians who were fully alerted when the main body of commandos attacked and they were repelled with heavy losses. The lesson was well learnt and thereafter the Greek resistance and the SOE agents would be enlisted to release weather balloons and submit weather reports.

Eighth Army was poised to take the counter-offensive at El Alamein. No effort was to be spared to sever the enemy's supply lines. We have seen earlier (see Chapter 9) that, on 26 August 1942, the RAF and USAAF Liberator bombers had attempted to block the canal but had failed. It was now SOE's turn to tackle the problem.

Chapter 13

New Plans: THURGOLAND and LOCKSMITH

Operation THURGOLAND

The Admiralty had never lost interest in blocking the Corinth Canal and the Commander-in-Chief in the Levant, Vice Admiral Harwood, reiterated this. British Intelligence knew that most of the supplies reaching Rommel were now passing through the Corinth Canal and to choke the waterway could have a major effect on the Desert War.

Major Quill RM, of Naval Intelligence, approached MO4 and suggested that they might use an acquaintance of his, Major Ioannis Tsigantes, who was described as 'an officer of enterprise and courage and could prove eminently suitable for such an operation'. Major Ioannis Tsigantes and his elder brother, Colonel Christodoulos Tsigantes, had been involved in the 1935 Venizelist coup d'état attempt and had been cashiered from the Army by the Metaxas government. In September 1942 Minister of Defence Kanellopoulos would appoint Colonel Tsigantes as the leader of the Greek Sacred Squadron. MO4 accepted the suggestion and allocated the sum of £4,000 for a Corinth Canal operation, which received the code name of THURGOLAND.

Panayotis Kanellopoulos, a university professor very respected for his political views, had been forced to flee from Greece following the Antiparos debacle and had joined the Greek government in exile. It was hoped that this would help make the king and his prime minister, Tsouderos, more palatable to the Greek people. The population was reported to be increasingly disenchanted with their king and his government, associated with the dictatorship of Metaxas, who had not shared in their suffering.

Appointed as Minister of Defence, Kanellopoulos had been informed of the THURGOLAND mission. He now asked MO4 if Tsigantes could contact the remnants of his organization in Greece in an effort to resurrect the resistance movement. He was to provide Major Tselos with money and contact the Kozani organization. This was accepted, provided it did not interfere with the Corinth Canal operation.

On 3 August HM Submarine *Proteus*, Lieutenant R. L. Alexander RN, landed nine Greek agents on a beach at Kalamata in the southern Peloponnese in Operation WATER MELON. They were led by Tsigantes, now known as SOE

agent A/H92, and his organization would be known as MIDAS 614. The original
team consisted of:

Major (Inf.) Ioannis Tsigantes
Captain (Inf.) Panayotis Rogakos
Lieutenant (Reserve Cavalry) Vassilios Zakynthinos (who later joined EAM)
Lieutenant (Reserve) Fotios Manolopoulos
Warrant Officer Dimitrios Gyftopoulos
Artillery Warrant Officer Spyros Kotsis
Sergeant Konstantinou Roussos (wireless operator)
RHAF Private J. Moraitis
Civilian J. Miltiadis Giannacopoulos (aka 'Aristides').

They were to find a way to block the Corinth Canal by sinking a vessel with
the use of limpets. At MO4 headquarters in Cairo, Captain Francis Noel-Baker,
who was fluent in Greek, was put in charge of the operation. THURGOLAND
had also been instructed to infiltrate Greek-speaking Serbs into Yugoslavia to
contact the Mihajlovic organization. A second group of agents was to follow in
September.

Unfortunately, during the landing at Nymfy (Laconia Bay in the southern
Peloponnese), one of the three wireless sets and the limpets, or 'toys' as they
were referred to in official correspondence, were dropped accidentally in the
water and could not be retrieved. The party was divided in two groups; the first
reached Athens after an exhausting trip by rowboat; in the meantime Tsigantes
had met Koulis Sideris from Paganea and had hired him with his caique *Aghia
Paraskevi* to bring the stores and the remainder of the party to Athens. The 26-
year-old Sideris had done some work for MI9 since August 1941 and would
prove a most resourceful fellow. He was destined to play a key role in the
attempt to block the Corinth Canal.

On 6 September they arrived at the capital. Major Tsigantes made various
contacts in an effort to unite Greek resistance but the lack of explosives put the
Corinth Canal operation on hold. On 29 September a caique carrying limpets
was sent to replace them. Tsigantes took advantage of this free time to involve
himself in Greek politics.

In retrospect, an officer of higher rank should have been sent, as the major
ruffled a few feathers by trying to order around colonels and generals. If his
courage was never doubted, discretion was not his foremost quality and, within
a short time, the presence and purpose of his mission was known throughout
Athens. It is surprising that the THURGOLAND organization survived so long
despite the lax security. Colonel Tselos, who had the trust of Kanellopoulos,
was so upset that he fled to Cairo to contact the Greek minister of defence.
Tsigantes felt obliged to send on his heels a courier to defend his own point of
view.

By this time Lord Glenconner had arrived in Cairo to take over the reins of MO4 from Maxwell. The organization was facing criticism from Greek Prime Minister Tsouderos that it was partial to republicans and communists and opposed to the return of the king in Greece after the war. Pirie was pointed out as the main culprit and, although his knowledge was judged essential for operations in Greece, Glenconner agreed to remove him by the end of the year. SOE's charter had been to carry out acts of sabotage behind enemy lines. It could be argued that the republicans and communists were carrying out the resistance to Axis occupation while royalists had been conspicuously absent in participating in any form of opposition, and some had even collaborated with the Germans.

On 26 August, with the fighting along the El Alamein line still raging, the RAF had made an effort to block the canal but without causing serious damage. The same day, London informed MO4 in Cairo that the RAF was unable to attack the canal for the next fortnight and that they should require their agents to sink or damage as many dredgers as possible to slow any attempt to clear the canal.

MO4 replied that no attempt would be made to sink any dredger, as the bombing had been ineffective. London then suggested that a caique should be hired to carry out as many passages of the canal as possible in bona-fide trade so as to allay the suspicions of Axis authorities and then could be used at the opportune time to carry out a sabotage operation. Cumberlege may well have suggested this idea in preparation for his own operation.

Designing a Suitable Mine

Blocking the Corinth Canal by using limpets was unlikely to be very effective. The limpets available at this time had about ten pounds of explosives and delay fuses of three hours, nine hours, or three days. The delay mechanism varied greatly according to the water temperature. With the transit of the canal done in as little as twenty-five minutes, it was difficult to time an explosion to occur when the ship was inside the waterway. The limpet could not be expected to sink a medium-sized ship and to sink a smaller vessel might not cause the Italians much difficulty in clearing. Mike Cumberlege thought that this method would only have blocked it for about a week; he sought means to produce more permanent results.

The Royal Navy had developed a human torpedo copied from the Italian design and the model was now ready for operational use. In October 1942 two of these torpedoes, known as 'chariots', had been attached to the Norwegian fishing vessel *Arthur* with the intention of attacking the German battleship *Tirpitz* anchored in the Trondheim Fjord. The vessel had managed to sneak in the fjord and successfully passed German control only to encounter bad weather that caused the two weapons to break adrift and sink to the bottom of the fjord. It was a frustrating turn of events with the target only ten miles away.

The operation against the Corinth Canal was also to use a fishing vessel that would enter the waterway and surreptitiously drop a mine in the middle of it. However, there is no indication that chariots were ever considered for the operation, although, by the time the LOCKSMITH team would sail, chariots had been used successfully at Palermo and Tripoli.

Under Cumberlege's instructions and, with the Admiralty's approval, a special mine was built at the Admiralty's Mining School in Havant; it weighed 45 pounds, of which twenty-five were high explosives. It would be detonated by the magnetic field of a ship at a distance of less than five feet and since the canal was twenty-six feet deep, this meant that it required a ship with at least a twenty-one-foot draught to work. It is quite possible that the device was designed with the assistance of Chester Beatty, the mining magnate, who had assisted SOE in the past with similar problems. The LOCKSMITH party was to bring five of these mines to be used for the operation. In addition, five counter-mines weighing 65lb each would also be added. They could be expected to detonate in sympathy with the magnetic mines to cause maximum damage to the target.

The mine and counter mine were believed to be powerful enough to break the back of the vessel which could not be patched up and raised but would have to be cut by acetylene torches, a long process. However, Cumberlege hoped that a large ship, sunk in the middle of the canal, could block it long enough for the RAF to complete its destruction. The Admiralty now sponsored this scheme; it is highly probable that the Director of Naval Intelligence, Admiral Godfrey, a personal friend of Mike, helped push it through. It was proposed that LOCKSMITH might work in tandem with THURGOLAND to achieve its objective.

Selecting the Team

Agent D/H.89, as Mike Cumberlege was known, initially proposed that the LOCKSMITH team should consist of four agents, a British officer, two Greeks and himself; he revised his estimate later to at least five agents and suggested the following as suitable for the operation:[15]

- Captain Michael Lowe RE, an expert in sabotage and keen mountaineer.
- Lieutenant Beckinsale RNVR, a veteran of two Crete trips.
- Rhodesian Sergeant James Cook Steele MM, of the Black Watch, who had made two trips with him to Crete. Steele was born in Meltsetter, in the Eastern District of Southern Rhodesia on 29 October 1918. He would be the youngest member of the quartet. He had married Patricia Alice Dennis on 4 September 1939 and had enlisted the same day in the 1st Service Battalion. In April 1940 he

was posted to 2nd Battalion The Royal Highland Regiment (Black Watch). We have seen in previous chapters that he had served with Mike on *Dolphin II, Athanassios Miaoulis, Hedgehog* and *Escampador*. For his role in para-naval activities, he had been awarded the Military Medal in September 1942. But Steele had temporarily disappeared and was listed as a deserter. He would make the final selection. It is possible that Cumberlege had interceded in his favour as charges of desertion appear to have been dropped.

- Sergeant Crook MM who had escaped from Crete with Commander Pool and had made two trips to Crete with Lieutenant Campbell DSC.
- A Free French officer, Captain V. Attius, who spoke fluent Italian and would be the radio operator. (This was actually Captain Victor Attias who had belonged to the Mounier/Breuillac network in Tunisia. In 1941, the organization had carried out sabotage missions on Italian ships, see Appendix H.)
- A Czech corporal in charge of consumable goods and food.
Cumberlege was thinking of Jean [Jan] Kotrba who had worked for six years as a deckhand on his yacht in the Mediterranean before the war. He would describe him as having 'an intimate knowledge of the Mediterranean where he has spent many years as a sailing yacht hand. He speaks a number of languages. He knows particularly well the area in which the proposed operation is to take place and which, naturally at the moment, it is impossible to divulge. He is a very sound loyal young man with plenty of initiative and the typical Czech mechanical mentality and interest in all kinds of engines and gadgets.'
Kotrba was born in Dresden on 11 August 1913. He had sailed with Mike on the yacht *Landfall*. In November 1939 Kotrba, who was then working as a cook at Juan-les-Pins in the south of France, had joined the Czech Army in exile and was now a corporal serving at the Driving School of the Czech Independent Brigade. He had married in 1941 and would use the pseudonyms of John Davies, his wife Eileen's maiden name, or Scott, to hide his Czech origin in case of capture. He spoke Czech, English, French, German and Italian. He would also make the final selection.
- A Greek naval petty officer who was a personal friend, Antonios Fakaros, had been used by Admiral Sakellariou for a special mission in Crete and would be invaluable as none of the others spoke Greek.
- A sixth member (optional) could be a Greek seaman who could act as general hand. Cumberlege suggested Strati Bournakes who had lived near the Corinth Canal and had sailed with him on the *Athanassios Miaoulis* during his escape from Crete.

By 26 September the team consisted of Jan Kotrba in charge of food supplies, Captain Michael Lowe of the Royal Engineers, who was to take care of the sabotage equipment, and Captain Attias, responsible for the wireless equipment. That same day Major Boxshall spoke to Cumberlege and asked him to provide a timetable for the operation. For unknown reasons Lowe was unable to join. The selection of Attias did not work out either as the Free French were short of manpower. Cumberlege would use instead Corporal Handley of the Royal Signals. The reasons for picking him are obscure, as he does not seem to have been known by Cumberlege, as were his other choices. Thomas Edward Vasey Handley, son of Frank and Mary Handley, was born on 23 September 1914 in Sedbergh, Yorkshire. He was described as six foot tall and weighing 170lb. He had been a librarian before the war and, by coincidence, had attended the same Sedbergh School as Major Michael Ward of SOE who would later investigate the fate of the agents of LOCKSMITH.

The Czech minister of defence released Kotrba for a period of six months at the salary of £25 per month, starting from 5 October. Cumberlege had also thought of inserting with the team a political officer and suggested Second Lieutenant Stott, a New Zealander who had escaped from Greece in 1941 and had made valuable contacts. He thought that Stott might accompany them and could be used to procure a caique instead of THURGOLAND. It is likely that, in December 1941, Cumberlege had met Stott in Alexandria when the latter was debriefed following his escape from Greece.

Donald J. Stott, then a sergeant of 5th New Zealand Field Regiment, had been wounded and captured on Crete in 1941. Brought to the Kokkinia prisoner of war camp near Athens on 4 August 1941, he managed to escape with his friend Bob Morton by pole-vaulting over the wall. They went into hiding and eluded the vigilance of German and Italian police for several months. On 24 November both men were picked up with nineteen other escapees by the submarine HMS *Thorn*, an operation organized by Lieutenant Atkinson who would later lead the ISINGLASS operation and cause the Antiparos disaster. In 1943 Stott would play an important part in the destruction of the Asopos viaduct and make contact with the Gestapo in Athens, carrying out a reconnaissance of the Corinth Canal in the process, but more on that later. Stott's selection did not work out as he had already left on a mission behind enemy lines.

While Mike was busy finalizing his team, his friend Rear Admiral Godfrey, Director of Naval Intelligence, was promoted to vice admiral on 15 September, but dismissed the same day from his post. Godfrey had always been very supportive of Mike and his absence from the scene came at an awkward time; nevertheless the operation would proceed without his blessing.

Selection of the Landing Area

An important question to be resolved was the selection of a suitable landing spot in Greece. The vicinity of the Corinth Canal was desirable but at the same time could be heavily patrolled. Cumberlege had suggested the nearly deserted island of Kyra, seven miles north of Methana and near Nea Epidavros, where he had many friends. A British escapee who remains anonymous appears to have been heavily questioned; the questionnaire is included in the LOCKSMITH papers. He had been extricated from Greece by the caique *Athanassios Miaoulis* near Cape Skyli after walking in the hills all the way from Corinth. This was most likely the Australian Johnny Sachs, who had escaped from the Poros area at that time. *Athanassios Miaoulis* was the same caique that Cumberlege had used to make his getaway from Crete in May 1941.

It appears the Eastern Peloponnese was heavily favoured and the areas considered were:

(1) The Methana Peninsula, to the west of Poros.
(2) Nea Epidavros, mid-way between the Corinth Canal and Poros.
(3) Ermioni area on the Hydra Channel with Cape Skyli.

Since the commandos were to be landed by submarine, it was vital that an absolutely safe landing place was found. The Methana Peninsula and Nea Epidavros were certainly more dangerous for a submarine approach and the Ermioni area was more suitable.

Cumberlege had personally made a thorough reconnaissance of the Cape Skyli area on 8 April 1941 and had frequently sailed between the Kelevini islands before the war. In his report he described the area as

> treeless and consists of broken limestone covered with bushes and heather. The small bay, protected on its southern side by the Kelevini Islands is sometimes used as a harbour of refuge for caiques temporarily weather bound. There are no buildings and no communications to the point. There are quite fair hideouts among the rocks. Vessels use and sail through the Kelevini Pass. Northerly (Meltemme) winds prevail in summer and landing from folboats [kayaks] could be made, particularly inside of the Supia Islet 1½ miles westward of the cape. The water along the coast is deep and clear of danger [thus could safely be used by submarines].

In one of his trips to Greece, the courier ODYSSEUS had been landed at Tselevinia near Cape Skyli, apparently on the same trip made by *Athanassios Miaoulis* and this probably added weight to the final choice.

On 1 October, as preparations were taking shape, *Marinegruppenkommando Süd* was being informed of the imminent passage through the canal of the Greek transport *Petrarkis Nomikos* of 7,020 tons. However, the ship was drawing full load 8.24 metres and the canal maximum depth was reported at the time of being only 7 metres, it was suggested that she make the passage only half-loaded. This underlined the main fault in the design of Mike's mine. It was supposed to detonate when a ship would pass within five feet of it but the uneven bottom of the canal made the prospect more difficult.

Hundreds of miles away, on the German-occupied island of Sark (one of the Channel Islands), a British commando raid (Operation BASALT) had netted five German prisoners and some would be shot while in custody. Unbeknownst to the LOCKSMITH commandos, this seemingly unrelated operation would weigh heavily on their destinies.

The Team Departs
While in London Mike had been reunited with his family. He also took the time to meet with the widow of John Pendlebury to express his sympathies.

By 27 October he expected to have all the equipment tested and ready. The Admiralty had arranged for a special flight to take the stores to Cairo and, on 4 November, the leader of the LOCKSMITH party had met Wing Commander Vaughan, head of Movements V, Air Ministry, to make the final arrangements. He was told that he could bring up to 3,000lb of stores and the plane could take off on 7 November. For security reasons, the stores had to be marked with the code name TORCHLIGHT instead of LOCKSMITH, but this proved to be an error and they had to be re-marked; their weight was less than 2,000lb and included six wireless sets. More stores were to follow, but they arrived a few days later. Finally, the team was told that they could take off in the afternoon of 18 November but, upon arrival at the airfield, they were informed that they could not take all the stores. After some intense arguments they finally decided to leave behind three wireless sets.

On the morning of 19 November the LOCKSMITH team and stores took off from Lyneham airfield for Egypt via Gibraltar; they arrived in Cairo on 21 November. By this time Axis forces were in full retreat in North Africa, but this had not diminished the importance of the canal. The whole Desert campaign had been a seesaw affair and the pendulum could still swing back. British generals had the greatest respect for Rommel and he could still redress the situation. It was not realized at the time that the field marshal had made his last stab at Egypt and the Suez Canal. Yet, with Britain still bent on drawing Turkey into the war on the side of the Allies, the blocking of the Corinth Canal would significantly hinder the supply of Axis forces in the Aegean.

The tribulations of Major Tsigantes
By 27 September Tsigantes had cabled that the operation to block the canal was almost ready. The next day Cairo sent his report to London outlining eleven methods to achieve the operation but at the same time admitting none could be

counted on to achieve more than a temporary interruption. It was deemed that the operation must succeed or not be tried at all; any failure could only lead to increased security from Axis forces, making it more difficult for subsequent attempts. Finally, Tsigantes had already sent details of his own plan to block the canal by a courier through Turkey. The man was arrested by the Turks in Chesme on 27 September but was released a few days later and the plan reached Cairo on 9 October and was approved. The execution of the operation was still very important as British Intelligence estimated that nine tenths of Rommel's seaborne reinforcements came through the canal and the third and final battle of El Alamein was still two weeks away.

On 3 November the submarine HHMS *Nereus*, Commander A. Rallis, landed three agents at Kymi, Euboa Island, with the purpose of assisting the Tsigantes mission (this was Operation HOLLYM also known as THURGOLAND II). They were:

Lieutenant of the Reserve Afentarios Maraslis
Corporal Theodoros Liakos (wireless operator)
Matthaeou Andronikos (wireless operator)

Maraslis had been trained at the weapon school in Maadi, a suburb of Cairo, and had volunteered for commando work. The three men had been briefed personally by Ian Pirie before their departure.

The operation encountered some difficulty right from the start as the submarine did not land the three men at the agreed point. The team brought two more wireless sets (one for THURGOLAND and one for the Myers mission) and one and a half ton of stores (sixty-four cases) for THURGOLAND, including small arms, hand grenades, explosives and limpets. They linked up with MIDAS 614 in Athens. Lieutenant Maraslis had been trained in sabotage with the express purpose of blocking the Corinth Canal and had been ordered to remind Major Tsigantes of his mission, but the latter refused to use him and substituted Lieutenant Vassilios Zakynthinos and Warrant Officer Gyftopoulos.

In North Africa the remnants of *Panzerarmee Afrika* were withdrawing from the El Alamein positions, followed very cautiously by the British Eighth Army. Most Italian divisions were being sacrificed; they lacked trucks as their own had been commandeered by the Germans.

On 6 November one last convoy sailed from Piraeus for Tobruk; it consisted of the Italian transports *D'Annunzio* and *Foscolo*, escorted by the destroyers *Geniere* and *Camicia Nera* and the torpedo boats *Orsa* and *Aretusa*. It had sailed from Brindisi via the Corinth Canal. It never reached its destination as it was recalled early the next morning. Tobruk was being abandoned. The submarine *Antonio Sciesa*, carrying stores and ammunition, was one of the last vessels to reach the base; she had been hit by three bombs during a USAAF raid and had to be scuttled. From now on, convoys to Africa would find their destination consistently changing until the long retreat of Axis forces stopped in Tunisia where they would make their last stand. The Corinth Canal traffic would no longer play a role in supplying North Africa, yet its importance in supplying Crete, the islands of the Aegean and the Dodecanese had not diminished.

On 11 November Tsigantes was pressed by Cairo as to the status of THURGOLAND; the operation was now of the utmost importance as Rommel was in full retreat and it was essential to prevent reinforcements from reaching him. By this time Anglo-American forces had landed in Morocco and Algeria and the battle for North Africa was about to enter its final phase.

The Greek Resistance and Gorgopotamos
PROMETHEUS II, Commander Koutsoyannopoulos RHN, brought together the bands of ELAS (Communist), led by Ares Veloukhiotis, and EDES (Republican), led by Colonel Napoleon Zervas. With the help of Colonel Myers of the Royal Engineers, this collaboration brought about the destruction of the Gorgopotamos viaduct on the night of 24/25 November in Operation HARLING. This was an important success for SOE but the communist partnership with Zervas was short-lived. Within a few weeks, ELAS, which had cleverly included moderate republicans in its ranks to masquerade its true intentions, was busy eliminating all other Greek resistance organizations in an effort to pave the way for a communist takeover of Greece at the end of the war. At the same time, the increasing strength of EAM/ELAS had made it the main opponent to the occupation forces. Threatened with extinction, some of the independent resistance bands formed a tacit but unholy alliance with the enemy and reinforced, at least in some quarters, the view that EAM/ELAS was the sole valid resistance movement. The communists were disciplined and well organized but collaboration with SOE would prove difficult. They distrusted the British government who favoured the return of the king while the majority of Greeks, communists or not, opposed it. At the same time, Prime Minister Churchill could not turn his back on King George II, who had steadfastly stood by his side at a time when Great Britain was alone.

Shortly after the Gorgopotamos success, the courier ODYSSEUS, a supporter of EAM/ELAS, was forced to flee from Greece as the Germans had discovered his hideout and he felt he could no longer operate safely. SOE had lost a reliable courier but traffic with occupied Greece was now established, with several caiques, and would continue uninterrupted to the end of the war.

Internal divisions were not confined to the Greek Resistance. Caiques arriving in Turkey could be met by representatives of ISLD, MO4 and MI9 who were often at each other's throats. Although used to their own internal strife, the Greeks were often puzzled by the bickering of the different branches of the British Intelligence Service.

PROMETHEUS II warned Cairo to beware of EAM/ELAS and ODYSSEUS, but basking in the success of the Gorgopotamos action, MO4 did not immediately appreciate the threat that was developing. Commander Koutsoyannopoulos' opinion was much valued at SOE headquarters, as he had always shown discretion as well as sound and impartial judgement. Unfortunately, his days were numbered, as he would not escape the attention of the German Secret Service. PROMETHEUS II was also warning that Tsigantes was talking too much and all Athens was aware of his visit. He mentioned that the Gestapo was circulating a paper presumed to come from the British Secret Service and signed by Maxwell but this was an obvious fabrication. German Intelligence was unaware that Lord Glenconner had now replaced Maxwell. The Nazis were trying to show that some degree of co-operation with the British was being achieved to fight the communists in an effort to drive a wedge between the Allies.

Tsigantes reported on 2 December that he was concentrating on the Corinth Canal operation but could not achieve permanent blocking with the available material. So far, his main tasks had been to organize the Greek resistance and he had made valuable contacts. He also appeared to have lived lavishly, inciting the jealousy of the agents working for ISLD who were on a tight budget. At the urging of Cairo, the major had despatched Lieutenant Zakynthinos and Warrant Officer Gyftopoulos to reconnoitre the Corinth Canal. For unknown reasons, Zakynthinos declined to carry out the operation; Tsigantes reluctantly proposed to Maraslis that he take his place on condition that he followed Zakynthinos' orders.

Maraslis, who felt that he should have been in charge of the operation in the first place, was upset at the lax security – the operation appears to have been widely known in Athens – and the Italians had discovered the limpets and increased security around the canal. He now told Tsigantes that the operation was unlikely to succeed, but within days Cairo had advised MIDAS to refrain from undertaking any action as a naval expert, Cumberlege, was soon coming from London with a new device that would ensure permanent blocking of the waterway. Tsigantes, perhaps irritated at being put aside, replied that if the THURGOLAND plan to block the canal failed, it was unlikely another plan would succeed. Cairo remonstrated that it was more important to block the canal permanently than to block it for a short time. Maraslis was sent to Smyrna to bring back explosives to be used in the Piraeus area.

Did Italian Intelligence get wind of these machinations? This is possible as, on 11 November, it was proposed to interrupt the navigation in the canal every Wednesday to carry out minesweeping. In Kalamaki, while surveying the canal, Lieutenant Zakynthinos (alias MIKY) had met a lady named Pagona Mikha and her two daughters Elleni and Penelope; one of them fell madly in love with him. Pagona was later suspected to have worked for the Italians and to have alerted them of what was afoot. Zakynthinos had used the daughters as couriers and imprudently sent them with their mother to the Kyriakides Apartments on 86 Patission Street, which was the hideout of Major Tsigantes. His colleague Gyftopoulos, alias GYPSY, had sent back one of the daughters to Kalamaki with a message from Tsigantes recalling Zakynthinos to Athens as the Corinth operation was put on hold due to the arrival of an expert [Cumberlege] with a special mine.

This message is reported to have reached 2 Italian Brigade based at Xylocastro. In February 1943, when the THURGOLAND mission was being evacuated, the two Pagona daughters are reported to have led *carabinieri* to the hideouts of the Greek agents but fortunately they had already changed their addresses. Yet, when the death of Tsigantes was later investigated, there was no hard evidence that Pagona and her daughters had played a role in it. In his subsequent report Lieutenant Maraslis was highly critical of Zakynthinos and his lax attitude while the latter, who later joined EAM, would try to shift the blame onto Tsigantes.

Tsigantes made another signal to Cairo on 10 December that traffic in the canal had almost stopped and it was difficult to find a ship large enough to apply limpets. However, he enquired if he could still proceed with the plan, as he did not believe that with the present conditions a new type of mine could be dropped. At about 1800 hours on 15 December, a German report mentions that an ambulance with Red Cross markings was stopped by a mixed patrol of two German GFP (*Geheime Feldpolizei*, the equivalent of the Gestapo for occupied territories) and two Italian *Carabinieri* in the suburb of Tamburia. There was a shoot-out and the German policeman Burgdorf collapsed, hit in the right hip. The three Greeks managed to escape on foot but they left behind their vehicle with a number of weapons and explosives, including hand grenades and twenty-four limpets of British manufacture. Tsigantes reported to Cairo that the vehicle had been stopped, but all his men had escaped after killing a German and an Italian which was not quite true. He added that twelve limpets had been lost as well as the Lyakos wireless set brought by the HOLLYM party and destined for Colonel Myers. When this was learnt, it raised some eyebrows in Cairo and there were doubts as to the veracity of his reports; this was the third time a precious radio set had been lost. Three days later Tsigantes reported that his attempt at blocking the canal was postponed indefinitely, pending the arrival of the British expert. It is not inconceivable that the loss of these explosives had eliminated any possibility of participation from his side.

Shortly before midnight on 4 January 1943 the Italian transport *Hermada* was rocked by an explosion in Piraeus harbour and sank at her moorings. According to PROMETHEUS II, this was the work of naval Captain Levides from the MIDAS 614 organization and he had managed to attach a limpet to the hull of the vessel. The explosion made a hole 1 x 1.5 metres; the vessel was raised on 7 January and docked but repairs were fairly quick and she could return to service in early February. Curiously enough, MIDAS 614 does not appear to have made much of it and PROMETHEUS II may have been mistaken when he attributed the sabotage to this organization. An unsuccessful attempt at sabotaging a searchlight at Salamis was made two days later; one saboteur was severely wounded and captured but he died of his wounds. Captain Levides fled to Turkey on 23 January; he was replaced by Emmanuele Vernikos, the same man suspected by Mike Cumberlege of sinister designs during the Antiparos disaster.

Death of Major Tsigantes
In the meantime Major Tsigantes tried to arrange the escape of Captain Atkinson who had been captured during Operation ISINGLASS. The Scottish officer had been seriously wounded – there was even talk of amputating his leg – and was held at the Athens Municipal Hospital. A male nurse named Dimitrios Manousakis was working there and was known to the organization; it was hoped he could arrange the escape. Unknown to the leader of MIDAS 614, Manousakis was working for the Italians and was later convicted for his betrayal. Kapetanides, one of Tsigantes' bodyguards, was given money to bribe Atkinson's captors but, despite promises that this would be done, nothing happened. Tsigantes began to suspect that he was being duped and requested Flying Officer Niarchos of the RHAF to take over the operation from Kapetanides. They do not appear to have known that agents from MI9 were also working on a similar scheme and were actually closer to bringing it to fruition. On 14 January 1943 Niarchos met Kapetanides and Manousakis at the restaurant Solonion and told them to wait for him there while he went to the hospital to see if Atkinson was still held there. Niarchos, who was distrustful of the two men, asked a waiter to watch them during his absence and, upon his return, was told that Kapetanides had left briefly and met a man near a kiosk on the opposite side of the street. The description of this man appears to match that of Parisis but was inconclusive.

Niarchos asked Kapetanides to come along to meet Tsigantes at his hideout on Patission Street. They were about 500 metres from the location when Kapetanides told him that there was a crowd gathering there and he was reluctant to go. Niarchos, who had excellent eyesight, was startled by the comment, as he could see nothing; he would later suspect that Kapetanides had foreknowledge of what was happening.

That same morning Tsigantes had left his mistress, the Belgian Marie-Louise 'Malou' Bertrand, and, accompanied by his bodyguard Parisis, had gone to his apartment on 86 Patission Street where he had met with his aide de camp Lieutenant Zakynthinos and Major Malaspinas. Parisis appears to have left them and it was then observed that the Italian police had drawn a cordon around the edifice. Was Tsigantes betrayed or were the events that followed purely accidental? Apparently a woman had twice called the Italian police to report that a New Zealand officer was hiding in the building; this was apparently false. Malaspinas was told by Tsigantes to leave and the Italians did not bother him. Tsigantes could also have left as he had papers in order, but as the police appeared to conduct a thorough search of the building, he told Zakynthinos to leave and began burning his papers. The smoke alerted the Italians and Tsigantes was stopped as he was trying to leave the building. Ordered to raise his hands, he drew a pistol and shot an Italian *carabiniere* before he was himself cut down. Zakynthinos managed to leave without interference.

Any attempt to free Atkinson from the hospital was now doomed and the Scottish captain was transferred to the Averoff prison. On 20 January Atkinson, the Cypriot Arvanitopoulos, aka Kipriadis, and twenty-five Greeks, some of them in absentia, including Alexandros Zannas, were tried by an Italian military tribunal. Atkinson, Arvanitopoulos and six Greeks were condemned to death and executed by firing squad on 23 February 1943. At about the same time an Italian court had also condemned to death the 25-year-old Englishman Antony Hadkinson and the 29-year-old New Zealander, Private John Stuart, both suspected of espionage. SOE made efforts to prevent their execution and even threatened to execute Italian prisoners in retaliation but the efforts came too late.

The death of Major Tsigantes was a serious blow to the THURGOLAND organization and it could not have come at a more inopportune time. The previous day Lieutenant Cumberlege and his three commandos had landed near Cape Skyli.

Operation LOCKSMITH was under way.

Chapter 14

Operation LOCKSMITH

The urgency to carry out the Corinth Canal operation was underlined when Admiral Harwood, Commander-in-Chief Mediterranean, ordered a submarine to be put at the disposal of the commandos and the Greek *Papanicolis* was selected. The British submarine *Taku*, Lieutenant A. J. W. Pitt RN, had sailed from Beirut on 9 December 1942 for the north-east coast of Euboea to carry out a special operation (Operation SATURN) consisting of landing three Greek agents near Nisia Rocks. This was carried out on 20 December but one of the agents was captured by the Germans and gave away the identity of the submarine. *Taku* had also been ordered to carry out a preliminary reconnaissance of Cape Skyli and the Peloponnese coast facing the island of Hydra, which had been selected as a suitable landing area for Operation LOCKSMITH. The submarine closed the coast on 26 December and at dawn carried out a periscope reconnaissance of the area. No enemy activity was observed, confirming that the area was suitable for the landing of the SOE team. *Taku* had made her presence known by carrying out several attacks, notably sinking the Italian transport *Delfin* and had eluded the German submarine chaser *UJ-2102* sent to hunt her. The submarine returned to Beirut on the first day of the new year.

On Thursday 7 January 1943, Operation LOCKSMITH was finally put in motion and the four commandos, Lieutenant Michael Claude Cumberlege, Company Sergeant Major James C. Steele, Sergeant Thomas E. Handley (radio operator) and Czech Corporal Jan Kotrba, boarded the submarine *Papanicolis*, Lieutenant Nikolaos Roussen RHN, at Beirut and sailed in the evening. Cumberlege's superiors had rejected the insertion of a fifth man, Antonios Fakaros; the lack of a man speaking Greek would prove to be a great hindrance to the operation. The SOE war diaries indicate that the departure had been delayed by ten days. The reason for the delay may well have been that they had waited for the return of *Taku* to get the latest intelligence on the area.

Since the ISINGLASS fiasco and the loss of HMS *Triumph*, the Royal Navy had been reluctant to lend submarines for special operations in the Aegean, but the ageing Greek submarines appeared quite suitable for this purpose. It is certain that Greek crews were reluctant to attack Greek shipping even if it was controlled by the Axis. However, their good knowledge of these coastal waters made them especially fit for clandestine missions.

Papanicolis was the most famous submarine of the Royal Hellenic Navy and her conning tower is preserved in front of the Piraeus Naval Museum. During the war with Italy, under the command of Lieutenant Commander Miltos Iatrides, she had sunk the schooner *Antonietta* and the transport *Firenze* before escaping with four of her sisters to Alexandria in April 1941. The French-built submarines were old and difficult to maintain and tremendous efforts were made to keep them operational. *Papanicolis* was no exception, requiring a long refit before being able to resume patrols. In June 1942 she was back in the fray, this time led by Commander, later Rear Admiral, Athanasios Spanidis, sinking several caiques and landing a commando which was to attack the Maleme airfield in Crete, Operation ALBUMEN. In September 1942 she landed another commando on the island of Rhodes in Operation ANGLO.

Lieutenant Roussen took over command on 12 October 1942 but clandestine operations were not new to him and he had brought an SOE party to Crete the following month, Operation OXFORD. Early in December *Papanicolis* was ordered to be available for the LOCKSMITH operation. When she sailed from Beirut in January she was also carrying three British Army officers who were to be used as a boarding party with the intention of capturing a sailing vessel.

In the early hours of 13 January the submarine arrived without incident in the Hydra Channel and spent the day at periscope depth, exploring the area where the LOCKSMITH party was to be landed. Roussen had been instructed to pick a suitable landing area as close to 37°25.1' N, 23°31.2' E as possible. At about noon two landing barges were observed east of Hydra and, shortly afterward, two caiques were passed but left unmolested. *Papanicolis* surfaced after dark just off Boufi Cove, weather conditions were good and, by 2015 hours, the operation was completed without a hitch.

The selection of the landing area had been carefully thought of. The THURGOLAND party had reported that they found a suitable landing spot for a submarine but the final selection was probably made after the courier ODYSSEUS (Gerasimos Alexatos) had used it on 14 November 1941 when he arrived from Smyrna. The Ermioni peninsula was sparsely populated and a landing could be carried out relatively unseen. Cumberlege had reconnoitred the area in April 1941 and had come to the same conclusion.

Boufi Cove is located in 37°25'43" N, 23°30'24" E, in an area known as Tselevinia. It is almost as deserted today as it was during the war. It can only be accessed through a dirt road. To locate it was no mean feat and it was thanks to the help of Rear Admiral Ioannis Maniatis (Retired), the local historian, and Ioannis Sambanis, cousin of Dimitrios Sambanis who assisted the sabotage team, that the author managed to visit it in 2010.

Contrary to many reports, the four men did not land on the island of Hydra. The *Papanicolis* patrol report mentions discreetly, as was common in Allied submarines involved in special operations, that she entered the Hydra Channel without giving any exact details. This has led some official documents to assume that they had landed on the island of the same name. Boufi Cove is in the Hydra Channel but on the mainland.

The four commandos paddled their way to the cove on the Peloponnese coast. They must have felt relief at leaving the cramped quarters of the submarine. They took two tons of stores with them. These included:

Ten mines and spares (five mines and five counter-mines)
Four folbots
Six 0.303in Vickers machine guns
2,000 rounds of ammunition
Three sets of personal gear
250lb of special stores

Papanicolis, her mission accomplished, retired towards Milos. In the following days she would capture the large German-controlled caique *Aghios Stephanos* that would be brought to Alexandria by her boarding party. The submarine would also sink by gunfire and ramming the caique *Aghia Paraskevi* in Italian service, before returning to Beirut.

According to a report produced by a Greek enquiry commission after the war and provided to Major Michael Ward of SOE, the LOCKSMITH party made contact with Theodoros Philippopoulos; his modest house was barely 200 yards from the beach where they had landed. The Greek initially thought they were agents provocateurs and appeared very scared about this sudden intrusion in his secluded life. They managed to allay his fears and brought their stores close to his house where they stayed for four days. The stores were then moved to a ravine about 200 yards from the farm and some of them hidden under a large stone. Two tons of stores could not be carefully camouflaged and they were quickly noticed by Ioannis N. Hadjidimitrou, alias 'Kareklas' or the 'chair maker', and later by the shepherd Panayiotis Kokalas. In his postwar testimony at a court of enquiry, Philippopoulos referred to the area as Avlaki. He also added that, after two to three days, Ioannis Kareklas (Hadjidimitrou) arrived by a German caique and asked him to show him the boat with which the British had arrived but he did not. There is no evidence in German documents to confirm this.

In the meantime Cumberlege had his team build a small hut where one of his two radio transmitters was installed. They made their first signal to Cairo on 17 January 1943; the text does not appear to have survived. This was followed by another on 23 January:

FROM LOCKSMITH. ONE OF 23 STOP YOUR NUMBER THREE REGRET TIME USED CAIRO LOCAL STOP A FISHERMAN HAVING BETRAYED OUR APPROXIMATE POSITION CAUSES

SOME UNEASINESS, REQUEST YOU ASK JOHNSON [codename of Major Tsigantes] TO MAKE RENDEZVOUS SOONEST, NO CONTACT WITH JOHNSON TWENTIETH OR TWENTYFIRST. ENDS.

Other signals would follow, some concerning local intelligence; others appear to have been weather reports, weather balloons being sent apparently on a daily basis. The SOE papers reveal that valuable meteorological information was provided.

The presence of the British team had been reported by the shepherd Kokalas to the 36-year-old Dimitrios Sambanis who lived in a house less than a mile to the south of Boufi Cove in the Foulkhari area. His wife, Elli, was born in Cairo and could speak English; she still had relatives in Egypt and in time they would be contacted to help vouch for the veracity of the LOCKSMITH team. Sambanis met with Cumberlege who reported him to be 'very helpful' and he was asked for the use of his motor caique. The Greek did not own a caique but used to rent one to sell his crop of lemons to Athens. Sambanis introduced Mike to Kleanthis Porfyropoulos, who had recently been released from prison for his part in helping Captain McNabb (see Chapter 11). He disclosed to him the fate of McNabb and also that of Alexandros Zannas and Captain Kondouriotis and others who had been incarcerated after the Antiparos fiasco. We know that Cumberlege was well aware of Operation ISINGLASS though he appears to have wrongly suspected Emmanuel Vernikos for its failure.

In his postwar report to SOE, Dimitrios Sambanis, a civil policeman by profession, confirmed that he had put his caique at the disposal of the LOCKSMITH commandos but that orders were then received to wait. He described that Cumberlege had produced a paper signed by Admiral (sic, General) Wilson, then Commander-in-Chief Mediterranean. Written in Greek, it stated that the mission was of the utmost importance and Greeks were exhorted to help it at all costs.

They attempted to make contact with the THURGOLAND organization, but, for security reasons, they could not contact them directly and had to go through Cairo to arrange a meeting. Cairo contacted THURGOLAND on 17 January for this purpose. They were told to send a representative to *Gefyra tou Diavolo* (Devil's bridge) in the hills behind Damala and to arrange for a caique to be at Galatas, a town on the Peloponnese coast facing the island of Poros. Damala is known today as Trizinia (ancient Troezen) and is the birthplace of Theseus, the hero of mythology. It is likely that Mike had visited it in April 1941 before the first canal operation.

Unfortunately, as related earlier, Major Tsigantes had been betrayed and killed on 14 January by Italian *carabinieri* who had stumbled on his hideout in Athens. When Cairo was informed of this turn of events, it was feared that LOCKSMITH had been compromised. After learning that Tsigantes had been busy burning his papers when he was surprised, it was hoped that the operation could still succeed. Lieutenant Fotios Manolopoulos was now in temporary command of MIDAS 614 and the organization had two wireless sets still in contact with Cairo, one from the original THURGOLAND mission and one that had been brought by the HOLLYM mission and operated by Matthaeou Andronikos.

When the men of MIDAS 614 were informed of the arrival of the LOCKSMITH team, a meeting was arranged at the house of Doctor Kokevis. Major Georgios Angelides, Lieutenant Manolopoulos, Warrant Officer Kotsis and Colonel Psaros, who was later murdered by ELAS, were reported present. They decided that Kotsis would be sent to meet them although he was not familiar with the area. It is not clear why Manolopoulos assumed command of MIDAS 614; Tsigantes had let it be known that, should anything happen to him, he wished Major Angelides to succeed him. Maraslis, who returned to Athens after a visit to Smyrna to pick up explosives, thought that Zakynthinos, who was Tsigantes' aide-de-camp, should have been put in command. Maraslis was arrested on 18 February 1943 after being denounced by a certain Kolokotronis. He was imprisoned for nine months. Manolopoulos' stint in charge of MIDAS 614 was to be a short one, though he was to play an important part in Operation LOCKSMITH.

The end of PROMETHEUS II
Another setback beset SOE when, on 2 February 1943, PROMETHEUS II's luck ran out. He was caught by the Gestapo with two of his assistants, Elias Deyallis and Antonios Papayannis, while they were transmitting a message from his flat at 3 Simantara Street in Athens.

This was the end of Station 333, which had sent no less than 1,200 messages to Cairo and PROMETHEUS II had proven to be the most reliable agent they had in Greece. Commander Koutsoyannopoulos did not believe he was betrayed but most likely he was caught through radiogoniometry. This is confirmed by German sources, as the *Funkabwehr* in the Kato-Patissia neighbourhood detected a radio transmitter and the raid had netted twelve Greek agents, including four former officers. Two radio transmitters were found; seventeen limpets, twenty-three bombs with detonators and other explosive materials, 16 million drachmas and 1,262 sovereigns were also seized. A successful radio operator had to make his messages short and be constantly on the move. Both Deyallis and Papayannis were executed by the Germans. Transmitting from the same location for a long period of time was bound to have fatal consequences. The APOLLO (Peltekis) organization would later rent a number of flats in Athens to allow their radio operators mobility. Fortunately, two of Koutsoyannopoulos' most important collaborators, Timoleon Louis and Ioannis Peltekis, managed to escape to Smyrna, bringing news of the demise of the organization.

On 6 February Cairo appointed Tsigantes' bodyguard, Sub-Inspector of Police Leonidas Parisis, aka agent Z27, to temporary command of MIDAS 614, despite reservations from some of the members of the organization who suspected him of having been behind the assassination of their leader. Parisis had offered his services to the British as early as November 1940 and had acted as an informant. He had stayed behind in April 1941 and continued his work in the anti-communist division of the Athens Police. Parisis contacted Tsigantes when the latter arrived in Greece and we must assume that SOE selected him to succeed as the head of MIDAS 614 in recognition of his past services. At about the same time Major Ioannis Kiphonides arrived from the Middle East to take over command of the political aspect of THURGOLAND and report on the situation. Due to the security risks caused by the death of their leader, most of the original members of the mission were now ordered out of Greece at the first opportunity.

LOCKSMITH contacts THURGOLAND

From 20 January Cumberlege and Sergeant Major Steele went daily to the Devil's bridge where contact with agent JOHNSON (Tsigantes) was to be made. This natural bridge, barely three metres long, spans a narrow gorge from where flows the Panas River; it is almost invisible in the dense vegetation in the hills above Damala. The two men found the inhabitants fearful of German reprisals and a small element of them were pro-German. It is probable that they hid in the area rather than making a daily trip from Tselivinia, because Nikolaos Manzaris, who owned a mill in Damala, later testified that he had purchased food for them.[16] He was the same man who had assisted Johnny Sachs and Roy Natusch in 1941.

It was not until 4 February that Warrant Officer Spyros Kotsis arrived in the area and was met by Cumberlege at the bridge. A handkerchief spread on the ground and covered with a few pebbles was the secret signal. He was to meet the Englishman with the password 'Are you from Ithaka?' The date recorded is possibly an error as Cairo relayed the following signal from THURGOLAND on 3 February:

NUMBER 92 I HAVE MET D/H89 [CUMBERLEGE] EVERYTHING IS IN READINESS FOR BLOWING UP OF X. SUCCESS IS ASSURED ON CONDITION THAT APPARATUS AND PERSON BRINGING IT WILL BE AT 41 LAND CAPITAL [ATHENS] BY FEB 8. DELAY BEYOND THIS DATE WILL MEAN LESS CHANCE OF SUCCESS.

Kotsis later wrote of his part in the episode and that Cumberlege startled him with a resounding 'Hullo!' instead of the prearranged password. This was all the more disconcerting as two villagers happened to pass by at the time. Kotsis described Cumberlege as hatless, in summer white naval uniform, wearing a pistol and a pair of binoculars; he also made note of the golden earring in the right ear. To allay the fears of the two villagers, Kotsis had to tell them that Cumberlege was Italian and that he was searching for British soldiers believed to be hiding in the neighbourhood. They went away, although Kotsis feared they were not convinced. He was brought to their hideout in the bushes about 100 metres from the bridge and after dark they moved to the watermill owned by Nikolaos Manzaris.

They did not linger long and during the night they left for Tselevinia to join the other commandos. Kotsis stayed with them for six days in their tent located near Ermioni. The Greek was surprised to watch weather balloons being sent up twice a day. True, the area was fairly isolated but he feared that this would attract the attention of shepherds who might report them to the Italians. Every day he went down to Galatas to look for the caique of Doctor Tsakonas. It had been allocated for their needs and was to have been brought by Lieutenant Vassilios Zakynthinos, but it failed to show up. This vessel was especially sought because it had Italian papers and could transit the canal but Tsakonas kept on making outrageous demands for compensation and later the caique was reported to have temporarily lost its access to the waterway. Tsakonas had initially asked to be paid 100 sovereigns for the operation but then changed his mind and asked for 1,000 sovereigns, a considerable sum for the times. Tsakonas was suspected of a double game and is reported to have been 'taken care of' (i.e. liquidated) but the exact details of his fate are unknown.

Kotsis, one of the nine original members of THURGOLAND, spoke only a little French but somehow the operation was explained to him. He had not been informed that the commandos required a caique that had papers for Poros and Ermioni. He was sent back to Athens to arrange for the purchase of another boat. On 15 February Cumberlege reported to Cairo:

No.31 OF 15. PROGRESS REPORT. CONTD. AT NOON ON 4TH FEBRUARY I CONTACTED SPYRO KOTSIS. HE SPOKE NO ENGLISH AND PRACTICALLY NO FRENCH. HIS ONLY COMMUNICATION WITH REFERENCE TO THE MEETING WAS YOUR TELEGRAM NO.70 TO THURGOLAND. OUR CONVERSATIONS, THEREFORE, WERE SOMEWHAT LIMITED BUT A CLEAR UNDERSTANDING ON ESSENTIAL DETAILS WAS REACHED. HE HAD NOT RECEIVED OUR MESSAGE REQUESTING THAT HIS BOAT SHOULD OBTAIN PAPERS FOR ERMIONE IN ADDITION TO POROS. HE HAD ARRANGED TO RENDEZVOUS AT THE BRIDGE WITH THE PARTY DETAILED TO CARRY OUT THE MAIN OPERATION BUT AS THEY HAD NOT MATERIALISED THE 9TH FEBRUARY HE RETURNED TO ATHENS TO RE-ARRANGE HIS BOAT'S PAPERS AND ENLIST AN

ENGLISH-SPEAKING FRIEND. HE INTENDED TO RETURN ON THE 11TH BUT DUE TO BAD WEATHER HE HAD NOT ARRIVED ON FEBRUARY 15TH. CONTINUED.

Cairo had received a similar confirmation from THURGOLAND on 14 February:

106 OF FEBRUARY 14. CONTACT WITH EXPERT HAS BEEN ACHIEVED. SPYROS WILL BE NEAR HIM TUESDAY 16 INSTANT TIME MIDNIGHT. SEND FISHING BOAT CONTINUED.

107 OF FEBRUARY 14. CONTINUATION. POSTPONEMENTS ARE DUE TO VERY GREAT DIFFICULTIES. INFORM EXPERT THAT HE MUST HAVE PATIENCE. FOR MEETING HE CAN LEAVE MESSAGES UNDERNEATH THE STONE (remainder of the message corrupt).

Kotsis returned on 17 February with Lieutenant Fotios Manolopoulos of THURGOLAND who spoke both English and Italian, and together with Cumberlege, they reviewed together their different options for the upcoming operation.

Two days later, the LOCKSMITH team was required to suggest suitable dropping areas for the infiltration of the CUMBERSOME mission in the Peloponnese. This mission, led by Captain Mickelthwaite, was to bring a wireless set to establish communications between Cairo and the various resistance organizations operating in the area. This was not the last time that such a request would be forwarded; a similar one would be made on 26 March. It is not known what information was supplied if any but it is unlikely that Mike was in a position to offer much advice. The lack of a Greek interpreter in the LOCKSMITH party greatly hampered their exchange with the locals and the four men would operate on Greek soil in almost complete isolation.

The *Abwehr* closes in
Admiral Arturo Riccardi, Italian Chief of Naval Staff, in a memorandum dated 18 February 1943, had underlined the importance of the Corinth Canal.[17] By this time, Libya had been lost but Axis forces still held a foothold in Tunisia. Reviewing the strategic situation in the Mediterranean, he wrote that if the canal were closed, the Axis military situation in the Aegean would be fatally compromised. This was echoed by a contemporary study made by the Kriegsmarine which pointed out the danger of the enemy landing a strong force of commandos in the Gulf of Navplion, perhaps coupled with an airborne attack, which could easily reach the canal and cause irreparable damages. The defence of the Canal Zone was deemed insufficient. Unknown to Admiral Riccardi, an attempt to block the canal was just two weeks away.

The anti-sabotage defence of the canal had been entrusted to two Luftwaffe battalions of the 2nd Division, while the Italian 26^ *Compagnia Chimica* was to cover the area with smokescreens in case of air attack. Italian forces in the area were under the command of Admiral Giuseppe Lombardi (*Marimorea*). In the spring of 1943 the main threat to the canal was perceived as coming from the west (i.e. Malta) and from the air; the installation of Freya radars on Cephalonia and Corfu was being discussed.

Cairo had in the meantime received information that THURGOLAND was being hunted by the Gestapo and issued the following warning to LOCKSMITH (1 March 1943):

NUMBER 21 OF FIRST STOP UNDERSTAND GESTAPO NOW HUNTING FOR MANOLOPOULOS, KOTSIS, TETARIS, GYFTOPOULOS, ZAKAS OF THURGOLAND PARTY STOP HAVE INFORMED THURGOLAND AND PASS THIS TO YOU SO THAT YOU CAN ENSURE LIAISON IS CARRIED OUT BY REPRESENTATIVES OTHER THAN THESE.

The THURGOLAND mission had initially used the small caique *Aghia Paraskevi* (16.5 tons) to travel with their stores from Mani, on the southern tip of the Peloponnese, to Piraeus. This caique, owned by 26-year-old Kiriakoulis Sideris, had to be sold hurriedly when the Germans took an interest in the vessel. To replace her, on 2 October 1942 they purchased the 20-ton caique *Anastasia* which was given to Sideris who was to prove a very resourceful man. His father owned a small farm at Paganea near Gythion but the young man had always sailed on caiques. The caique was renamed *Aghia Varvara* but she had a speed of only 4 knots and her engines had to be changed at Piraeus on 22 February 1943. This was the vessel destined to play the central role in the Corinth Canal operation. It was an appropriate name for Saint Barbara is the patron saint of those dealing with explosives because her pagan father, who beheaded her, is reported to have been struck by lightning. In the French navy the 'Sainte Barbe' and in the Italian navy 'Santa Barba' were the names given to the powder magazine.

There is conflicting information concerning *Aghia Varvara*'s registration number; one SOE document identifies her as Mytilene 658 and another as Piraeus 1050. One states that she was lost at Samos when David Pawson was captured, the other that she survived the war.

Abwehrstelle (AST) Athens, headquarters of German Intelligence in Greece, was working closely with the GFP 640 Unit and they were on the trail of MIDAS 614. Early in December 1942 they had found out that weapons were being smuggled at Mesta on the south of the island of Chios. On 14 January 1943 the GFP at Salonika replying to an enquiry from their station at Chios stated that the sailing order 09218 and sailing paper 267 had never been issued to the caique *Aghia Varvara*, Master Leonidas Dongas. The only *Aghia Varvara* known to Kuest Salonika was a vessel of 200 tons, Master Konstantinos Karlovolos, with a crew of eight.

The other *Aghia Varvara* was singled out as having forged papers. They had noted that its crew included 'Kulis Sideris and Fotis Manolopoulos'. The two men belonged to the MIDAS 614 organization and were indeed on this vessel. The Germans had not yet connected this boat with the Mesta incident. On 25 January GFP Chios advised the *Abwehr* IIIM section in Athens that a party had been organized to seize *Aghia Varvara*. *Feldwebel* (Sergeant) Auerbach with an interpreter was proceeding to Athens on board the caique *Evangelistria* (Syros registry no. 698). He would then take over the caique *Lambrini* whose crew was suspected of espionage and bring them back to Chios. In a signal made on 10 February from Athens to the Chios branch of the GFP, Auerbach confirmed that the papers of this *Aghia Varvara* were indeed falsified. Apparently the principal person concerned had been arrested but had managed to break out of a Wehrmacht prison on 29 January.

On 24 February the *Abwehr* station at Chios made a signal to their colleagues in Salonika and pointed out that the Greek officers Kulis Sideris and Fotis Manolopoulos were connected to arms smuggling. They requested Salonika to supply them with any information possible on the case. Had these two men applied for travel permits since December 1942? However, they added, 'Do not arrest them. Carry out the investigation so as not to interfere with our stratagem.' What was this stratagem? We do not know, but it is possible that they had pinned their hopes on surveillance of the two men taking them to their leaders.

On 2 March 1943 the Italian Naval Command based at Patras and in charge of the Corinth area, issued a study on the defence of the Corinth Canal against insidious and assault weapons, '*mezzi insidiosi e d'attacco*', and sent a copy to Rome. Was this prompted by some foreknowledge of the impending operation, or was it merely routine? The next day the caique *Aghia Varvara*, ex-*Anastasia*, arrived from Piraeus at Tselevinia. According to the testimony of Philippopoulos, the 'ammunition' was loaded on the caique at Boufi Cove. On board were Kiriakoulis Sideris, owner and skipper, Michael Morakeas, engineer, and Second Lieutenant Fotios Manolopoulos, who was in charge of the operation. Papers for passage through the canal had been obtained thanks to Corporal Constantinos K. Levantis of the Royal Hellenic Air Force who had won the confidence of the Germans.

The next day *Abwehr* Chios was informing their colleagues in Mytilene that a connection had been found between the falsified papers of the caique and the weapons smuggled at Mesta. They would take no immediate action as they added the cryptic remark: 'the last stratagem is still going on'. The caique was under surveillance in the hope that it would lead them to the rest of the organization. They appeared to have been unaware that the caique was to be used in an important covert operation. Considering that the caique had been at Piraeus certainly for some time if her engines had to be changed, it is surprising that *Aghia Varvara* travelled to Tselevinia without interference.

All these signals from *Abwehr* or *Geheime Feldpolizei* were being read by Bletchley Park, albeit with a delay sometimes of two to three weeks. But there is no indication that the references to the caique *Aghia Varvara* were fully understood. In the first place, SOE had not yet been informed that the caique had been purchased. At this time the *Abwehr* decrypts were distributed to four members of MI6 (Colonel Vivian, Colonel Dansey, Lieutenant Colonel Cowgill and Captain Trevor-Roper), one member of MI5 (Mr Hart), and the representatives of the Intelligence branches of the three services: Major Harris of the Royal Marines or Lieutenant Commander Ewen Montagu[18] for the Navy (DNI), Wing Commander Williams for the RAF (D of I) and Major Melland for the Army (DMI). It will be noted that SOE was not represented and would have to depend on the goodwill of the members of these intelligence branches to be kept informed and warned.

The Operation
Blissfully unaware that their caique was the object of such unwanted attention, the LOCKSMITH party loaded the four mines, each with 30lb of explosives, and the four counter mines, each with 80lb of explosives, on the vessel. They had been disguised to look like ordinary petrol tins. The fifth mine was not used, perhaps because it had been found to be defective. Had the mines been damaged during transport? Cumberlege had sent a signal on 7 February, to be relayed to SMD Havant, reporting that the mines had been found to have some form of defect at Alexandria and were believed to have been not well packed by the RAF. Some repairs had to be done and the retaining lugs for the magnetic units had to be soldered again. In fact, on 17 February, Cumberlege once again wired Cairo stating that the five mines and counter mines had been carefully examined and several defects had been found but all had been repaired.

Mike Cumberlege and James 'Jumbo' Steele embarked on *Aghia Varvara* and at 0800 hours on 4 March they sailed for their mission. The alert from Cairo that they should make no contact with Manolopoulos and Sideris was ignored. As they were proceeding east of Poros, unknowingly they avoided a defensive minefield laid on 23 December 1941 by the Italian auxiliary minelayer *Barletta* between Poros and Aghios Georgios, just two or three miles to the east. Another defensive minefield, laid by the German *Bulgaria*, between Aegina and Phleves on 4 December 1942 was also avoided. In both cases the risk would have been small as the mines were probably too deep to do any harm. They now passed to the north of Aegina, evading enemy patrols until they reached the Diaporoi Islands at dusk.

Mike Cumberlege going through the Corinth Canal before the war.
(Photo courtesy of Eunice Cumberlege-Ravassat)

View of the Corinth Canal taken from a RAF reconnaissance aircraft (12 May 1941).
(detail from photograph in ADM199/806, © TNA)

The bridge which was blown up during the German airborne assault in 1941.
(Hellenic Naval Archives)

An Italian submarine making the passage through the canal before the war.
(author's collection)

The Corinth Canal today: a view from the approximate spot where the mine and depth charges were laid in April 1941.
(photo by author, 2010)

Mike Cumberlege in the 1930s.
(Photo courtesy Eunice Cumberlege-Ravassat)

Mike Cumberlege during *Landfall*'s Adriatic cruise (1939).
(Photo courtesy Marcus Cumberlege)

James 'Jumbo' Cook Steele.
(Photo courtesy Jenny Ludick via Alan Harris)

Mike Cumberlege (facing the camera)
during the escape from Crete on
Athanassios Miaoulis (May 1941).
(Photo courtesy Marcus Cumberlege)

Escampador on a clandestine trip (1941).
(Photo courtesy Marcus Cumberlege)

Major Cleland Cumberlege, killed in action
on 31 May 1941.
(Photo courtesy Marcus Cumberlege)

Escampador hiding in the cave of the 'Remarkable Cascades' (Crete 1941).
(Photo courtesy Marcus Cumberlege)

At Tres Eklesias – Escapers and friends (1941).
The Abbot of Preveli flanked by a Greek wing commander (left) and Jack Smith-Hughes (right),
Captain Harris (with pipe) and Sergeant Steele behind him.
(Photo courtesy Marcus Cumberlege)

Atkinson escape party in Cairo (October 1941).
From left to right (standing) 2/Lt John Atkinson (UK), Cpl Bert Haycock (NZ),
Harry Grammatikakis, Sgt Fleming (RAF), Flt Lt Henry Daston (RAF) (seated),
2/Lt Edward Cooper (NZ), Lt Jim Craig (NZ).
(Photo courtesy Robyn Molloy)

The German transport *Maritza* in the canal (probably on 20 June 1941).
(Photo courtesy Reinhard Kramer via Theodor Dorgeist)

The Italian torpedo boat *Alcione* going through the canal (1941).
(*courtesy Kostas Thoctarides*)

The tug *Titan* towing a ship through
the canal.
(*courtesy Kostas Thoctarides*)

The new bridge replacing the one
destroyed in the airborne assault.
(*courtesy ΙΣΤΟΡΙΑ magazine*)

The conning tower of the submarine *Papanicolis* preserved in front of the
Piraeus Naval Museum.
(photo by author, 2010)

Lt Nikolaos Roussen, RHN,
Commanding Officer of
Papanicolis, killed by mutineers
in Alexandria in 1944.
(courtesy Hellenic Naval Archives)

The bust of Major Ioannis Tsigantes at Plateia
Aigyptou in Athens.
(photo by author, 2011)

North side of Boufi Cove where the LOCKSMITH team landed.
(photo by author, 2010)

At Boufi Cove – From left to right: Dr Alex Stratoudakis, Admiral Ioannis Maniatis (retired), Ioannis Sambanis and author.
(photo by author, 2010)

Tselevinia area overlooking the Hydra Channel with the island of
Hydra in the background.
(photo by author, 2010)

Nikolaos Manzaris,
the miller who assisted
the LOCKSMITH team
in Damala.
*(courtesy Panayotis
Manzaris)*

2/Lt Fotios
Manolopoulos who
carried out operation
LOCKSMITH in March
1943.
*(courtesy Kostas
Thoctarides)*

Dimitrios Sambanis, the
landowner who assisted the
LOCKSMITH team in
Tselevinia.
(courtesy Admiral Ioannis Maniatis)

Motozattera landing Italian tanks in North Africa (1942). Their poor seakeeping
qualities made their trip via the Corith Canal essential.
(Cigala Fulgosi Collection, Ufficio Storico Della Marina Militare)

Vesta scuttled at the eastern entrance of the canal in October 1944.
(©Australian War Memorial, SUK13345)

Post-war clearing of the waterway.
(courtesy Kostas Thoctarides)

The Corinth Canal re-opened after the war.
(courtesy Kostas Thoctarides)

The courtyard at the *Zellenbau*, showing part of the T-shaped compound which was razed to the ground. *(Photo by author, 2011)*

The cell at the *Zellenbau* commemorating the seven men of operation CHECKMATE. *(Photo by author, 2011)*

Mike's last letter to Nancy smuggled from Sachsenhausen on 30 January 1945. *(photo by author with permission from Marcus Cumberlege)*

Dead South Lakes soldier was a hero

FIFTY five years after his execution at notorious concentration camp Sachsenhausen, the name of a Sedbergh soldier is to be commemorated.

Attached to the Special Operations Executive, Sgt Thomas Edward Handley was captured in Greece in May 1943.

A member of the Locksmith party, which was trying to blow up the Corinth Canal, the old Sedbergh School day boy was sent to Sachsenhausen and tortured by the Gestapo.

— by

Karen Barden

Sgt. Handley was held in solitary confinement before his execution on April 10, 1945, and a prisoner in a nearby cell got to know of the brave soldier.

He was Bertram James, a former RAF squadron leader, who recently set out to trace any surviving members of Sgt Handley's family to tell them of the memorial plaque, dedicated to the 29 British servicemen shot at Sachsenhausen.

Henry, saw a notice in *The Westmorland Gazette* appealing for information about his brother and got in touch with Military Cross holder and retired diplomat Mr James.

"I am so pleased Thomas's name will be remembered," said Thomas's 82-year-old

in a precious parcel. They starkly state former librarian Thomas was a prisoner-of-war, and later say he had to be presumed dead.

"We were never really told anything. I didn't even know about the Corinth Canal connection until now," Mr Handley told the Gazette.

His wheelwright and undertaker father Frank never got over his eldest son's death and

Mr James had taken part in the great escape from Sagan prison in Silesia, immortalised in the film starring Steve McQueen.

Captured near the Czech border, he was sent to Sachsenhausen, where 100,000 perished between 1936 and 1945.

After getting out of a high security compound and fleeing 100 miles before recapture, Mr

MEMORIES: Henry Handley looking at the only letter received from his brother Sgt Thomas Handley (left) when he was a PoW in Germany.

A newspaper clipping commemorating Sergeant Handley. *(via Sedbergh School)*

Captain Michael Ward of SOE at Veneton (Christmas 1943). He tried to solve the disappearance of the LOCKSMITH team. *(Courtesy Robin D'Arcy Ward)*

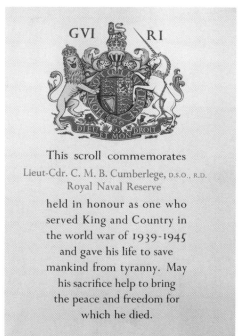

GVI   RI

This scroll commemorates
Lieut-Cdr. C. M. B. Cumberlege, D.S.O., R.D.
Royal Naval Reserve

held in honour as one who
served King and Country in
the world war of 1939-1945
and gave his life to save
mankind from tyranny. May
his sacrifice help to bring
the peace and freedom for
which he died.

The DSO and Bar awarded to
Mike Cumberlege.
*(photo by author with permission from
Marcus Cumberlege)*

Commemorative Scroll.
*(photo by author with permission from
Marcus Cumberlege)*

The award of the Greek War Cross Third Class.
(photo by author with permission from Marcus Cumberlege)

Seventy-one years later at Boufi Cove:
Marcus Cumberlege and daughter Eunice Cumberlege-Ravassat (May 2014).
(Photo courtesy Eunice Cumberlege-Ravassat)

The Memorial Plaque at Sachsenhausen.
(Photo courtesy Sami Suttill via Francis Suttill, 2001)

While the Corinth Canal and the Peloponnese came under Italian jurisdiction, the waters of the Saronic Gulf were under German control. The following day at dawn, the mines and counter mines were checked and prepared for the operation. In his book *Midas 614*, Spyros Kotsis wrote that holes were drilled near the waterline in the hull to attach the mines, and water slowly seeped into the boat. At about 0900 hours, while the process was going on, a German patrol vessel with a crew of seven appeared suddenly. Mike was in the water attaching the counter mines to the *Varvara*'s bottom but he managed to climb back unseen and joined Sergeant Steele hiding in a narrow space behind the false bulkhead. When the Germans came on board, the primed mines were still on deck disguised as petrol cans and, although they made a thorough search of the vessel, the camouflage was effective and they were overlooked. The three Greeks tried to act normally which must have worked as the Germans left without further ado. The Greeks had managed to give a suitable explanation for their presence in this area. In his report Mike praised the coolness displayed by Sideris during the proceedings.

The identity of the German vessel has not been found. Was German control lax enough to have missed the opportunity to seize the occupants of the caique? The *Abwehr* already knew the correct identity of two of the three Greeks. Did the German crew deliberately look the other way as instructed by the *Abwehr*?

Why did they fail to notice the mines hanging over the side? After all, GFP Salonika had warned that Greek fishing vessels might smuggle material for the Greek resistance by attaching rubber bags to the anchor chain, so the counter mines should not have escaped their attention. No mention was found in the German naval records that *Aghia Varvara* was stopped by a patrol boat on that date and it is possible that, through a mix-up, the correct authorities were not informed at that time. It is also true that the German patrol boats of the Sea Defences of Attica seldom recorded their encounters with caiques which were routinely made. Most probably, if the Germans were indeed trailing *Aghia Varvara*, they would have had some GFP personnel on board but this does not appear to have been the case.

German records do show that two patrol-boats, *GA-55,* (*Steuermannsmaat*, [Quarter Master] Bremer, and *GA-68*, *Steuermannsmaat* Hader, were patrolling on the axis Cape Turlo–Cape Kellivini (Skyli) and went to Poros on 2 March but they had returned to Piraeus on the next day. Two other boats *GA-53*, *Obersteuermann* [Navigator] Jens, and *GA-59*, *Bootsmannsmaat* [Petty Officer] Stuckmann, had taken refuge in Hydra because of the bad weather and on 6 March proceeded to Piraeus after carrying a sweep between Cape Zourva, east end of Hydra, and Cape Turlo. It is possible that one of them was the vessel involved.

The three Greeks were now left to carry out the actual operation. Cumberlege and Steele could not pass effectively for Greeks and it would have been a pity if their presence on board had given the show away. The four counter mines now lashed to the bottom of the caique were to have been dropped by cutting the ropes while the actual mines were to be dropped simultaneously over the stern. At the entrance to the canal, *Aghia Varvara* was to embark an Italian guard for the crossing and Sideris' task was to keep him distracted while the operation was carried out.

Cumberlege and Steele were disembarked some seven miles from the entrance of the canal, probably near Katakali. According to Spyros Kotsis, who was not present but must have heard accounts from the participants, the two men were seen climbing a hill from where they could have a better view of the canal and could watch the operation unfold.

Cumberlege wrote that the task was to have been completed by noon on 5 March. He appears to have been mistaken as the THURGOLAND report shows the operation occurring on 6 March. Why this delay? Or was it just a typographical error by one of the parties? This has not been explained. Manolopoulos, for security reasons, decided to ditch three of the four mines with their counter mines before entering the canal. He may have felt that four mines might increase the chance of being detected and one would be enough to do the job. Considering the unreliability of the mines, this act reduced the chance of success significantly. Why did he not inform Cumberlege of his concern? The leader of the LOCKSMITH team would remain convinced that four mines and four counter mines had been used. The remaining mine was reported to have been dropped some 700 to 800 metres east of the bridge, without drawing the attention of the Italian guard.

The excuse given for the passage of the canal was that *Aghia Varvara* was going to Corinth to fetch a cargo of fish for the Germans in Piraeus. After a two-hour stop, the caique returned along the canal, surprisingly without arousing suspicions, and stopped at Aegina to take its load of fish before returning to Piraeus.

Traffic in the canal does not appear to have been heavy at this time of the year. No vessel of any consequence made the crossing on 5 March. The next day the German *Bergit*, carrying 2,713 tons of stores, transited from Corinth to Piraeus. On 7 March the Italian torpedo boat *Castelfidardo* made the passage from Patras to Piraeus; she was followed shortly by the old naval transport *Cherso*. The same day the Swedish relief ship *Yarrawonga* arrived at Piraeus carrying Canadian wheat. She did not use the canal as her safe-conduct allowed her to round up the Morean coast without interference from the Royal Navy or RAF. Three days later, the steamer *Salvatore* in ballast made the passage from Piraeus to Patras and Sibenik. A procession of vessels followed without detonating the mine.

Sideris would later claim that the operation had failed because Cumberlege and his team had divulged the details to the Germans after they were captured.

This is unlikely as they were caught several weeks after this attempt, ample time for the mines to detonate.

On 4 March, the very day *Aghia Varvara* was being loaded with the mines, apparently through administration mishaps, GFP at Chios was informed by AST Athens of an attempt at arms smuggling at Mesta the previous December and that forty-two weapons had been confiscated. *Aghia Varvara* returned to Piraeus without being disturbed. The same day she had laid her mines, GFP Chios was being asked by their Salonika counterparts to be kept informed of the *Aghia Varvara*, Captain Leonidas Dongas, developments. Chios replied the same day that the forged papers were probably procured in Turkey and the captain was not Leonidas Dongas but Panayotis Manolopoulos.

Had the minelaying operation succeeded, *Abwehrstelle* (AST) Athens would have had some explaining to do. They had deliberately let go the caique in the hope of catching bigger fish. The opportunity to capture the caique was there, or perhaps the whole thing was a deliberate smokescreen arranged with a Greek traitor? *Feldwebel* (Sergeant) Auerbach from GFP Chios had gone to Athens to bring documents showing that Koulis Sideris and Fotios Manolopoulos and a third man were using *Aghia Varvara* for some illicit action since they had forged papers for their vessel. The third man was later said to be Theologos Tsalmetsoglou, at least according to Drakos Moskowis who was their fourth companion and was arrested in Piraeus on 10 March. Moskowis was now talking. They knew that Sideris and Manolopoulos had been at Mesta where they had been seen in the house of Serios, a cafe owner and Manolopoulos had met a certain Georgios Masarakis.

The coincidence was too much to be ignored and, on 22 March, the GFP raided Mesta, arresting Serios and twelve fishermen. They informed GFP Salonika and radioed Athens, alerting both AST Athens and GFP Piraeus that Sideris and Manolopoulos were to be arrested immediately. It is certain that German Intelligence and Security forces were understaffed in Greece and policing the Greek isles was quite a challenge to any occupier. They had a serious shortage of interpreters and, in a signal of 4 April, AST Athens confessed that they were unable to carry out preventive measures against sabotage.

We have also seen that Cairo had already warned the LOCKSMITH party that the Gestapo was on the trail of several members of THURGOLAND including Manolopoulos.

Cumberlege and Steele came back overland on the morning of 11 March, when they renewed contact with Cairo. How they trekked back the forty miles to their hideout at Ermioni without raising suspicions is not known. They perhaps stopped at Nea Epidavros where Mike had made contacts in April 1941.

They now waited for new instructions from Cairo. On 13 March Cumberlege wrote a second progress report, stating that 440lb of explosives had been used and describing in detail the operation. He was unaware that Manolopoulos had only used one fourth of the explosives. Two days later he summarized that the operation did not present serious difficulties but apparently there were no results, probably due to defective detonators.[19] He was disappointed to have been so close to success but now that collaboration with THURGOLAND had been successful, a repeat operation could be made, provided that new mines could be delivered to them.

In a signal made on 22 March, Mike proposed the use of a caique to capture and destroy some of the many sailing vessels plying the waters. He may have reflected on this for some time and it could explain his choice of bringing Vickers machine guns with his stores. His buccaneer instinct gave him confidence enough that should a German armed caique attempt to stop them he could surprise it and dispose of its crew, as they were seldom more than four or five.

We do not know of any other activities the commandos may have undertaken. According to the testimony of Georgios Drivas from Poros, one of the commando named 'Tom' (Thomas Handley) and a Czech (obviously a reference to Jan Kotrba), 'blew up the fascist building on Patission Street' in Athens, but there is no other evidence to confirm it and, if Cumberlege made a reference to such action, it has not been found in the archives.

In Tunisia the military situation for the Allies had improved considerably since the battle of Kasserine Pass. But in Egypt and Palestine all was not well with the Greek government in exile. During March two Greek brigades had mutinied over the issue of the return of King George II to Greece after the war. The Greek government had moved from London to Cairo and the Defence Minister Kanellopoulos had to resign. The Greek army in exile was believed to have been infiltrated by left-wing elements and the fragile unity that the Greek resistance had tried to achieve was crumbling. The communists in Greece were now openly eliminating all forms of opposition suspected of working to reinstate the king. Cumberlege and his men were poorly informed of the storm brewing around them.

SOE agents had been taught to keep their signals brief to avoid detection. Plutarch tells us that, at the end of the Peloponnesian war, Lysander sent a message to the *ephors* of Sparta to inform them of the capture of their rival city: 'Athens is taken'. They rebuked him by informing him 'Taken' would have been enough. Cumberlege would have better adhered to the laconic traits of the region. The signals from the LOCKSMITH party had been numerous and some were unusually long and it is not surprising that they were discovered. According to Lieutenant Colonel Jack Churchill who befriended Mike Cumberlege at Sachsenhausen, the LOCKSMITH team was located on 23 March through RDF (Radio Direction Finding). The *Abwehr* station in Athens was not in an ideal geographical position to triangulate effectively the origin of the signals and they believed that the signals came from the island of Hydra. It was not long before a more exact location could be pinpointed.

Geheime Feldpolizei had still not given up. On 25 March GFP Chios in a signal to Mytilene informed them that Koulis Sideris and Fotios Manolopoulos in the small caique *Aretouse* or *Aretousa* (four tons) had visited the small harbour of Passalimani near Mesta on the first day of December and had claimed to be going to Mytilene to buy oil. Chios wanted to know whether this was true and what their destination was. The net was closing.

Cairo received further confirmation from THURGOLAND on 28 March, stating that the caique had gone through the canal on 6 March and had dropped seven devices (three mines and four counter mines). This was rectified in another signal on 1 April, stating that 60 kilos of explosives had been dropped successfully 700 metres east of the bridge. On 2 April they reported that nothing had yet happened as no large ship had made the crossing on account of the bad weather.

Canal traffic appeared to have gone on unimpeded. The German destroyer *Hermes* (ex-Greek *Vassilefs Georgios*) used it on 2 April 1943 on her way to Italy and eventually to meet her final fate in Tunisia. The freighter *Marie Maersk*, the same vessel that Admiral Turle had briefly considered as a blockship for the canal in 1941, was finally raised and towed by the tugs *Instancabile* and *Tenax*. She was to have entered the canal on 21 April 1943 but her bad luck had not deserted her and she ran aground near the entrance. She had to be disengaged with the help of additional tugs *Samson* and *Cyclops*. Her size would have made a perfect target for the British mines.

At this time an attempt was also to be made to block the Levkas Canal and force coastal traffic into the Ionian Sea. If the Corinth Canal had been effectively blocked, the immediate problem to tackle would have been the severe shortage of coal in the Dodecanese islands. The transport *San Luigi*, that was to have brought a cargo, had been the victim of a collision and no other vessel could take her place before mid-April when the transport *Rubicone* would be available. Requests to Admiral Aegean (German Naval Command) had only yielded a small amount of coal. *Rubicone* would have to unload 2,500 tons of coal at Patras in order to transit the Corinth Canal. After nearly three years of war, the Italian merchant navy had shrunk considerably, due to the depredations of the RAF and Allied submarines.

Why the Mission Failed

We know that two weeks before the operation, the Italian Naval Command in Patras had issued orders forbidding sailing vessels from arriving at Isthmia (eastern entrance of the waterway) after sunset as a security measure to prevent a surprise attack on the Corinth Canal. In case of delay, sailing vessels were to keep eastward of the meridian of Aghios Theodoros Point. This order had been disclosed by an ULTRA signal but its significance was probably ignored at the time. At MO4 headquarters in Cairo only Brigadier Keble was privy to ULTRA signals and, if he had read this specific signal, he failed to pass any form of warning to the LOCKSMITH party. Did the Italian Secret Service have knowledge that such an operation was afoot? In December 1945 an enquiry made by Ioannis Kokoretsas of the Higher Military Judicial Council even raised some doubts that the mine had ever been dropped.

According to Spyros Kotsis, Doctor Tsakonas had warned the Italians that an operation was afoot and they had found the mines. As we have seen earlier, Tsakonas had been approached by MIDAS 614 to lend his caique to the organization but had demanded a lot of money in return. Apparently he had been having second thoughts on his involvement with the Greek resistance and was now anxious to ingratiate himself with the Italian authorities. He was unaware that the operation was already underway but he thought that by alerting the Italians this might relieve some of the pressure that MIDAS 614 was putting on him to lend his caique. He is reported to have been 'liquidated' by the Greek resistance.

Dimitrios Sambanis, who talked to Cumberlege after his return from the operation, related after the war that news was anxiously awaited from Cairo to confirm that the operation had succeeded. As the days went by without any result, he was told by the mission leader and the 'specialized soldier saboteur' (Steele) that the mines had probably been damaged on their way from America; there is no evidence that the mines were American-built. Later, it was thought that since the mines had been designed for a vessel of 5,000 tons or more, they had not exploded as no vessel of this size had transitted the canal during the subsequent three months and by this time the mines would have become ineffective. We know that the magnetic mechanism had been found to be unreliable and that it would only work if the mine was tilted.

The true reason for the failure lay elsewhere. An ULTRA decrypt dated 5 April 1943 can be found at the National Archives and refers to a signal from *Supermarina* to the Italian Patras-based Naval Command enquiring about the magnetic mines located in the Corinth Canal.

In fact, two mines had been found; one was reported as of the 'standard type' and perhaps referred to a mine laid by the RAF; the other mine was found floating and was recovered intact. The mine described as '*Englisch Kanistermine*' was carefully studied and its characteristics passed to the Italian High Command (the Italians referred to it as '*Torpedine inglese a forma di latina di petrolio*'). Obviously the mine had been defective as it was not supposed to float but to sink next to the counter mine. However, its true purpose appears to have eluded the Germans who examined it and thought that it was designed as a floating mine. Drifting mines had been banned by the Hague convention of 1907 as they could indiscriminately harm neutral vessels. Most mines were supposed to be anchored and de-activated if they became detached through bad weather. Ground-laid magnetic mines were accepted as their weight made them unlikely to drift even in a strong current. Why did the mine designed by Mike float? Was this a flaw in the design that had escaped its inventors? To German scientists, examination of the mine revealed that it had an ascending force of one kilo and was 'undoubtedly' designed as a floating mine. The mine was described as externally identical to an old petrol can of a red rust colour, the explosive charge estimated at about 15 kilos and the magnetic mechanism to operate at a distance of about one metre. To mask its content, the explosives were covered with a layer of grease. The magnetic mechanism was in a bakelite box with an oil-filled sponge and two small batteries supplying the current. A warning was distributed that in case similar mines were encountered they ought to be destroyed with small-arms fire from a safe distance (at least 100 metres). Mike's mine appears to have aroused the interest of the Axis High Command. We can find correspondence relating to it from the Italian Chief of Naval Staff, Admiral de Courten, and the *Ispettore Armi Subacqua* (Inspector of Underwater Weapons) as late as August 1943, barely a few days before the Italian Armistice.

Collapse of MIDAS 614
While Mike and his men waited for developments, the THURGOLAND/ MIDAS 614 organization began unravelling. Lieutenant Maraslis had decided to leave Greece but was captured by the Italians on the very day of his departure, 18 February; he was tortured but survived. After the Italian Armistice, Spyros Kotsis would manage to secure his release through briberies (he was reported to have paid a German officer 50 million drachmas). On the morning of 18 March, Theodoros Liakos, who had rented a room in the apartment of Kyriakos Gunelas at Piraeus Street 169, was operating his wireless when the Germans surprised him. Kyriakos and his brother Michael were also arrested. On 31 March the *Geheime Feldpolizei* had homed in on the wireless operator Roussos who was still transmitting when they burst into his flat at Dodecanessou 15 in Nea Smyrni. He managed to draw his pistol and kill Corporal Schmidmeier of the GFP before he was himself cut down. It was later reported that it was his girlfriend who had betrayed him. His hosts, Christos and Eleni Giannakea and their two daughters, were arrested by the Germans. Unaware of what had happened, the other operator, Matthaeou Andronikos, walked into the flat the following day and was promptly arrested, a pistol and a poison pill were found in his possession. It is likely that the *Abwehr* had penetrated the organization. Some blamed the policeman Kapetanides for having failed to warn Andronikos in time. . Liakos and Andronikos were condemned to death and were executed on 20 May. The life expectancy of clandestine radio operators was very short indeed.

Christos and Eleni Giannakea were also condemned to death but this was later commuted to a 15-year prison sentence and they were sent to a concentration camp in Germany. The two daughters got four years each. The

Gunelas brothers were luckier; they managed to plead that they were unaware of the transmissions made by their lodger and were acquitted due to lack of evidence.

On 20 March, Cairo had received this cryptic message:

BEWARE OF DANGER. SETS 59410 AND 463 HAVE BEEN CAPTURED BY GERMANS AS A RESULT OF TREACHERY. WE ARE IN DANGER. GOD HELP 463. IT IS LIAKOS. ZIRELIS.

This ambiguous signal was from Parisis who had assumed control of MIDAS 614 and used the pseudonym of Zirelis. Cairo was uncertain if the traitor was Liakos or the wireless operator and demanded clarification.

By 27 March Parisis, who had succeeded Tsigantes at the head of MIDAS 614, handed over the reins of the organization to Captain Miltiadis Kanaris RHN and the next day escaped to Smyrna on board the caique *Aghia Varvara* of Koulis Sideris. Zakynthinos, Gyftopoulos and Moraitis also came along, but as stowaways, and were unaware of the presence of their chief until they reached their destination. Yet the small caique carried about forty refugees and must have been overcrowded. An *Abwehr* agent in Turkey, 'ALADIN', reported the arrival of forty-five refugees at Chesme on 6/7 April via Mytilene. This prompted the *Abwehr* IIIF (counter-espionage) section at Salonika to inquire of GFP Mytilene how this could have occurred. Manolopoulos and Sideris appear to have made another trip from Athens to Smyrna at the end of May. On 22 April *Aghia Varvara* is recorded as having sailed back from Smyrna with a wireless set and the sum of 1,000 sovereigns.

Upon leaving Smyrna, Greek caiques returning to Greece had to sail between the German-controlled islands of Chios and Mytilene where they had been instructed since 12 February 1943 to follow strict routes. They had to make mandatory stops for inspection at Mytilene if they were sailing towards northern Greek ports and at Chios if they were sailing towards southern ports. How *Aghia Varvara* managed to elude both the *Abwehr* and *Geheime Feldpolizei* is a mystery that has not been solved. Both services were now hot on her trail.

On 12 April a strange signal from *Abwehr* IIIM Athens, the section of *Korvettenkapitän* Meincke, informed GFP Chios that *Gefreiter* (Corporal) Euler Karystos had confused in the darkness the certificate of the caique *Rini* with that of *Aghia Varvara* so that the crew of the latter was entered as if belonging to the former. Did this help the escape of *Varvara*? Was bribery involved? This cannot be totally discounted. According to Captain G. A. Harris of the Smyrna SOE section, *Aghia Varvara* reached Turkey and was then given to an individual named Sophian.

At the end of the war Sideris forwarded a claim of ownership of *Aghia Varvara*. Major Michael Ward of SOE, who had been put in charge of closing the SOE accounts in Greece, expressed some scepticism as to its validity and made further enquiries. The caique papers were found showing *Aghia Varvara* had been purchased in the name of Second Lieutenant Michail Petrolekas. This officer, with Second Lieutenants Gyftopoulos, and Manolopoulos and police officer Parisis, were contacted by SOE. All four men were full of praise for Sideris and confirmed that the caique had been given to him. There were some conflicting reports as to the fate of the caique; one stated that she had been sunk at Samos in October 1943 while Sideris reported her in Mytilene. Yet an SOE memo, dated 3 March 1945, shows that the caiques *Aghia Varvara*, *Spiros* and *Niki* were sold to a certain Synodinos for the sum of 350 sovereigns, *Aghia Varvara*'s actual cost was 150 sovereigns; this was perhaps the vessel reported by Sideris. Eventually his ownership of the vessel was recognized but the engines were claimed as SOE property. Although Captain Harris had recommended that the claim be turned down, he admitted that Sideris should get some compensation for his ill health. SOE records show that Sideris, who suffered from tuberculosis, received a payment of 50,000 drachmas on 20 August 1945 and another 100,000 drachmas on 10 October 1945.

Following the escape of *Aghia Varvara* to Smyrna, the Italians arrested Kanaris on 7 July 1943 and he joined Maraslis in prison. The arrest had nothing to do with his part in MIDAS 614 but was in a connection with an illegal newspaper he had helped publish. Kotsis was now the only original member of the organization left at large in Athens and he assumed temporary command. The following month, through bribery (he paid 207 sovereigns), he managed to secure the release of Maraslis. Kanaris was also freed in similar circumstances but MIDAS 614 had effectively ceased to exist. At the end of 1943, Kotsis and Maraslis would flee to the Middle East.

Captain Skelly of SOE interrogated Kiriakoulis Sideris on 9 August and again on 19 August. Was the LOCKSMITH operation discussed? We know that it was not raised during the first meeting but no record of the second meeting appears to have survived.

Later Major O'Toole and Captain Harris would try to find out what had caused the demise of the organization and were highly critical of the group of men who had gone with Tsigantes. Harris found that only Gyftopoulos was reliable. He affirmed that the money used to bail out Kanaris had been ill spent. The leader of MIDAS 614 had not been actually appointed by SOE, nor was he in their employ. Since he had been arrested on a minor offence, he would probably have been released within a month or two.

Invasion threat

Axis Forces in Greece were now on the alert expecting an Allied invasion of the Peloponnese to be imminent. This was part of the deception scheme known as Operation ANIMALS. It does not appear that Operation LOCKSMITH was part of this attempt to draw enemy forces away from the upcoming invasion of Sicily.

Already the increasing incursions of enemy bombers in the Aegean had forced the Axis High Command to forbid sailing vessels from travelling during daylight hours south of the 37°35' N parallel (just north of the island of Poros). On 3 April the German South East Command had enquired from High Command Greece if suitable ferries would be available to carry trains across the Corinth Canal should the bridges be destroyed. Provisions were being made in case troops had to be rushed south to oppose an enemy landing.

On 15 May the German High Command, citing 'very reliable sources', had warned that an invasion of the western coast of the Peloponnese was planned with the British 56th Infantry Division to land near Kalamata (southern Peloponnese) while the 5th Infantry Division would land south of Cape Apoxos. This 'information' was certainly part of the deception initiated by Operation MINCEMEAT, the plan devised by Lieutenant Commander Ewen Montagu to draw Axis forces away from the impending landing in Sicily. The Germans were not keen to divert many forces to the defence of the Peloponnese as the risks of being cut off were great but units from the Brandenburg Division were despatched. The Corinth Canal could be an obstacle to any reinforcements rushed to attack the landing areas and plans had already been drawn up by the Italians to use ferries in case the bridges were destroyed. The only immediate defensive measures taken were the laying of a defensive net and minefields off the harbour of Kalamata.

The other Allied missions in Greece would be used in due time to reinforce the enemy's belief that Greece was to be invaded by increased guerrilla activity but Cumberlege and his team were left out of the scheme. They had now practically no communications with their Greek contacts. It is possible that, when Axis Intelligence learned that an attempt had been made to block the Corinth Canal, they had deduced that this was part of a general plan against their Peloponnese position, but this was not the case. The Navy and Army had different views of the Corinth Canal. For the Navy the canal was seen in terms of east-west movements and it was an important waterway essential for carrying out their task of keeping the lines of communication open with the Aegean. For the Army the canal was seen through the prism of north-south communications; it was a ditch that could become a hindrance to any movement of troops to defend the Peloponnese.

In June 1943 work on the bridges across the canal led to the use of lighters and ferries to keep the railway traffic going. On the 26th, the dredger *Calabria* was slightly damaged by incendiary shells and had three wounded as she was alongside the freighter *Quirinale* which was the target of an air attack. At the same time, the Levkas Canal which could be used by vessels drawing up to 5.5 metres saw an increase in traffic as enemy air attacks became more frequent.

The dredgers *Axinos*, *Calabria* and *Ionia* were available for both the Levkas and the Corinth canals.

The torpedo boat *Sagittario* had been one of the first vessels to pass through the canal following its seizure in April 1941. On 30 June 1943 she led a convoy from Piraeus to Patras, and eventually to Brindisi, consisting of the steamers *Argentina* and *Italia* and escorted by the torpedo boat *Lince* and the auxiliary *Pola*. Her mission report illustrates well the difficulties that any attempt at sabotage by limpets with delay mechanism would have encountered. She arrived at the eastern entrance of the Corinth Canal at 1130 hours. It was not until 1302 hours that she embarked a pilot and the canal was entered at 1335 hours and exited at 1350 hours followed by *Pola*. At 1457 hours *Argentina* came out of the waterway but *Italia*, which appeared ready to enter the canal at 1647 hours, did not complete the crossing before 1842 hours, followed by *Lince*. In his report, *Capitano di Corvetta* Antonio di Montezemolo of *Sagittario* complained of the slowness in making the passage which made his stationary vessels vulnerable to air attack. This was due to the larger ships being towed by a tug through the waterway. It also created problems in timing the detonation of any explosives attached to the hull of a ship passing along the canal. The detonation could have occurred well before the ship entered the canal. Initially, some of the limpets had a delay of only an hour. Since some ships took as little as twenty-five minutes to make the passage, it would have been extremely lucky to time the explosion to occur inside the waterway. The method implemented by Cumberlege may have been the best, but it took several months to prepare. By this time the initial objective, which had been to deny Rommel's reinforcements to North Africa, was no longer required. The canal itself remained an important objective but if the mine devised by Mike was intended to be used against a large ship, it is possible that the ship, because of its size, could only have been damaged and perhaps successfully towed away before sinking. Unfortunately, these questions will remain forever unanswered.

Chapter 15

Capture

The LOCKSMITH party was now waiting for further developments; the four men might be evacuated by submarine or remain and carry out a second attempt, but they needed more mines. On 18 March four Italian secret service men from Xylocastro arrived at the house of their contact, but they were not betrayed.[20] Someone in Damala must have talked. The Italian SIM (Secret Service) and the German *Abwehr* seldom shared information. To complicate matters, the land areas of Poros and the Peloponnese coast were under Italian control, but the Germans controlled the waters of the Gulf of Athens.

The following signal was sent the next day:

From: LOCKSMITH
To: CAIRO.
NUMBER 91 OF 19. FOUR ITALIAN SECRET POLICE ARRIVED AT HOME OF OUR CONTACT HERE [Sambanis], AND DEMANDED WHEREABOUTS OF ENGLISHMEN IN VICINITY. POLICE FROM XILOCASTRO. THEY HAD FULL DETAILS OF DEVIL'S BRIDGE AND OUR HIDEOUT THERE. SITUATION REMAINS OBSCURE, BUT ARE TAKING EVERY PRECAUTION. ALL OUT TELEGRAMS TO 90, AND IN TO 28 DESTROYED. PLEASE CONGRATULATE MANOLOPOULOS ON HIS ACHIEVEMENT ON OUR BEHALF. ENDS.

Cairo replied that they could:

(1) move to Kefkas if they had sufficient stores
(2) leave to Turkey by caique if available
(3) go to the Parnon mountains where they could be supplied by parachute drops until an evacuation by sea could be arranged; (a party of three agents was parachuted on 23 May on Mount Parnon, in Operation STADHAMPTON). Their wireless set was to be left behind in a safe place, as it could be most valuable for future operations.

Greeks always feared that Germans were posing as Englishmen to test their loyalty to the regime. Elli Sambanis, née Porfyropoulos, the wife of Dimitrios, had relatives in Port Said. On 21 March Cumberlege sent a signal to Cairo requesting to have them send a message to the Sambanis in Greece through the Red Cross; this would establish in their eyes the credentials of the commandos. He concluded that 'Sambanis most valuable to us. Short answer from family would further cement our relationships as our position here depends largely on their good will.'

Days passed and the mines appeared not to have caused any damage; by 28 March LOCKSMITH sent the following signal to Cairo (the first part appears to have been lost):

NR 114 CONTD.
PLEASE PASS GIST OF ABOVE BY TELEGRAPH TO S.M.D. HAVANT, ASK THEM THEIR REACTIONS AND SUGGEST THEY SEND A FURTHER FIVE RPT FIVE M RPT M UNITS PLUS FIVE STANDARD MINES CONTAINING M UNITS SET FOR SIMILAR CONDITIONS EITHER WITH OR WITHOUT EXPLOSIVE DEPENDING ON WEIGHT TO EGYPT BY AIR IMMEDIATELY. YOU COULD DROP THESE SUPPLIES TO US AT AN AGREED POINT. WE CAN FIT THE M UNITS TO THE 4 MINES AND SEE WHETHER WE GET A POSITIVE TEST. INFORM HAVANT THESE UNITS WOULD HAVE TO BE DROPPED. WE HAVE AMPLE GELIGNITE FOR A REPEAT CANAL OLUS (?) LEVKAS. OTHER REQUIREMENTS WILL FOLLOW.

The following day, London having been informed of the above, Major Boxshall of SOE contacted Commander A. E. Jennings of Naval Intelligence to discuss the developments. Boxshall suggested that since over three weeks had elapsed since the laying of the four mines and four countermines (actually only one of each had been laid), it was obvious that either no ship large enough had passed through the canal or the mines had been defective. He also asked Jennings what size of ship the mechanism was designed for and if the changing strategic situation warranted another try at the operation.

The reply to the first question was provided by Lieutenant Colonel Pearson who explained that the mines had been intended to break the back of the ship and could have resulted in blocking the canal for a period of up to six months.

The *Abwehr* in Greece

With all the signals sent from the LOCKSMITH party, it was inevitable that Axis Intelligence had become aware that something was afoot.

The *Abwehr* in Greece was in the hands of the 47-year-old Bavarian *Oberstleutnant* (Lieutenant Colonel) Walter Sensburg, head of the Athens station (*Abwehrstelle* or AST Athens). The rival *Sicherheitsdienst* maintained only a small presence, although this was to increase steadily in the next months. Colonel Carlo Sirombo was the head of the Italian Secret Service (SIM) in Greece, assisted by his deputy Lieutenant Colonel Bassignano. Contacts between the two services were cordial but actual collaboration was practically non-existent. The Germans distrusted the Italians, suspecting them of anything from careless leaks to downright treason. In fact, the main sources of information available to the British were their own signals which were now regularly deciphered.

The *Abwehr* station in Athens had been constituted in May 1941 and initially led by *Korvettenkapitän* Franz Maria Liedig (code name HAGEN). He had been working under the cover of assistant naval attaché at the German embassy in Greece. Liedig was a friend of *Oberst* Hans Oster and had been involved in the early attempts of the German resistance to dispose of Hitler. In April 1940 he had travelled to Copenhagen just a few days before the invasion of Denmark and may have been the source of the leak regarding the imminent occupation of Narvik. This information was received by the American Embassy in the Danish capital and quickly passed to the British Admiralty but was not taken seriously. The German resistance had hoped that a show of force by the Royal Navy might have dissuaded Hitler from invading Norway.

At the end of 1941 Liedig was replaced by *Oberst* Ludwig Dischler who had been chief of *Abwehr* station in Brussels. Dischler was himself succeeded by *Oberstleutnant* Walter Sensburg in June 1942. Liedig would remain in Athens as Chief of Gruppe I-M SO until the spring of 1943[21] when he was succeeded by the Viennese *Korvettenkapitän* Hans Sokol who had liberal views and abhorred the Nazis; the Austrian *Korvettenkapitän* Rudolf von Call, alias KELLERMANN, acted as deputy. Prior to this, von Call had been in charge of German para-naval activities with the assistance of Walter Fuerst, alias Vassilios Vassilou, an Austrian Jew who had lived in Greece since 1924 and had converted to the Greek orthodox faith. Von Call and Walter Furst had used several Greek caiques to insert spies in Cyprus and Syria.[22]

Gruppe I-M SO dealt with naval matters but it was specifically Gruppe III, under the 47-year-old *Oberstleutnant* (Lieutenant Colonel) Otto Hoffmeister, that was responsible for dealing with enemy sabotage, among other tasks. Hoffmeister's subordinate was *Korvettenkapitän* Meincke, in charge of section III-M (1942-1943) dealing with naval counter-intelligence and anti-sabotage. These two men would become the nemesis of the LOCKSMITH mission. Intercepting enemy signals and sending deceptive information (*funkspiel*) was the task of *Funkabwehr* Athens (a sub-section of *Abteilung* III-F) under *Oberleutnant* Bauer.

Gunfight

On 7 April Cumberlege had made a signal mentioning that if he could not make contact with the THURGOLAND party, it would be essential to get a reliable Greek agent sent over; he reiterated his personal choice for Fakaros. The Directorate of Special Operations (DSO), in a memorandum dated 14 April 1943, finally approved the sending of a British or French-speaking Greek agent but still rejected the choice of Fakaros, in any case it was too late for the LOCKSMITH mission. Mike wished to have another try but lacked suitable mines. He had great misgivings about the mines as the magnetic test had failed when they were standing upright but did work when they were tilted. He thought that perhaps they had been demagnetized inside the submarine but had decided to carry out the operation nonetheless. Cairo estimated that a new set of mines could be supplied in June but the operation could not be undertaken before mid-July.

This lengthy signal may have helped the Germans pinpoint the approximate position of the transmitter. *Kapitän zur See* Hans-Paul Leithäuser, in charge of the coastal defences of Attica, was asked to put some of his vessels at the disposal of Meincke. The GFP in Athens, under *Kriminal Inspektor und Komissar* Torkler, was collaborating closely with the *Abwehr*. On the evening of 6 April three German patrol-boats, *GA-51*, *GA-54* and *GA-67* sailed from Piraeus towards the island of Hydra from where the transmission was believed to come. These boats were auxiliary minesweepers from the *Minensuchgruppe* (eighteen boats under the command of *Kapitänleutnant* D. R. Oesterlin) belonging to the *Küstenschutzflottille Attika* (Coastal Defence Flotilla Attica under *Kapitänleutnant* D. R. Dr Brune). The mission was organized by Meincke and included a detachment of the GFP 640 unit. The three boats were being used to triangulate the radio location. Once they reached the area it was realized that the transmission did not come from Hydra but from the mainland in the area of 'Furgari' (Fourkari) in the Tselevi Bay.

At about noon on 8 April – the date is confirmed by Cumberlege in the report he later entrusted to Jack Churchill and by Sambanis and Philippopoulos in their testimonies – a party of five Germans landed at Soupias, about 700 metres from Boufi Cove, near Pergari. According to the enquiry made after the war, they were guided by Ioannis N. Hadjidimitrou and his brother-in-law Nikolaos Skhizas, a close friend of Sambanis. The German report of this action does not mention the presence of the two Greeks but this may be an oversight. The landing party began searching the area, cautiously making their way towards Cumberlege's hut. They were examining the bushes when, about fifty yards from the hideout, they suddenly came across Cumberlege and Handley. Most of the area is covered with low vegetation and very few trees, making it difficult to understand how the two parties were surprised. The first one to react was Mike; he quickly drew out his pistol and shot *Feldwebel* Rautenberg severely wounding him in the thigh. Strangely enough, the Germans appear to have been taken completely aback. After an exchange of gunfire, they fled, abandoning their wounded comrade.

The two commandos ran back to their hut where Cumberlege quickly grabbed a submachine gun before escaping in the opposite direction. But they had made a fatal mistake: they had left their codebooks and transmitter behind. About an hour later the Germans had composed themselves and began searching the area thoroughly. They found the transmitter with a battery, two Italian-made machine pistols with five magazines, one pistol and a camera with three exposed films. They arrested a suspect – his identity is not known but this may have been Philippopoulos – and returned to Piraeus the next evening, reporting the mission completed.

Dimitrios Sambanis witnessed the gunfight. He recalled that there were eight Germans and they were about sixty metres from the LOCKSMITH hideout and would have probably missed it but for the unfortunate fact that Cumberlege and Handley were seen outside, moving stores. He confirmed that the officer, Cumberlege, immediately shot one of the Germans, seriously wounding him, and that his companions, after hearing several shots, turned in flight leaving the wounded man there. About ten minutes after the gunfight, Sambanis met Cumberlege who had run back to pick up an automatic weapon and was making off in the opposite direction. He was urged by the Englishman to join him by escaping in the hills. Sambanis replied that he would comply but he had to assemble his whole family, eighteen persons, and it would take some time. He then saw Mike and the radio operator, Handley, escaping towards Damala to join their two companions. About an hour after the encounter, he observed about sixty Germans disembarking from the patrol-boats and combing the area. They discovered the radio transmitter and some of the stores.

After the war Sambanis, who had received £1,000 from Cumberlege for safe-keeping, came under suspicion of betraying the commandos, but no concrete evidence was found. His friendship with Skhizas did not help but then it would have been easy for him to arrange a trap for the commandos had he been inclined to do so. For his part in the demise of the LOCKSMITH party, Hadjidimitrou, aka 'Kareklas' or 'the chair maker', was arrested by BCIS Salonika (Balkan Counter-Intelligence Section) on 27 May 1945. He does not appear to have suffered much from his supposed collaboration and may have even benefited from some of the loot of the LOCKSMITH party. After the war he purchased and ran the boat *Elleni* which was the largest ferry linking Poros and Galatas. Skhizas disappeared and was rumoured to have been executed by the Andartes but his true fate is uncertain. According to Ioannis Sambanis, he was most probably liquidated by the Germans.

In the meantime Cumberlege and Handley had slipped through the net and joined up with Steele and Kotrba in the village of Damala where they had set up the second transmitter. Cumberlege went about using the cover name of Cabelis but the fact that none of the four commandos spoke Greek was a great handicap for further operations.

It was not long before this transmitter was used to warn Cairo of the commandos' predicament, but AST Athens intercepted the signal and the Germans realized that another station was now emitting. Cairo appears to have suspected that the LOCKSMITH party may have been captured. According to Panayotis Manzaris, son of Nikolaos Manzaris, the 'man with the golden earring', (Mike Cumberlege), went about the village barefooted and in Greek clothing and used the name of 'Tsabis'.[23] The four men from LOCKSMITH were fed by his father who owned a mill near Devil's Bridge. They used a bicycle to power up the transmitter but reception was bad and they had to move it to the top of the hill to be able to reach Cairo. They hid in a cave, a few hundred metres above Devil's Bridge. Nikolaos had emigrated to Australia in 1918 but had decided to return to Greece in 1928. He spoke good English and was thus a valuable asset to the commandos as none spoke Greek. Although Panayotis was too young to remember any event, his father told him that 'Tsabis' had agreed to become his godfather at his coming christening and even donated his gold earring as a gift.[24] Panayotis was under the impression that 'Tsabis' had been killed by the Germans at Tselevinia but we know this was not the case.

In his account, Sambanis stated that, six days after the gunfight, he was visited by a strong German force that searched for the British assisted by an aircraft which flew at low level. The next day an Italian boat arrived and removed all items from his houses and sheds.

At 2240 hours on 13 April the German patrol-boats *GA-52*, *GA-57* and *GA-62* sailed from Piraeus for the island of Hydra again under *Abwehr* orders but they returned to Piraeus at 2300 hours the following night, after cruising in vain off Cape Kellevini. This was probably the 'visit' mentioned by Sambanis.

About fifteen days after the gunfight, Cumberlege and Steele returned to the area and met Sambanis in the hills above his property. The Greek showed them a place where he had hidden some of the stores they had entrusted to him and these had not been discovered by the enemy. They transferred them by night to another spot but then disclosed to Sambanis that they had failed to find 2,000 gold sovereigns they had previously hidden. Suspicions immediately fell on Philippopoulos as Sambanis told them that, four or five days before, he had been approached by him and disclosed that the British had hidden a box under a large stone and that they should go and get it. Sambanis had told him not to interfere with the British.

Cumberlege asked Sambanis to get the money back but Philippopoulos had disappeared after he had divided the spoils with another accomplice, D. Bisias, also known by his nickname 'Harbilas'.[25] The theft was greatly distressing as it could limit their future operations. Sambanis was asked to arrest Philippopoulos and, if he refused to hand over the box, to execute him.

After the war Philippopoulos would testify that Skhizas, one of the Greeks who had guided the German party on 8 April, arrived one evening at Sambanis' house to get information on the British. He tried to infer that the commandos were betrayed by Sambanis but if this was so it would have been easy for the Germans to have them arrested at the time.

Later it would transpire that another 1,000 sovereigns had been left in the care of Sambanis for safekeeping. This would leave 1,000 sovereigns unaccounted for, plus the diamonds, some of which may have been given to the MIDAS 614 group and to the Greek inhabitants of the Poros area, who had supplied the mission with food and lodging.

The Trap
From 22 to 24 April the auxiliary minesweepers *GA-53*, *GA-57* and *GA-62* had made a sortie to track the LOCKSMITH party but their radio appears to have been silent at this time and again the Germans returned empty-handed.

On 26 April the radio operator, (Handley) arrived from Damala and brought two signals to the two commandos stating that a submarine would come to fetch them at 2130 hours on 29 or 30 April at Fourkari, at the same place where they had landed. Cumberlege ordered him to go to Damala and fetch the radio set and the other commando, (Kotrba). Unbeknownst to them, the message actually originated from the *Abwehr* Athens section where *Korvettenkapitän* Werner Meincke was preparing a trap. Using the codebooks captured on 8 April, the *Abwehr* now carried out a *funkspiel,* mimicking signals from Cairo in an effort to trap the commandos.

There was now an unexpected interference to these plans. The Greek resistance had shown some teeth and the area of Euboa had long been a stronghold of the communists of ELAS/EAM. On 14 April an Italian postal boat travelling from Volos to Stylis had been captured by partisans and towed to Volos. The German patrol boats *GA-02* and *GA-26* had tried to intervene but were hit by gunfire which had caused some casualties.

In concert, the German and Italian high commands decided to clear this area with the largest scale operation the Aegean had witnessed since the occupation. In the early hours of 20 April, the Italian destroyer *Turbine* sailed from Piraeus to take over command of a force consisting of the torpedo boats *Solferino* and *Castelfidardo*, both already on the scene, the fast motor patrol boats *MS-41* and *MS-26,* the minesweeper *RD-9* and the tug *Elias.* The Germans had provided the auxiliaries *Drache* and *Bulgaria,* the submarine chaser *UJ-2102* and the patrol-boats *GA-03, -05,-06,-08, -09,43,-53, -55,-57,-59,-69, -59,-61,-66,-68* and *Aetos.* Their objective was to clear the Euboa Channel and the Volos areas from insurgents. By the time *Turbine* was on the scene, the naval operations were almost over. On 27 April the Italian *Pinerolo* Division (this division would join the Greek resistance after the Italian armistice) had sent four columns to converge on the partisans. The whole operation would net a number of prisoners, capture some twenty-five caiques and seize the steamer *City of Karachi* which had been beached since April 1941 and had fallen into the hands of the rebels.

This operation had practically emptied Piraeus of shipping and may have caused Meincke some difficulty in obtaining the three vessels required for his own use. Finally, at 1630 hours on 29 April, the patrol vessel *GA-04* under the command of *Obersteuermann* Schaefer and the motorboats *Könnern* and *Aegaeis* sailed from Piraeus to patrol off Tselevinia which was some thirty-five miles away. Cleverly, the Germans had chosen moonless nights when the commandos would not be able to distinguish in the dark that patrol boats were coming to the rendezvous instead of the expected submarine.

Why the radio operator Handley did not detect that the last signal was faked is not known. We have to believe that the German radio operator had done an excellent job in mimicking the Cairo station. That same evening, the four men of the LOCKSMITH party donned their uniforms and, carrying their transmitter, went to the appointed rendezvous. Sambanis and a party of Greeks who wished to be evacuated came along, but no boat showed up. Meincke's boats missed the first rendezvous; possibly rough weather had slowed down the patrol boats and they had sailed too late to reach Tselevinia in time. The following morning, the three boats most probably cruised along the coast out of sight. In the evening Cumberlege signalled again with his torch; this time it was answered, but, according to the Greek witnesses, something was wrong and the British officer did not appear convinced and feared a trap. After exchanging signals for about three hours, the four commandos decided to risk it and took to a rubber boat but the Greeks wisely refused to join them. About ten minutes later a searchlight illuminated them and a machine gun opened fire; they could not put up any resistance and surrendered. One magnetic mine and their radio transmitter were also seized and the patrol boats returned to Piraeus with their prisoners. The four men were disembarked at 0730 hours on 1 May. The mine found was most likely the fifth mine which was defective and had not been used. Mike had probably taken it back so that experts could study the flaws in the design. The Germans noted that a similar mine had been found floating in the Corinth Canal the month before (see previous chapter).

After the war Sambanis related how Cumberlege had appeared at first agitated and believed the 'submarine' to be German. Sambanis had then taken away his family but, half an hour later, Mike had returned and told him that everything was all right; the submarine was British but could not see his small torch. He then said goodbye and the British began to row away in their boat. After about ten minutes there was the sound of gunfire. Sambanis was helpless; he could only return to his family and they fled to the hills. They eventually made their way to Athens where he claimed to have signalled Cairo of the fate of the LOCKSMITH party; the signal does not appear to have reached Cairo. About a month later, he learned that they had been taken to Averoff prison.

In 1945 the Greek investigator Prossalendis who led the enquiry on the LOCKSMITH party was highly suspicious of Dimitrios Sambanis, recording that he had feigned illness at the last minute to avoid sailing with the LOCKSMITH party. He was suspected of collusion with the Germans but nothing could be proven. Cumberlege himself appeared to have trusted him completely and had given him the considerable sum of 1,000 sovereigns for services rendered and safe-keeping. Major Michael Ward, who was the recipient of the Prossalendis report, did not judge that there was enough evidence to accuse him. Sambanis was located in early 1944 by the Andartes and roughed up to obtain some money. After the war, he rented a caique to sell lemons from his farm to Salonika. For his return trip, he took passage on the steamship *Heimara*, also known as *Chimara*, which sailed for Piraeus. His decision was fatal as the ship either hit a floating mine or hit a reef—versions differ— and sank on 19 January 1947. The vessel was the former German *Hertha* (1,257 grt, 1905) ceded as reparation to Greece and was carrying members of EAM/ELAS being exiled to the Aegean islands; 389 lives were lost. Although Sambanis was not on the casualty list, Poros records indicate that he was drowned on his return trip.

In March 1945 a German deserter, Emilius Katt, was caught and it was discovered that he had been in the boat that had seized the commandos. Unfortunately, through a misunderstanding, he was shipped to a PoW camp in the Middle East before he could be properly interrogated. Although SOE documents showed that there was a keen interest in finding out what Katt really knew, no information has been located of a follow-up.

The only positive aspect was that the capture of the men probably reinforced the Germans in their belief that the Peloponnese was to be invaded in the near future. This played well in the general deception plans devised by the Allies to force the German and Italian forces to be dispersed away from the future invasion of Sicily. We know that, in the middle of May, the German Admiral Aegean was much concerned about his defences of the western Peloponnese and had requested all mine-laying efforts be concentrated in this area and off Kalamata in an effort to improve their defences. However, any suggestion that the LOCKSMITH party would have been deliberately sacrificed to reinforce this deception must be rejected. The plan to block the Corinth Canal pre-dated any of the deception plans.

In a few days Axis forces would surrender in Tunisia and nearly 300,000 men would be taken prisoner. The whole of North Africa was now in Allied hands. During the same month Allied anti-submarine forces would sink over forty U-boats; it was the turning point in the battle of the Atlantic. Admiral Dönitz was forced to withdraw his boats from the North Atlantic theatre until a solution could be found to offset Allied anti-submarine measures. Following the victories at El Alamein and Stalingrad, the tide of the war had definitely turned, but final victory was still two long years away.

By coincidence, on 8 May the German-controlled *Aghia Varvara*, registered in Volos as No. 205, (this was not Sideris' boat) was intercepted north of Crete and sunk by gunfire from the submarine *Papanicolis.*

Tselevinia was in the Italian-controlled area and the Germans should have informed their allies of their raid. Apparently they declined to do so, perhaps from fear that the Italians would leak the information and jeopardize the operation.

Following the capture of the LOCKSMITH party there were no German reprisals on the inhabitants of the Poros area, which later led to the belief that they had been betrayed. However, it appears most likely that the presence of the three boats was to triangulate their position as a result of the interception of their signals. In Cairo there was no immediate awareness of what had happened and it is probable that German radio operators were scrambling their signals.

On 4 July 1943 Brigadier Keble of MO4 would recommend the commandos for awards. In the case of Sergeant Handley, he mentioned that he was captured on 9 April with another – Kotrba – while Cumberlege and Steele managed to escape. Keble was under the impression that they had moved to the island of Hydra. We do not know the source of these errors as German documents show clearly that the commandos were all captured on 1 May at Tselevinia and there is no indication that they ever went to Hydra. Keble added that Handley had operated his wireless under German control until mid-June but had managed to insert clues in his messages to indicate he was working under duress. Since Keble was the only SOE officer in the Middle East to have access to ULTRA messages, it is possible that he made use of these but was induced into error by a false interpretation. If he did get his information from an ULTRA signal, this has not been found in the documents released so far at the National Archives. It was also believed that Handley was used by the Germans to send false signals to Cairo as three radio operators in the Egyptian capital recognized his touch, or perhaps the German operators had succeeded in imitating it. The signal of 19 April is certainly genuine and no mention is made of the earlier capture of two commandos. Did Handley collaborate with the Germans? He may have told them about the security check but the use of odd wording helped Cairo recognize that the messages were fed by the enemy. For example the messages referred to 'baggage' instead of 'stores'.

Later it was found out that the LOCKSMITH party had been sent to Germany on 11 May. The same day, Group South, the German high command in charge of the Black Sea and Aegean areas, had enquired from Admiral Aegean if precautions had been taken for the defence of the Corinth Canal. Was this a coincidence or as a result of their capture? A few days later, 617 Squadron RAF carried out a successful raid on the Ruhr Dams by using four-ton mines with hydrostatic fuses. This raised the concern that similar attempts might be made against important objectives but it does not appear that the Corinth Canal was ever considered for this type of attack.

The LOCKSMITH men were brought to Averoff jail in Athens. If Hitler's *Kommandobefehl* was to be followed to the letter, the commandos should have been handed over to the *Sicherheitsdienst* and on no account kept under military guard as ordinary prisoners of war but treated as common criminals. From information later acquired, it was known that *Oberstleutnant* Hoffmeister, head of the *Abwehr* Group III in Athens, had resorted to 'unlawful' means to extract information from the four men. What form this torture took, and what information he got, we do not know. Once the interrogation was terminated, they should have been liquidated to conform to German policy at this time but this was not done, possibly since their names had been released to the Greek Red Cross. This was either done through an administrative error or perhaps it was done deliberately by a member of the *Abwehr*, some of them being quite opposed to the methods used by the Nazis.

PROMETHEUS II escapes

Commander Koutsoyannopoulos, who had been caught by the *Abwehr* in February 1943, was also an inmate of Averoff jail. He caught a glimpse of the LOCKSMITH team but was unable to communicate with them.

Following the capture of PROMETHEUS II, his most important collaborators, Ioannis Peltekis and Timoleon Louis, had fled to Smyrna. On 23 February they had been interviewed by Major Pawson, with Captain C. J. Harris, his assistant, acting as an interpreter.[26] Louis expressed the wish to join the Royal Hellenic Navy while Peltekis, who now took the codename of APOLLO, agreed to return to Greece and try to form a new organization, YVONNE. This organization would take over from LOCKSMITH/ THURGOLAND, but ironically one of their final tasks would be to protect the Corinth Canal from destruction. Peltekis received elementary training in explosives and SOE methods, and the sum of $20,000 US for his own use and $50,000 US for Colonel Angelos Evert, Chief of the Athens Police, to bribe prison guards and secure the release of PROMETHEUS II. Colonel Evert played an essential role throughout the war by providing help to SOE and the Greek resistance. After the war Major Michael Ward wrote a letter of commendation and gave him a gold cigarette case as a token of appreciation from SOE. Yet he was not universally liked as he had ordered the Athens police to shoot during a left-wing demonstration.

On 6 March Peltekis sailed from Smyrna on the caique *Evangelos Panayotou*, reaching Athens three days later. He had made a brief stop at Euboa where he recruited a fisherman, 26-year-old Nikolaos Adam, who was to become his best underwater saboteur and is described in his SOE Personnel File as 'the most exceptional of APOLLO's collaborators'. He made his first contact by radio on 27 March; some reports also give the date as 2 or 3 April.

On 8 May 1943 Koutsoyannopoulos was released from Averoff, thanks to the cunning of Ioannis Peltekis who managed to bribe one of the jailers.[27] He reached Smyrna on 28 June and brought the first news that the commandos were in German hands. He stated that an English reserve naval lieutenant and five other Englishmen had been brought to Averoff prison; they were in uniform and were well treated. Later, he was shown a photograph of Cumberlege and confirmed that he was the officer he had seen and was fairly sure he recognized Sergeant Steele. It was bad luck that Peltekis did not know of the incarceration of the LOCKSMITH party at Averoff or he could have arranged for their escape at the same time as Koutsoyannopoulos.

Were Cumberlege and his men aware that Axis forces had capitulated in Tunisia and the whole of North Africa was now in Allied hands? Perhaps. Such news had a way of travelling fast even in prisons, and the morale of the incarcerated men would have been boosted. The tide of the war was turning but their ordeal was just beginning.

News from the LOCKSMITH party
On 10 May 1943 Cumberlege was allowed to write a message, limited to twenty-five words, to his wife Nancy; the Greek Red Cross would transmit it through Geneva. He wrote:

MY DARLING LOVE IN THIS FIRST LETTER TO YOU MY MARCUS AND BIRA ALL IS WELL WITH ME DON'T WORRY YOUR LOVING HUSBAND MICHAEL.[28]

Patricia Steele had not heard from her husband since January and had written from Rhodesia to the authorities on 12 July 1943 to enquire about his silence. She got an answer from MO4 dated 27 July, stating that he was missing in action and believed to be a prisoner of war as of 30 June.

Despite repeated requests from his father, it was only on 25 January 1944 that Sergeant Handley's relatives would receive a Red Cross cable from him. It was dated 11 May 1943 and read:

DEAR MOTHER, PRISONER OF WAR BUT DO NOT WORRY. WELL, AND TREATED ALL RIGHT. NO MAIL SINCE LAST DEC DATE ATHENS 11 MAY 1943 LOVE, EDWARD.

It is probable that these messages contained a hidden text but this has not been revealed. Military personnel operating behind enemy lines were usually taught a basic cipher to use in case of capture so that they could insert messages in ordinary letters that would get through the enemy censorship.

The day that Handley had written this note he was transferred with his three companions to Austria. Any chance that Peltekis could arrange their escape was gone.

Cumberlege's message was withheld as the *Abwehr* was determined to keep the capture secret in the hope of luring other SOE agents into their nets. It was only on 3 August that the message reached the British Red Cross. On 1 July Nancy Cumberlege had been informed that her husband was missing in action; she finally received his message on 7 August. Through unofficial channels she had already received some information that he was kept in Averoff prison, apparently from her sister Nora Wooler, who was a WRNS (Women's Royal Naval Service, known as Wrens) petty officer and worked at Queen Anne's Mansions. The vivacious Nora, known for her shapely legs, which had been used in Wren advertising posters, had by chance come upon confidential information concerning Mike's capture. Nancy disclosed her knowledge to the authorities but made sure that her sister would not be in trouble; the capture of Mike was then confirmed.

At this time Lieutenant Commander Hugh Bevan RNVR, from the Naval Intelligence Division, took a special interest in finding out the fate of Michael, perhaps at the instigation of Admiral Godfrey who may have pulled some strings, although he was no longer the Director of Naval Intelligence. This was pursued even after the war had ended.

Lord Glenconner was informed that no effort should be spared to affect the release of the LOCKSMITH party and to buy them out if need be and by concluding 'the tariff cannot be too high'. Unfortunately, it was recognized that the success of the PROMETHEUS II escape could not be easily repeated as security would now have undoubtedly been tightened.

Greeks who escaped to Turkey were usually interrogated and a number of their reports can be found in the National Archives. Copies were usually forwarded to, among others, David Pawson, Professor Alan John Bayard Wace, who worked for ISLD, as MI6 was known in the Middle East, and sometimes to Ellis Waterhouse of the Foreign Office; the latter would prove to be the nemesis of APOLLO.

The PROMETHEUS organization would eventually be resurrected. In the summer of 1944, when Captain (later Major) Michael Ward of SOE despatched a team consisting of Harilaos Louis (younger brother of Timoleon Louis, a Venizelist naval officer who had been active in the PROMETHEUS organization), Takis Andricopoulos and an unidentified third man, but their tasks appear to have been confined to the collection of intelligence.

In the meantime, Peltekis created the YVONNE organization and it would become one of the most important resistance groups of the war. It would be responsible for many attacks on Axis shipping and regularly supplied the Allies with information on the movements of enemy vessels and other intelligence. Peltekis, now known by his code name of APOLLO, had difficult beginnings.

Through a misunderstanding, his first signals failed to use the security check and he was believed to be in the hands of the Gestapo. The escape of PROMETHEUS II had been a great coup and SOE in Cairo were extremely pleased that their 'star' collaborator had safely reached Turkey. Soon, the YVONNE organization could report the sabotage of the Italian transport *Città di Savona* that was limpeted on 12 June and sank in shallow waters; sixty-nine horses were drowned but the ship was later raised. This was the first of a long string of successes by APOLLO and his men (see Appendix G).

On 21 July 1943 Smyrna sent the following signal to APOLLO:

WOULD IT BE POSSIBLE TO FIND OUT AND INFORM ME, BRITISH RESERVE NAVAL OFFICER CUMBERLEDGE (sic) AND THREE OTHER ENGLISHMEN, STEELE, HENLEY (sic) AND COTTAS (sic), ARE STILL IN AVEROFF PRISON. PROMYTHEUS SPOKE TO YOU ABOUT THESE MEN WHO WERE TOGETHER WITH HIM IN PRISON. THEY WERE HELD AS PRISONERS OF WAR AND SENT TO GERMANY.

Within a few weeks Italy had signed an armistice and the Badoglio government, who had taken over, joined the fight on the Allies' side. Prime Minister Churchill now decided that the Dodecanese Islands were ripe for occupation since it was hoped that the Italian garrisons would welcome British troops and this might induce Turkey to join the alliance. If most Italian forces were indeed willing to throw in their lot with the Allies, there were still some diehard fascists and the Germans were not yet ready to yield. Major Pawson was himself captured in the Dodecanese during the night of 18/19 September 1943. He had sailed from Samos for Ikaria on board the Italian motor torpedo boat *MAS-522*, along with Major Michael Parish of MI9 and Captain Levides of the Royal Hellenic Navy and a pro-Badoglio Italian officer. The Italian *MAS* captain had a change of heart and, during the night, the four men were overpowered – Parish was shot and wounded – and delivered to German authorities. According to the interrogation of a German agent, one of the British officers provided the *Sicherheitdienst* with a lot of information. Based on this knowledge, a plan was drawn to use a Brandenburg unit to carry out a raid on the British Intelligence mission in Cesme and abduct officers residing there. The raid was cancelled as it was a clear infringement of Turkish neutrality and this was to be avoided at this time.

Another signal follow dated 22 September:

... PLEASE OBTAIN ACCURATE AND FULL INFORMATION REGARDING FATES OF THE FOUR ENGLISHMEN WITH CUMBERLEDGE (sic) ...

The APOLLO organization replied on 24 September; they had correctly identified the four men:

MICHAEL CUMBERLEGE JAMES STEELE JOHN DAVIES [Jan Kotrba] AND THOMAS HANDLEY SENT TO CONCENTRATION CAMP IN POLAND SINCE MAY ELEVENTH.

They also informed Smyrna in the same signal that Pawson, Levides and Parish, captured earlier in the Dodecanese, were held in the Averoff jail.

Another signal from Smyrna followed on 13 October:

WE BELIEVE CUMBERLEGE IS IN SOME ORLAG. CAN YOU CONFIRM.

This was due to a message that Cumberlege had smuggled to an airman and was received by MI9 sometime in October. It was not clear from the message if the LOCKSMITH leader was located in a *stalag* near Barth on the Baltic coast, probably Stalag Luft I, or if the airman had been transferred there. The content mentioned that the task had been accomplished but that the Germans were working the wireless set to Cairo.

The APOLLO organization had in fact answered on 27 September:

CAMP OF CONCENTRATION WHERE CUMBERLEDGE (sic) AND OTHERS ARE IS MARKED IN GERMAN STALAG EIGHT SCHLESIEN.

There is no evidence to confirm this information and the four commandos were probably in Austria at this time. After the war enquiries made through the Swedish Red Cross revealed that the prisoners had been held at Mauthausen for eight months before being transferred to Sachsenhausen and this appears to be correct. The APOLLO organization had just been dealt a severe blow when three of their saboteurs were condemned to death and were executed on 9 October. SOE had sent money to secure their release – corruption was not unknown in Greece – but it arrived too late.

Chapter 16

Double-Cross Attempt

Radio Game

Double-cross attempts were not rare in the Second World War; British Intelligence had created a special XX (for double-cross) or Twenty Committee under John Cecil Mastermann to deal specifically with them. Most enemy agents who were captured in Britain during the war were either hanged or used as double agents, feeding the Germans with false information. This became especially important as the landings in Normandy were near and every attempt was made to draw enemy forces away from the area.

German Intelligence was not novice at the game and their most successful operation was Operation NORDPOL in the Netherlands (1942-1944) when they successfully penetrated the Dutch underground and captured a number of SOE agents. The *Abwehr* operated their radio sets initiating what was known as a *funkspiel* (radio game) or, in this particular case, the *Englandspiel.* One after the other, SOE agents parachuted into the Netherlands fell into the welcoming hands of the *Abwehr*, most of them being executed within a short time. The operation had been directed by *Abwehr* Major Hermann Giskes who later wrote an account of the operation. The blame could be laid directly on the lack of observance of security procedures by SOE. Critical security checks had been missing from the first messages and this had gone unnoticed by the SOE operators in London. Security checks were usually deliberate errors in spelling which were pre-arranged and confirmed that the signals were genuine. Their absence indicated that the signal was being sent under duress and that the operator had been captured.

The operation was terminated on 3 April 1944 when Giskes sent an ironical message to London, telling them that this was the last time they would be making business in the Netherlands and concluding with the chilling sentence:

NEVER MIND WHENEVER YOU WILL COME TO PAY A VISIT TO THE CONTINENT YOU MAY BE ASSURED THAT YOU WILL BE RECEIVED WITH SAME CARE AND RESULT. ALL THOSE YOU SENT US BEFORE.

It is certain that the AST Athens station entertained similar ideas and the capture of the radio sets and codes from the LOCKSMITH mission made this possible. They had successfully lured the four commandos into a trap and now they turned their attention to bigger games.

On 6 May Cairo sent a signal enquiring about the LOCKSMITH party and this was replied to two days later by the AST Athens station, now directing their deception directly to SOE headquarters and initiating the *funkspiel*. The following signal No.158 was sent in two parts:

158 STOP AT NEXT CONTACT THURGOLAND IS TAKEN UP SHOULD REPLY TO YOU SOON AS WISH TO TERMINATE CANAL ENTERPRISE STOP IF CONTACT WITH THURGOLAND IS LOST COMMUNICATIONS FOR THEM CAN BE ARRANGED BY MY MEDIATION STOP

WAITING FOR MANOLOPOULOS AND SPIRO KOTSIS ONE TWO REPEAT ONE TWO MAY STOP WAITING ALSO FOR VICTUALS AND ASSISTANCE FROM THURGOLAND AS SITUATION IS VERY SERIOUS NOW AS BEFORE STOP

We know that, by this time, all four members were in German hands and *Abwehr* Athens knew quite a few details about the operation. They had cleverly used the names of Manolopoulos and Kotsis, whom they knew to be connected to *Aghia Varvara* and were known to be at large. The identity of the two men did not have to be extracted through the torture of the LOCKSMITH team since they had already been identified several weeks before in connection with the false papers of this boat. The rendezvous of 12 May was fictitious. At the end of the war Sambanis made a statement that he gave a message for transmission on that very day (8 May) to a man named Kokorellis (probably Kareklas, an alias of Hadjidimitrou), warning Cairo of what had happened to Cumberlege. If so, the message does not appear to have gotten through. Did the *Abwehr* manage to use one or more survivors of the MIDAS 614 organization as a double agent? This is a possibility but no concrete evidence has been found. When pressed by Cairo as to the whereabouts of Cumberlege, the Germans tried to buy time by replying that he was in the hills and would return only on 11 May, although the signal was dated the same day.

From a report on the operation compiled at the end of the war, it is stated that Cairo received the following signal on 16 May:

THURGOLAND AND REPRESENTATIVES HAVE NOT APPEARED TILL TO-DAY. TRIED TO GET A BOAT FROM ELSEWHERE UNFORTUNATELY WITHOUT ANY SUCCESS. OUR POSITION IN THE WHOLE AREA HAS BECOME UNTENABLE AND I THINK

OUR REMAINING HERE ANY LONGER WILL BE OF NO VALUE. PLEASE GIVE INSTRUCTIONS URGENTLY.

This signal contained the security check known only to Cumberlege and Handley, so it appears that someone had talked. Cairo replied that a caique would be sent to evacuate the party and leaving it to Cumberlege to arrange for the rendezvous.

On 28 May another signal, No.163 from Athens, was sent to Cairo:

NR ONE SIX THREE OF TWENTY EIGHT STOP FROM HANDLEY STOP REGRET ANNOUNCE D.H. EIGHTY NINE [*D/H89 was the SOE code name for Lieutenant Cumberlege*] SHOT BY ITALIAN PATROL AFTER HAVING KILLED TWO OF THEM STOP CONSIDERING OUR EXTREMELY SERIOUS POSITION WE BEG URGENTLY YOUR ASSISTANCE STOP IF POSSIBLE SUGGEST RENDEZVOUS WITH SUBMARINE AT BEACH OF OUR LANDING KNOWN TO BOTH PAPANICHOLAS AND TAKOO STOP PLEASE REPLY WITH INSTRUCTIONS SOONEST STOP ENDS.

Cairo was disturbed to learn of the alleged death of Lieutenant Cumberlege but realized that this was a fake message and still entertained hope that he was still alive. The reference to the submarines *Papanicolis* and *Taku* meant that at least one of the commandos must have been talkative, although we know that the *Taku* mission had already been known since the capture of a Greek wireless operator during Operation SATURN. This was not the first time that an attempt to entrap an Allied submarine was made by the *Abwehr*. In September 1941, a French agent had been landed by the submarine HMS *Urge*, Lieutenant Commander E. P. Tomkinson RN, near Palermo. He was caught and turned by the *Abwehr*. An attempt to destroy the submarine as it was returning to pick up the agent almost succeeded. HMS *Urge* barely managed to extricate herself from the clutches of the Italian torpedo boats *Cascino* and *Dezza*.

Two independent reports reached Cairo before the end of May stating that a British party had been captured by the enemy in their area during the first week of May.

Cairo cautiously replied on 1 June:

NUMBER (48) OF FIRST STOP DEEPLY REGRET NEWS STOP WHERE IS JUMBO STOP YOU SHOULD NOW MOVE TO AREA GIVEN OUR LAST TELEGRAM STOP TRY TAKE W/T SET WITH YOU STOP IF THIS IMPOSSIBLE TRY TO OBTAIN SAFE ADDRESS OF PERSON NEAR CAPE THROUGH WHOM WE MIGHT BE ABLE TO CONTACT YOU AND INFORM US BEFORE

YOU LEAVE STOP THEN HIDE SET IN SAFE PLACE STOP IF NO
ADDRESS IS AVAILABLE GIVE US YOUR ESTIMATED TIME OF
ARRIVAL IN AREA OF CAPE STOP GOOD LUCK.

'Jumbo' was a nickname of James Steele and the Germans were not likely to
know about it. It was a test to verify the authenticity of the signal.

The 'Cape' was a reference to Cape Trikeri on the Peloponnese coast west
of Spetses, apparently made in an earlier signal from Cairo which was not found
at the archives. It is about seventy miles over land from where the commandos
were located.

The post-war report also cites a signal made by Handley on 1 June (actually
dated 31 May):

FROM HANDLEY STOP GOING TO TRIKERI WITH RADIO AND
BAGGAGE WOULD BE TOO DIFFICULT. AND DANGEROUS
HAVING LOST CIVILIAN CLOTHES. IMPOSSIBLE TO GET
SUITABLE BOAT STOP PLEASE SEND CAIQUE TO THAT
MENTIONED SMALL BEACH ABOUT TWO MILES WESTWARD
OF KELEVINI ISLANDS STOP IT IS THE SAFEST PLACE WE
KNOW AS ENEMY NIGHT PATROLS OR SHIPPING NOT
OBSERVED STOP PLEASE GIVE IMMEDIATE NOTICE OF
ARRIVAL CAIQUE FOR HELP IS URGENTLY NEEDED STOP
CAIQUE MIGHT LAY UP BEFORE AT POROS ENDS.

This message and the one before were regarded with suspicion as the name of
the operator was never mentioned in previous signals and because of the
reference to the word 'baggage' instead of 'stores'. Did Handley collaborate
with the Germans? If he did, this was very briefly and he appeared to have left
clues for Cairo to find their fate.

The next day Major Boxshall of SOE London informed Commander Jenning
at the Admiralty that it had been obvious for some time that the wireless radio
used by LOCKSMITH had fallen into enemy hands. That no submarine was
despatched reveals that Cairo treated these signals with suspicion; for we know
that submarines were available. During May *Papanicolis* was involved in a
special mission in Crete and, in June, the submarine *Katsonis* landed another
party in Euboa. They could easily have been diverted to pick up the
LOCKSMITH team if needed. As *Abwehr* ciphers had been read by British
Intelligence, there is a possibility that the capture of the commandos was already
known but, for security reasons, was not disclosed. Cairo informed Major
Boxshall in London that Cumberlege had most likely fallen into enemy hands.
Nevertheless Cairo played along and on 3 June issued one last signal to
LOCKSMITH:

NUMBER (49) OF THREE JUNE STOP WE REFER TO CAPE
TRIKERI EIGHT MILES NORTH OF LEONIDHION STOP VERY
SORRY WE CANNOT REPEAT NOT SEND CAIQUE TO PLACE
YOU MENTION STOP YOU MUST EITHER MOVE TO AREA OF
CAPE TRIKERI OR REMAIN WHERE YOU ARE STOP IF YOU
CHOOSE TO STAY WE WILL TRY SEND HELP TO YOU BUT THIS
WILL BE DIFFICULT. AND WILL TAKE TIME STOP ENDS

This signal was to eliminate any doubt that LOCKSMITH may have thought
that the rendezvous was on Trikeri Island, a small island between Hydra and
Spetses, and therefore could only have been accessible by boat.

No further message purported to be from LOCKSMITH was received and
it is likely that *Abwehr* Athens was nonplussed at the reference to 'Jumbo' and
realized that the game was up. The *Funkspiel* was terminated. MO4 in Cairo
does not appear to have been subtle enough to keep the communication channel
open. A unique opportunity to feed the enemy with false information was
perhaps missed. Sometimes this could help the survival of the agent who was
caught as the Germans might be induced to keep him alive for their own use in
deception.

Hitler had already given his infamous *Kommandobefehl* which instructed
that captured Allied commandos, even in uniform, should be summarily
executed (18 October 1942). Somehow the four members of LOCKSMITH had
survived thus far and were brought to Mauthausen concentration camp near
Vienna. They had had a very 'unpleasant' time at the hand of an *Oberst*
Hofmeister (sic) in Athens, and now their tormentor was H. I. Seidl of the
Gestapo. This was known through a message transmitted by Cumberlege to Jack
Churchill in February 1945:

OBERST HOFMEISTER [SIC] DEFENCE [ABWEHR] ATHENS
HERR SEIDL GESTAPO VIENNA BOTH USED UNLAWFUL
MEANS TO PRESS A CONVICTION.

Oberstleutnant Otto Hoffmeister was head of *Abwehr Gruppe III* in Athens and
the superior of *Korvettenkapitän* Meincke. There is a reference dated 1 August
1942 to Major Hoffmeister from Freiburg im Breisgau in connection with
Operation ISINGLASS, the Atkinson affair, in the captured *Abwehr* papers, very
likely the same person. Seidl may have been *SS Hauptsturmführer* Siegfried
Seidl who was in charge of the Theresienstadt concentration camp and was
executed for his war crimes in 1947, but more probably this was *SS
Hauptsturmführer* Fritz Seidler who operated at the Mauthausen concentration
camp and was known for his brutality. Seidler's fate is uncertain, but he is
believed to have shot himself in May 1945.

Under duress Cumberlege was forced to sign a confession that they were saboteurs, even though the party had been captured in uniform which had been confirmed by German reports. In August 1943 the Greek Red Cross informed British authorities that the party had been captured on 1 May, which was correct. Why their lives were temporarily spared is not clear. While in captivity, Cumberlege would be promoted to acting lieutenant commander on 30 September 1943 and finally to lieutenant commander with seniority as of 22 November 1943.

No further information was received from the Red Cross despite several enquiries. Nancy Cumberlege believed that her husband appeared in a photograph of the April 1944 issue of *The Prisoner of War*. It depicted the theatre staff at Stalag Luft III and the second man from the left on the bottom row was apparently Michael. No evidence was found that he had ever been held in this camp and this was expressly forbidden by Hitler's *Kommandobefehl* as saboteurs were under no circumstances to be held in prisoner of war camps.

After the war Nancy Cumberlege would learn from a woman who had acted as an interpreter during her husband's interrogation in Austria that he had been held there until December 1943. Cumberlege confirmed it when he confided to Jack Churchill that he had been moved to Sachsenhausen in January 1944.

Chapter 17

APOLLO and the Don Stott Episode

SOE in London had been very critical of their Cairo headquarters as they were slow in forwarding copies of their signals due to a shortage of typists and cipher clerks. Security had not been the best, as code expert Leo Marks would find out when he visited them later in September. But mistakes were not one-sided; on 3 August SOE in Cairo was informed that documents relating to the LOCKSMITH operation had disappeared in London. With some embarrassment, it was revealed that they were lost on 23 July, while being transferred from the Naval Intelligence Division to SOE headquarters on Baker Street. Measures were to be taken in case these documents had fallen into enemy hands, such as changing the operation code name in case further attempts would be made.

By June 1943 it was obvious that canal traffic was unperturbed; Cairo had considered another blocking attempt by using a new team, but not until Axis surveillance had diminished. A new batch of mines was now available at Havant, but the strategic situation had changed and the urgency had waned. The mines could now be sent by sea rather than by air. The whole North African coast was now in Allied hands and there were no Axis reinforcements to be shipped through the canal and Crete. However, the canal was still essential for controlling the Aegean; German units garrisoned most islands while the Italians heavily defended the Dodecanese. With the invasion of Sicily imminent, it was still essential to foment trouble in Greece to draw Axis forces away. At the same time, any weakening of the Axis position in the Aegean might induce Turkey to enter the war on the Allies' side and affect the whole Balkan situation.

Sabotage in the Piraeus area would now be taken over by the YVONNE organization led by APOLLO (Ioannis Peltekis), who proved to be a brilliant organizer. Peltekis was born on 25 July 1904 in Chanak, Turkey, and had worked for the PROMETHEUS II organization before escaping to Turkey. Lieutenant Colonel Julian Antony Dolbey, commanding officer of Force 133 as SOE in the Balkans would be known, described him as the 'most efficient and the most successful' of all the resistance leaders under British command, and recommended him for the DSO decoration.

The YVONNE organization kept a steady stream of information with Smyrna, the SOE station in Turkey. A number of apartments were rented in

Athens and the radio operators were moved around constantly to avoid being pinpointed by the enemy's efficient radio direction finders.

The saboteurs of YVONNE had been very successful in using limpets and claimed to have sunk or damaged fifty-eight Axis ships (about 56,000 tons) during the war, while providing a steady stream of information on Axis shipping movements. Already, by the summer of 1943, their activities were causing alarm at the headquarters of the German Sea Defences Attica. But no further attempt was made to block the Corinth Canal and no special mines were provided, although a new set of mines designed by Cumberlege had been sent to the Middle East by sea.

The success of the APOLLO organization led to the recall of Peltekis to Cairo where he arrived at the end of August. He was to receive a new set of instructions and this time met with Lord Glenconner, Brigadier Keeble and Colonel Tamplin of SOE. Before returning to Greece, he was also interviewed by Mr Reginald 'Rex' Leeper, the British ambassador to Greece and Mr Waterhouse of his staff. Peltekis did not have much respect for the Greek monarchy and made his views clear in his communications. This could not have endeared him to the Foreign Office, but his work was too valuable to be ignored.

The Italian armistice of 8 September 1943 radically changed the Mediterranean situation. The Greek communists took the opportunity to seize as many weapons as possible from Italian forces that were being disarmed. They were now less inclined to co-operate with the British who appeared bent on restoring King George II to his throne. They had certainly not been encouraged when a delegation of EAM had nearly been imprisoned during a visit to Cairo the previous August. SOE missions in Greece were caught in the middle and had to make the best of a difficult situation.

The strange episode of Captain Donald John Stott followed. This enterprising New Zealander had been captured in Crete but escaped with his friend Bob Morton from a prisoner of war camp in Greece and reached Egypt. Both men had joined SOE in Cairo and were to have parachuted behind enemy lines at El Alamein but their aircraft was hit and Morton seriously wounded. Stott had already returned to Greece and taken a leading part in the destruction of the Asopos bridge in June 1943. The Asopos bridge was repaired by the Germans after four weeks but, at the first test, it collapsed again and needed another three weeks to repair. Stott had been suggested by Cumberlege as a suitable member for the LOCKSMITH team but was not available at the time. MO4 had sent him on a new mission to sabotage the aerodromes of Kalamaki, Tatoi and Eleusis (KINCRAIG mission), and to examine the possibility of blowing up the Asopos bridge a second time. Later he was also instructed to prepare counter-scorch tactics, and especially to prevent the Marathon dam from being destroyed should the Germans evacuate Greece.

Using the code name WEAZEL he was to be assisted by Captain H.

McIntyre RE, and the inseparable Sergeant (later Second Lieutenant) Bob Morton, the latter acting as his radio operator. He had contacted Captain Kanaris who was now in charge of the remnants of MIDAS 614 and through one of his contacts, Pavlos Bakouros, was informed that the mayor of Athens was interested in meeting him.

Stott was unable to attend the rendezvous but McIntyre did meet the mayor of Athens, Angelos Georgatos, on 17 October 1943 at his house on Homer Street and through him a meeting with Gestapo officials was arranged. The threat of communism and the possibility of an arrangement with Great Britain were discussed.

Two days later, Peltekis, who had not been informed that Stott had returned to Athens, was surprised to receive a message from him informing that he was in hiding. The APOLLO organization had been busy monitoring and reporting the German build-up which would result in the invasion of Leros and Samos.

On 4 November Stott met with *Oberleutnant* Roman Loos, chief of the *Geheime Feldpolizei* for the Balkans, and Major Welle of the civilian administration. Loos' adjutant, Karl Schurman, acted as a hostage. Loos was a native of Linz, Austria, as was Kaltenbrunner, the redoubtable head of the RHSA (German Security Services) and the two men had bonded, so it was hoped that the meeting would be sanctioned in high places. Another meeting occurred on 21 November. The SOE officer asked to be allowed to contact Cairo to forward their proposals. The Germans obliged, even supplying him with a side arm should partisans be encountered! He was driven to Corinth where he hoped to use a British transmitter to contact Cairo. He took the opportunity to examine the Corinth Canal and made mental notes of its defences. Stott later reported that an attack on the bridge across the canal would be too difficult to carry out on account of the strong defences. However, the two railway bridges running parallel to the canal were not well defended and could be destroyed at an opportune time and prevent German reinforcements from pouring into the Peloponnese.

Stott used APOLLO as a conduit and reported briefly to Smyrna that the Germans had approached him with proposals claiming to come directly from Hitler. The New Zealander had been non-committal, agreeing only to act as a courier and he was now waiting for more information from Berlin. This upset Cairo, as Stott had no such instructions and had acted on his own initiative. The event could be embarrassing if it became known publicly. The Germans could exploit it to drive a wedge between the Western democracies and the Soviet Union and divide the Greek resistance. To the Greek communists this could only confirm them in their opinion of 'Perfidious Albion' double-crossing them. Stott was told to restrict his activities to sabotage tasks and not to meddle in local politics. He replied that he had no such intentions and had raised a guerrilla force of 12,000 men, a gross exaggeration! In fact he had been promised the co-operation of right-wing elements whose loyalty was of doubtful value and who were more interested in fighting communism than liberating Greece from the German yoke.

Later Stott was given a safe conduct and sailed in a German caique via Chios, reaching Chesme, Turkey, without incident on 25 November.

The same day as Stott had communicated his initiative, Peltekis had quickly realized the damage that Stott's mission could do to the Allied cause and signalled his misgivings. When Stott returned to Cairo, he was severely criticized for his dealings with the Germans and he blamed APOLLO for his failure. The New Zealander was certainly a very brave man and had proven himself by surviving in occupied Greece for long periods of time, but he was politically naive. SOE opposed his return to Greece; he would remain in their employment but would be sent to a new theatre of operations. In March 1945 he is believed to have drowned when attempting to land from the submarine USS *Perch* in Borneo on another clandestine mission.

In contrast to Don Stott, Ioannis Peltekis, APOLLO, had all the tools to become an astute politician but he was himself under suspicion that he was working for the Germans. Peltekis was a republican and did not hide his opposition to the return of the king to Greece, but his organization appears to have been apolitical. A brilliant organizer, he had quickly established a large network of spies and saboteurs and they provided a steady stream of accurate information to MO4. Recalled to Cairo, he was forced to defend his actions but managed successfully to refute accusations that he was a double agent. His accuser was Mr Ellis Waterhouse of the British Embassy to Greece, who had heard allegations from a Greek contact with royalist sympathies.

This was not the first time that APOLLO had come under suspicion. His initial messages in April 1943 lacked the security check and for a time it was believed that he was in enemy hands, but apparently this was due to an oversight. On 1 June 1943 David Pawson wrote a message stating that he had received definite confirmation that APOLLO had been captured but did not disclose the source. According to Peltekis, Smyrna station had first accused him of being a Gestapo agent on 6 April 1943 and had received confirmation from the NIKO station, manned by ODYSSEUS. Yet, shortly after, the APOLLO organization embarked on a string of successful operations, beginning with the sabotage of the Italian transport *Città di Savona* carried out by young Niko Adam and a flood of signals describing the movements of Axis shipping. Even Enigma keys were provided which reinstated Peltekis as a member of good standing by MO4.

It became unavoidable that APOLLO would meddle in politics; he had hoped to unite various Greek resistance organizations regardless of their allegiance. He was treading a fine line and was accused of being a Gestapo agent by the left and a communist agent by the right. Peltekis was unruffled by the accusations; he would later mention that he had been charged of many crimes, among them being a communist, a Gestapo agent, a professional gambler (by Stott) and many others. Ironically, he added that he had still not been accused of being an American agent. When he had been recalled to Cairo to explain his views, he did not disguise his republican leanings and this did not endear him to royalist circles. The Greek government in exile had observed the growth of the EAM/ELAS communist-run organization with increasing panic and it was suspected that Peltekis sympathized with them.

After claiming eighteen ships, totalling 48,000 tons, sunk or damaged by sabotage, the YVONNE organization suffered a serious blow when Adam and two of his saboteurs were arrested and executed on 9 October 1943.[29] Adam is reported to have been submitted to terrible tortures but revealed nothing. He attempted to escape from his execution squad but was machine gunned 200 yards from the spot of execution. MO4 lost no time in replacing him with a trained saboteur, Kostas, who was parachuted in on 15 October. Peltekis had returned to Athens on 6 October and diligently engaged in reconstituting his organization. He was now informed that his main contact in Smyrna, Pawson, had been captured with Parish and Levides in the Dodecanese while attempting to induce Italian forces to join the Allies.

Fortunately, Pawson's assistant, Pamela Lovibond, proved to be an efficient collaborator and smoothed the transition when the inexperienced Major Alan W. Paton, codename DRAX, arrived to take over. Sabotage was resumed but in April 1944, with the Germans hot on his trail, Peltekis was again forced to flee to Cairo. The success achieved by his saboteurs was such that, on 22 December 1943, the Smyrna station relayed the following message:

FROM BRITISH C. IN C. LEVANT. BEGINS. THE ROYAL NAVY HAVE WATCHED WITH ADMIRATION THE MANY DARING ATTACKS UPON AXIS SHIPS CARRIED OUT BY YOUR GROUP. WE DEEPLY REGRET THAT THE NUMEROUS SUCCESSES OF YOUR GROUP HAVE NOT BEEN ACHIEVED WITHOUT THE SACRIFICE OF BRAVE LIVES. YOU MAY REST ASSURED THAT THE CASUALTIES YOU ARE INFLICTING ON THE ENEMY SHIPPING ARE MAKING A NOTABLE CONTRIBUTION TO THE COMMON CAUSE AND THE FREEING OF YOUR COUNTRY.

The Admiralty, with the First Lord's approval, had actually dictated the message. Yet success had not been achieved without some difficulty. In January 1944 APOLLO complained that a number of limpets were defective; he sent back one of them to Cairo for testing. A court of enquiry was convened at Force 133 headquarters and it was discovered that a whole consignment of limpets was indeed defective. But things were beginning to be too hot for Peltekis and the

Germans had put a high price on his head. A number of his collaborators were arrested and later executed. He managed to escape to the Middle East. In May 1944 he was invited to Beirut where Greek government officials were meeting at the Hotel Métropole to discuss the future of their country. He met Papandreou who sought his advice, and a few days later became prime minister. Peltekis was however barred from further meetings which occurred at Broumana, in the hills above Beirut. The order was apparently issued by Ellis Waterhouse of the British embassy to Greece, who appears to have held a special grudge towards APOLLO.

Waterhouse had accused him, at one time or another, of being a Soviet agent, a German agent and an EAM agent. At the urging of the British embassy, APOLLO was to have been arrested but this was resisted by his operators in Cairo. They could scarcely hide their disbelief that their star agent should suffer such an indignity. It must be added that Mr Leeper, the British ambassador to Greece, was highly distrustful of Force 133, suspecting it of meddling in political matters, contrary to the interest of the Foreign Office. Certainly Peltekis had no use for the Greek monarchy and dealt on occasion with EAM. He defended himself by stating that he could not have done otherwise as the supplies shipped to him from Smyrna had to pass through the island of Euboea, which was controlled by the communists and he had to maintain good relations with them. OSS agents, who later joined SOE in special operations in Greece, had similar experiences at Euboea.

Peltekis was staunchly defended by his colleagues, including the head of SOE, Lord Selborne, who were certain that there was a deliberate attempt in royalist circles to frame him. APOLLO's organization had several prominent right-wing members in its ranks and, under close scrutiny, the accusations fell apart in a court of enquiry held just as the liberation of Greece was occurring. Perhaps not mentioned directly, APOLLO's credibility had been enhanced by confirmation of his achievements through ULTRA intercepts. During his absence and through lack of funds, his organization had been badly decimated by the Germans but continued to provide the Allies with valuable information. No less than seventy-one agents were reported to have been arrested and the majority were shot. While away, Peltekis was succeeded by Costantinos Benakis, son of the founder of the well-known museum in Athens.

The organization was now to be called upon to act in a very different role, that of anti-scorching tactics and preventive sabotage as the Germans were evacuating Greece.

Chapter 18

Last Attempt: The Germans

The Canal Changes Hands

On 8 July 1943, a dredger belonging to the Corinth Canal Company and manned by Greeks was reported to have sunk in bad weather. It was also reported as sabotaged and sunk in the waterway, although it is not clear if this was due to the Greeks. An ULTRA intercept of 28 July showed that the dredger had been raised.

The Italian armistice on 8 September brought a change of occupants. The 24th Pinerolo Infantry Division joined the Greek resistance, providing much needed weapons to the EAM/ELAS formations. On the island of Cephalonia the Italian 33rd Acqui Infantry Division, after a fierce resistance to the German forces, paid a heavy price with some 4,750 men executed. The Badoglio government's need for secrecy about its intentions had kept the Italian Navy in Greece in the dark and the armistice took them by surprise. They offered little resistance in the Aegean and at 0315 hours on 9 September 1943, *68.Armee-Oberkommando* recorded laconically:

KORINTH-KANAL IST FEST IN DEUTSCHER HAND

A few hours later, the leader of the *21.U-Jagdflottille* (submarine chasers) reported the situation well in hand in Piraeus.

With little resistance, the minelayer *Morosini*, the destroyers *Turbine, Crispi,* the torpedo boats *Calatafimi, San Martino*, one *MAS* boat, sixteen auxiliary minesweepers and four minor warships had surrendered. The merchant ships *Adriana, Celeno, Città di Savona, Pier Luigi Salvatore* and *Tarquinia* had fallen intact into German hands. Only at the coal pier, the small Italian steamer *Arezzo* had been beached and *Archiango* was sunk. At the old customs pier *Vesta,* which lay there following her torpedoing by the submarine HMS *Trident* in July, was scuttled but later raised and the following year would be used to block the Corinth Canal.

Elsewhere in Crete and in the islands the scenario was repeated with little variation. The exception was the torpedo boat *Monzambano*: only three days earlier some of her crew had been suspected of holding talks with the enemy and the order had come for the arrest of two warrant officers and nineteen ratings. She now had the good fortune to sail from Piraeus at 0950 hours on

8 September and was probably the last warship flying the Italian flag to make use of the canal. Embarking the pilot at 1315 hours, she made the passage with two steamers from 1352 to 1427 hours and anchored that same evening at Patras where her commanding officer, *Capitano di Corvetta* Alberto Cuomo, was informed of the armistice.

At dawn the next day, having topped up with fuel, *Monzambano* was to have sailed and escorted the transport *Re Alessandro* carrying German troops to Zante. But the captain of this vessel, *Comandante* Pappalardo, alerted Cuomo that the Germans were preventing him from sailing. Shortly after noon, Cuomo decided to force the blockade and managed to take his ship to sea. About two hours later the destroyer was attacked by four Stukas, which dropped bombs and strafed her but she escaped damage. Her anti-aircraft guns claimed to have shot down two aircraft, one crashing in the sea, its two occupants having managed to jump while another was seen crashing into the mountain. German records confirmed the loss of a single Junkers 87. By that time *Monzambano* had managed to work up a speed of 25 knots and, next morning, reached Taranto where she joined Allied forces.

Passage through the canal was briefly blocked from 0900 to 1100 hours between 14 and 16 December as German sappers built a bridge to enable the movement of forces to the Peloponnese should an Allied invasion materialize. The waterway still had its use as it linked the Aegean with the ports of the Northern Adriatic which were in German hands; but traffic at their disposal had considerably shrunk. The Allied air forces now ruled the skies and the Piraeus area was now frequently bombed. Even the little harbour of Poros did not escape their attention and on 8 February a yacht and a caique were sunk there, fortunately without any loss of life. The garrison of the little island was reinforced during the following month, Poros being declared as a *Stützpunkt* (strongpoint) in the defence of the Piraeus approaches. From this time it figures frequently in German documents of the period. But the spirit of 'Bouboulina'[30] was still alive and, on 29 March 1944, three of four sailing vessels used to transport supplies to Crete were reported captured by 'pirates' off Hydra. The following June a strong German detachment was sent to clear the area of partisans from Ermioni to Spetses. For the Allies the canal was no longer a target as they now hoped to use it once Greece was liberated, but this was not to be. The Royal Navy had even planned to use the Danube River, the most important waterway left open for the Germans. In April 1944 they had informed Force 133 that no sabotage should be carried out there. Although no specific document has been found, it is probable that the Corinth Canal was similarly earmarked and was to be left open for navigation. The shoe was now on the other foot and, in the autumn of 1944, as the Germans were evacuating Greece, extensive demolitions of all facilities were carried out and the canal was not spared.

At the beginning of August the Germans had approached the YVONNE organization through their Greek Quislings and let it be known that they were ready to discuss conditions to evacuate Greece. YVONNE passed on the message to Cairo but was told in return not to engage in any discussion unless the Germans were ready for unconditional surrender and the negotiations were broken off.

On 27 September Admiral Aegean ordered that preparations for the blocking of the canal were to be carried out as it was feared that the Allies might attempt an airborne landing to capture it intact. Already sixty parachutists of the Special Boat Section had been dropped near Araxos airfield on 23 September and had seized it. In addition, three days later, a force known as BUCKETFORCE had been landed at Katakolo, had advanced to Patras, which was liberated on 2 October, and reached Corinth on 8 October. These were largely unopposed, the Germans already having evacuated the areas.

During the night of 29/30 September 1944, the German auxiliary *GA-79* blocked the Rhion Channel at the western entrance of the Gulf of Corinth with twenty-six EMC mines (minefield G-145) and the following day *GA-78* laid twenty RMH mines (minefield G-189) at the western entrance of the canal. As they were withdrawing, the Germans were multiplying their minelaying operations.

SOE had informed its agents in the field to prepare for anti-scorching operations and prevent any sabotage from the Germans as they were leaving the country. At the same time as Peltekis was being investigated by a court of enquiry, his saboteurs were ready to take preventive action. On 1 October Admiral Aegean decreed that the Corinth Canal was now closed to shipping. The same day, the YVONNE organization, aware that preparations to block the canal were under way, wired Smyrna:

BRIDGE OF CORINTH CANAL MINED SUCH A WAY AS EXPLOSION WILL CAUSE LANDSLIDE BLOCKING THE CANAL. ALSO SIDES OF THE CANAL MINED THREE PLACES. EMBRANCHMENT OF SPAP LINE LEADS EDGE CANAL AS PROBABLE INTENTION THROW ALL POSSIBLE SPAP [*SPAP stood for Piraeus, Athens and Peloponnese Railways (Σιδηρόδρομοι Πειραιώς-Αθηνών-Πελοποννήσου or Σ.Π.Α.Π)*] WAGONS AND ENGINES DESTROY THEM AND BLOCK CANAL. GUARD AND OFFICERS CHANGE CONTINUALLY.

The organization became aware that *Vesta* was towed to Palataki and had been earmarked to block the Corinth Canal but was powerless to intervene. The steamers *John Knudsen* and *Anna* were similarly prepared to be used as blockships. Two days later, another signal followed:

VESTA RPT VESTA OLD ITALIAN 3000 TON TUGGED [towed] 1/10
TOWARDS CORINTH CANAL. HAVE NOT YET CONFIRMED
ARRIVAL BUT PROBABLE PURPOSE IS SINK IT IN CANAL. WE
WILL TRY SEND MAN ATACK [sic] IT THOUGH SEEMS VERY
DIFFICULT. IF RECONNOITRED BY AIR MIGHT BOMB IT FOR
SURE RESULTS.

No action could be taken in time. A torpedo from the submarine HMS *Trident*
had crippled the former Italian freighter *Vesta* on 4 July 1943; she was now sunk
at the eastern entrance while mines were laid in the western entrance. *Vesta* was
not a lucky ship; eventually she was raised by the Greeks and renamed *Memphis*,
only to be mined south of Crete in 1948.

The YVONNE organization kept a steady stream of signals reporting the
destruction wrought by the retiring German forces and on 5 October, in their
message No 418 to Smyrna, noted:

CORINTH CANAL COMPLETELY DESTROYED. 2 BRIDGES
BLOWN. SPAP ENGINES & WAGONS THROWN IN THEN SIDES
BLOWN UP AND EARTH FILLED CANAL HIGHER SEA LEVEL.
VESTA SUNK IN KALAMAKI HARBOUR ENTRANCE. POWER
STA [Station] AND WT POST DESTROYED. ABOUT 2 YEARS
WORK RESTORE.

The information was quite accurate: the two bridges had been blown up, over
200 railway cars were toppled over the cliffs and about 350,000 cubic metres
of earth were dumped in the canal. At some points the landslides reached some
thirty metres above sea level. The German army carried out the destruction as
the surviving units of the German navy were busy evacuating the islands of the
Aegean. The APOLLO saboteurs had prepared for anti-scorching operations
but could not prevent the canal from being blocked. They would have better
luck at Piraeus.

At 2300 hours on 8 October saboteurs succeeded in crippling a big floating
dock reported to be carrying the German-manned torpedo boat *Francesco Crispi*
(renamed *TA-15*) (the warship was actually *TA-17*, former Italian *San Martino*),
as well as a smaller floating dock which were to be used to block the entrance
of Piraeus harbour. Each target had two limpets fixed to the hull; the large dock
capsized with *TA-17,* the smaller dock was damaged but did not sink. Later the
small dock was towed by the Germans and, along with the steamer *Carola*,
scuttled at the end of the Themistokles breakwater, but they could only partially
block the harbour. The APOLLO organization kept Allied forces well informed;
they were referred as the 'CX' (Intelligence) source.

During the afternoon and evening of 9 October all the seaworthy vessels that could be mustered evacuated stores and troops northward. They left Piraeus in four groups and included the steamers *Anna I* and *Lola* and the torpedo boat *TA-39*. The remaining troops would be evacuated by land.

The Norwegian steamer *John Knudsen* was strongly guarded and proved to be more difficult to attack; initially YVONNE suggested that she ought to be sunk by air attack. However, at 0200 hours GMT on 11 October, saboteurs succeeded in fixing four limpets to her hull, two in the stern section and the others on two different holds. They exploded in the morning as she was being towed near Psyttalia and she sank in the afternoon. German documents do not confirm any sabotage attempt; they do state that *John Knudsen* under the command of *Oberleutnant* Leers was to have blocked the entrance of Piraeus. She was loaded with eight large depth charges and a load of explosives when at 1100 hours on 11 October she was sunk prematurely, taking two hours to sink. The report does not explain the sudden sinking and why she was not sunk at the entrance of Piraeus as intended. British forces would find the wreck sunk just off the north end of Psyttalia. Smyrna was immediately informed of the success and told that the air force could cancel the operation. This was just in time as the destruction of Piraeus harbour installations began at 1500 hours GMT on 12 October.

The Hunt-class destroyers HMSs *Bicester* and *Oakley* arrived at Poros on 1 October to cover a force of minesweepers, motor launches and landing craft to setup an advanced base (Operation EDGEHILL). This was done without incident because of the poor visibility and the island was used as a base until 26 October 1944. The small armada was under the command of the 5th Minesweeping Flotilla, which was transferred from Kithera and included the 60th Motor Gunboat and 29th Motor Launch Flotillas. Elements of 9 Commando and the Greek Sacred Squadron were landed to provide security. They included Foxforce with Danish-born Major Anders Lassen of the Special Boat Service. Lassen's action during a previous raid on the island of Sark, although unrelated to LOCKSMITH, would bear heavily on the destinies of the four men (see next chapter). Nevertheless, German artillery on the island of Aegina could still fire accurately on Poros harbour and movements during daylight hours had to be curtailed. Eventually *Bicester* and *Oakley*, after bombarding enemy positions and attempting to interdict enemy vessels from leaving Piraeus, had to return to Alexandria. They were relieved by the Hellenic destroyer *Themistocles*. The Greek cabinet in exile was transferred to Poros in anticipation of the liberation of Athens. Operation MANNA was due to start on 15 October but ran into a minefield which damaged HM Ships *Larne* and *Clinton* and sank the minesweepers *GYMS-2070* and *-2191* and the motor launch *ML-870*. The future prime minister, Harold Macmillan, then Minister Resident in the Mediterranean, witnessed the event from the bridge of the light cruiser HMS *Orion*, flagship of Admiral Mansfield, and this evidently made an impression on him. The minefield had to be cleared but thanks to the work of the APOLLO saboteurs, Piraeus had not been successfully blocked by retiring German forces. This enabled the venerable armoured cruiser *Averoff* to bring the Greek cabinet from Poros and enter harbour on the morning of 18 October.[31] They were driven to Athens amidst an enthusiastic reception from the population. But the Greek Civil War would soon erupt.

John Peltekis had been vindicated and he was awarded the DSO in May 1945. He had meetings with Mr Leeper who offered him a portfolio in the Greek government and the hatchet was buried, at least on the surface. By this time, the government of national unity was dissolved and the Labour party was now in power and more forgiving of Peltekis' attitude towards the Greek monarchy.

Commander J. R. P. Morton RNVR surveyed the canal and submitted a report on 20 October. He reported that the blockage had been done by the railway bridge, 200 railway wagons and 350,000 tons of debris. It was estimated that the clearance would take nine months; but Greece had been devastated by the war and there were more urgent works to be undertaken. Initially the cost of clearing was estimated at £100,000 and, although enlarging the canal to a width of 42 metres and a depth of 12 metres was considered, the cost appeared prohibitive and was never implemented. A few months later, a more detailed study revised the figures to 600,000 cubic metres of earth and a cost of £500,000.

After the mammoth work of clearing the debris, the canal was successfully swept for mines by three minesweepers of the Royal Hellenic Navy in four periods: *GYMS-2190* (16-23 July 1947 and 20 August-3 September 1947), *GYMS-2066* (9-15 June 1948) and *GYMS-2229* (12-13 September 1948). No mines were found.

Normal crossings of the canal finally resumed in October 1948, the passenger ship *Nafsika* being the first one to pass through the canal on the 25th of the month.

Chapter 19

Sachsenhausen

Hitler's *Kommandobefehl*

But what about the fate of the four commandos of LOCKSMITH?

Irritated by the success of the British commando missions, Hitler issued his infamous *Kommandobefehl* on 18 October 1942. The decision appears to have been triggered by Operation BASALT, the raid on Sark, one of the Channel Islands. The operation had been carried out during the night of 3/4 October 1942 by a mixed force of SOE's Small Scale Raiding Force and 12 Commando, led by Major J. Geoffrey Appleyard. The raiders had sailed from Portland in *MTB-344* and they included the Danish Second Lieutenant Anders Lassen, who would later earn the Victoria Cross.

During the raid the commandos took five German prisoners and tied them up. One attempted to shout and alert the rest of the garrison; he tried to flee in the darkness but was caught and shot. The diversion enabled three of the remaining prisoners to attempt to escape; two were shot dead and the third was caught but then killed when a pistol was accidentally discharged. The fifth prisoner was brought back to England. Whether these killings constituted a war crime or not, German propaganda was quick to exploit it and accused the British of executing prisoners of war.

This would have tragic consequences for the LOCKSMITH party. The Führer was incensed by the incident. In August 1942, following the raid on Dieppe, he had been told that Canadian soldiers had tied up German prisoners, a direct contravention of the Geneva Convention. There were rumours that some of them had drowned when their boat sank. It did not take much to inflame a volatile situation and retaliation was at hand. Hitler issued the order that commandos should not be treated as prisoners of war, even if captured in uniform. They could be executed on the spot unless their interrogation could be useful, in which case execution could be delayed by a few days. Custody in prisoner of war camps was forbidden.

It must be said that, in a few cases, SOE agents condoned or even participated in the murder of German or Italian prisoners of war. Working behind enemy lines made the caring of prisoners difficult and it was sometime easier to 'dispose' of them. SOE agents and the resistance groups with which they worked could not expect much mercy from the enemy and in return did not give any.

It so happened that another commando had raided the Norwegian coast the previous month. Captain Graeme D. Black of the South Lancashire Regiment, a native of Ontario, had led a team of twelve men (two officers and eight other ranks of No.2 Commando, Special Service Brigade, and two Norwegians) who were landed on 15 September from the Free French submarine *Junon* to destroy the Glaamerfjord power station on Glomfjord, south of Narvik. This was Operation MUSKETOON that was successful though seven commandos, including Captain Black, were captured and another died of wounds, but the remaining four managed to reach Sweden. The seven men in enemy hands were Captain Graeme D. Black MC, Captain Joseph B. G. Houghton, Sergeant Miller Smith, Lance Corporal William Chudley, Rifleman Cyril Abram, Private E. Curtiss and Private Reginald Wakeham. They were initially brought to Colditz but when the *Kommandobefehl* was issued, they were transferred to the *Zellenbau* (cell block) at Sachsenhausen on 22 October 1942 and executed the next day. Their bodies were cremated and the Red Cross was just informed that they had 'escaped'.

Sachsenhausen/Oranienburg was one of the first concentration camps built in Germany. It was located some thirty kilometres from Berlin, next to *Amstgruppe D*, the administration centre of all concentration camps. Its first commandant was *Oberführer* Barowski, who died of natural causes in 1940. His successor was *Oberführer* Loritz, but his administration was tainted by accusations of corruption and, in 1943, he was replaced by *Standartenführer* Anton Kaindl. Kaindl would remain in command until 1945 when the camp was evacuated at the approach of the Soviet Army.

The four men from LOCKSMITH did not immediately share the fate of the MUSKETOON party. The *Abwehr*, who had proven to have been a formidable nemesis to the LOCKSMITH party, would now come to their defence. The Amt Ausland/*Abwehr* department under Admiral Leopold Bürkner was concerned with foreign affairs. Its International Law branch was led by Count Helmuth James Graf von Moltke, great-grandnephew of Helmuth von Moltke the Elder, the victor of the Franco-Prussian War of 1870-71. A jurist by profession and opposed to the oppressive measures taken by the Nazis, von Moltke was a founder of the Kreisau Circle that envisaged a new Germany after Hitler. Dr Otto Reichel, a judge by profession, was enrolled in the Ausland department in 1940 and worked for von Moltke. According to him, the count had prepared a study to denounce the harmful effect of the *Kommandobefehl* and attempted in vain to have it annulled. In February 1948 Reichel was interrogated by British Army Major Eric Alastair Barkworth at Wuppertal, specifically on the fate of the Bordeaux commandos. They were the men from Operation FRANKTON, the 'Cockleshell Heroes'. These commandos, Royal Marines of the Royal Marine Boom Patrol Detachment, had been launched from the submarine HMS *Tuna* on the night of 7/8 December 1942. They paddled their folbots up the

Gironde estuary and, using limpets, had seriously damaged several German blockade-runners loaded with rubber from the Far East. Some of the commandos had been captured and executed according to the *Kommandobefehl*. Reichel was shown exhibit 1487-PS, read the name of Cumberlege on page 10, and remembered that he had been incarcerated at Oranienburg. He had studied Mike's file and had read a request that the LOCKSMITH leader had made to be allowed to have a wood carving knife in prison to pass the time. Reichel, who was aware that Cumberlege was the recipient of the DSO, thought that such a request should be granted to a man of such distinction and recommended it to the RHSA which was concerned with these matters. RHSA or *Reichsicherheitshauptamt* was the German Security Service which included the Gestapo. It absorbed the *Abwehr* when Admiral Canaris fell from grace. Reichel professed never to have met the commando and was not aware of his fate. Count von Moltke, who had written arguments to denounce the *Kommandobefehl*, may have bought the commandos some time, but he was arrested by the Nazis in January 1944 and executed a year later.

In October 1943 MI9 received a message dated early June from Stalag Luft I, a prisoner of war camp for RAF personnel located at Barth on the Baltic coast. It is unlikely that the commandos were held there, and the note was probably smuggled to another prisoner who was transferred there. Its content mentioned that DH89 (codename of Mike Cumberlege) and S. M. Scott, an alias of Jan Kotrba, had been captured on 1 May, the task had been accomplished—an obvious reference to the Corinth Canal operation—but that the Germans had captured the codes and were working the radio to Cairo. The commandos could not have been held at a Stalag Luft camp as these were exclusively reserved for airmen. It appears they were held in Vienna at this time. How the message was smuggled remains a mystery.

At the *Zellenbau*
In January 1944, the four commandos were transferred to the Sachsenhausen concentration camp. As it would later transpire, the order apparently was signed on 19 January by none other than Ernst Kaltenbrunner, Chief of the RHSA, during one of his visits to Vienna. The Soviet war crimes trials at Kharkov had just occurred in the middle of December. German prisoners of war had been accused by the Russians of war crimes in the Ukraine and had been condemned to death. The RHSA had prompted the *Ausland/Abwehr* Department to study the commando cases in the hope that similar accusations could be made in retaliation. We have seen earlier that Judge Reichel had examined Mike's file to find some legal justification for the incarceration of the commandos. According to the 1487-PS file, there was no intention of conducting a staged trial but to gather evidence and have 'only a propaganda recital of violations of International Law by enemy soldiers'. A final list of ninety-seven men was

drawn up (seventy-nine British and eighteen Americans). Reichel's own boss, Count von Moltke, had been arrested by the Gestapo on the very day Kaltenbrunner had signed the order declaring the four LOCKSMITH men as 'Enemies of the State' but this was probably just a coincidence.

From a notebook retrieved after the war by the Russians, it appears that Sergeant Steele, and most probably his three companions, arrived at Sachsenhausen on 23 January. They were treated as common criminals and incarcerated at the *Zellenbau*. The *Zellenbau* was a T-shaped compound containing seventy-nine cells and had its own courtyard within the camp. Prisoners were held there in solitary confinement; they were not allowed to receive or write letters, nor did they receive Red Cross parcels. Which cells they occupied is a matter of conjecture, but Mike Cumberlege may have been assigned to cell 69 and Handley to cell 71. The other two were most likely in the same area.

A notorious *Zellenbau* inmate was Captain Sygmund Payne Best of the British Secret Service. The Germans kidnapped him in 1939 in neutral Holland during the notorious Venlo incident engineered by Walter Schellenberg, future head of the German Secret Service. Enticed by the promise of meeting German dissidents plotting against Hitler, Best and his colleague Major Richard Henry Stevens fell into a trap. They were forced at gunpoint across the German border in an incident that cost the life of a Dutch Intelligence officer. For a time, the two Englishmen were suspected of being behind Georg Elser's attempt on Hitler's life which had occurred the previous day in Munich (8 November 1939). His bomb had missed Hitler by only ten minutes. An investigation found that the two Englishmen had nothing to do with the Munich plot. Best got to know Elser, who was also incarcerated at Sachsenhausen, and it is puzzling that the German had been kept alive for so long. The man, who had come so close to altering the course of the war, was executed finally on 9 April 1945.

The 60-year-old Best appears to have been decently treated, unless he was afflicted by what was later known as the 'Stockholm syndrome'. He wrote a fascinating account of his life at Sachsenhausen. The Venlo fiasco was a blow to SIS and certainly played a part in the decision by Churchill to create the Special Operations Executive. Unfortunately, it also made British Intelligence very suspicious of subsequent attempts by the German resistance movement to approach them. On 20 February 1945 Best was suddenly transferred to the Gestapo headquarters in Berlin, along with RAF Flight Lieutenant Hugh Falconer and Vassili Kokorin, a nephew of Molotov. He was told that *Obergruppenführer* Müller (Chief of the Gestapo) had ordered that he would be well taken care of. It is unclear why this occurred and it is possible that the Germans entertained the thought of using them to make contacts with the Allies, as indeed would happen with Major Johnnie Dodge. The idea appears to have fallen through as the prisoners were then moved to Buchenwald and later evacuated southward. After many tribulations they were finally liberated by the Americans in northern Italy.

In August 1943 seven British commandos captured near Stavanger, Norway, were incarcerated at Sachsenhausen. The Norwegian *MTB-626* had dropped them off at Kopervik and, led by Sub Lieutenant John Godwin RNVR, and using folbots (kayaks), they had managed to sneak into the harbour and fix limpets on the hull of the German minesweeper *M-5207* which was sunk; this was Operation CHECKMATE in May 1943. But this success was not to be repeated. About ten days later, the commandos were captured and imprisoned at Grini in Norway. They were then transferred to Sachsenhausen.

Godwin and his men do not appear to have been held at the *Zellenbau* as the commemorative plaque in one of the cells implies, but in the general compound where Norwegian prisoners were also held. Initially, they were treated relatively well and put to work in the kitchen, a task considered relatively 'easy'. At the end of 1943 their *Rapport Führer*'s (a non-commissioned officer in charge of the disciplinary side of the block) family dwelling was destroyed during a RAF bombing raid and his attitude towards them changed drastically. He ordered them transferred to an SK section (*Strafkompanie*) or punishment section where they were treated very harshly. They were forced to carry sandbags and march forty-eight kilometres (thirty miles) per day to 'test' army boots. This punishment is reported to have gone on for thirteen months. Although the camp guards belonged to the SS, a number of German criminal inmates were promoted to *Block-Ältester* or block leaders. These were allowed to carry sticks and would often mercilessly beat their fellow prisoners with a ferocity not displayed by the SS guards themselves.

Not all SS guards were sadistic brutes and some of them displayed, discreetly, some compassion towards the inmates. In 2011 a Norwegian Sachsenhausen survivor described to this writer how a German officer had been kind to him and gave him an 'easy' job in a factory. In 1947 the tables were turned and the SS guards were being judged as war criminals. The sister of 21-year-old *Unterscharführer* Hans-Peter Raffel wrote to Captain Peter Churchill pleading for mercy on behalf of her brother. He obliged and wrote a letter describing how Raffel, in charge of Sonderlager A, had behaved decently towards the prisoners. When Wing Commander Day and his four companions had escaped they had made sure that he was not on duty to avoid getting him into trouble.

In July 1943 SOE Agent Captain John Ashford Renshaw Starr was taken prisoner in civilian clothes in Dijon where, known as 'Bob', he had organized the ACROBAT resistance network. Transferred to Sachsenhausen, he met Godwin and his men and shared their suffering in the *Strafkompanie* but was lucky to survive and provided some clues of what had happened. In contrast to the *Zellenbau* inmates, the seven CHECKMATE commandos were allowed a certain freedom of movement and could visit other barracks. Part of their stories was pieced together from Norwegian and Danish prisoners they had befriended. A Norwegian inmate, Isak Rygg, described them as always cheerful despite their harsh treatment.

At about midnight on 2 February 1945 Godwin and four of his men were led to execution with about a hundred inmates, including some twenty Luxemburgers who had refused enlistment in the SS and about forty-five Russian officers. According to eyewitness accounts, a Polish prisoner managed to stab a German guard and, in the ensuing scuffle, the prisoners were all mown down by gunfire. Other accounts also state that Godwin seized the pistol of the German officer who was leading the execution squad and killed him before he was himself shot down. A Norwegian prisoner, Rosenqvist, had access to the Camp Registry; he noticed that their deaths were recorded as '*tot wahrend des transports*' (died during transport). The other two ratings of CHECKMATE did not survive long; they were transferred to Belsen and murdered there a few weeks later.

Notable internees of Sachsenhausen had been the former French Minister President Paul Reynaud, Generals Gamelin and Weygand and other French officials. These prisoners were '*Prominenten*' and relatively well treated, but they were transferred to a castle in Tyrol before the arrival of the LOCKSMITH commandos. The main camp held a large number of Soviet, French and prisoners of other nationalities in appalling conditions. Jewish inmates had also been used to create counterfeit British sterling pound notes. This was a scheme devised by the *Sicherheitdienst* Amt VIF section in an effort to flood the market with these and bring about the collapse of the currency. The notes were notably used during the CICERO operation.[32]

Peter Morland Churchill, an SOE agent, was also held in the camp. He was captured in France with fellow agent Odette Sansom by Hugo Bleicher of the *Abwehr* and remained at Sachsenhausen almost to the end but never met the LOCKSMITH party. He later wrote a vivid account of his adventures and life in the concentration camp.[33] Churchill's life was spared because it was wrongly assumed that he was related to the prime minister and could be used as a valuable pawn. Despite having also been captured as a saboteur, and in civilian clothing at that, he was held in the '*Prominent*' section (*Sonderlager*) and his treatment was markedly better than that meted out to Cumberlege and his three men.

Churchill became acquainted with other '*Prominenten*' of the small international community who were the 'guests' of the camp: among others, there were the former Italian attachés in Berlin who were arrested following the Italian armistice: Colonel General Luigi Elfisio Marras (Army), Rear Admiral Carlo de Angelis (Navy) and Colonel Giuseppe Teucci (Air). Also present were Soviet Major General I. G. Bessonov, executed by the Soviets in 1952, and Lieutenant General Piotr Privalov and General Alexandros Papagos, Commander-in-Chief of the Greek Army.

The Great Escape

The *Prominenten* would be joined by five Britons who would succeed in escaping from the camp on 23 September 1944. They were Wing Commander Harry 'Wings' Melville Arbuthnot Day, Lieutenant Colonel Jack Churchill, Major Johnnie 'the Dodger' Dodge and Flight Lieutenants Sydney H. Dowse and Bertram A. 'Jimmy' James.

Wing Commander Day of 57 Squadron RAF had one of the longest captivities; he had been shot down on 17 October 1939. In March 1944, with Roger Bushell, he had taken a leading part in organizing the 'Great Escape' from Stalag Luft III when seventy-six PoWs had managed to tunnel their way out of the camp. Only three men had managed a 'home run', the rest being recaptured, most of them within days. They had caused such a disruption that an enraged Führer had ordered their execution. Reichsmarshall Göring, who was partial to his fellow airmen, pleaded in vain for their lives and could only ensure that a few would be spared. Eventually, fifty of the recaptured escapees, including Bushell, were executed. Their case would figure prominently during the Nuremberg trials. Luckily, Day, Dodge, Dowse and James had survived. With Jack Churchill, who had attempted to escape from another camp, they were sent to Sachsenhausen.

The five men were incorrigible. They had barely arrived at Sachsenhausen when they began to plan another escape. Held in *Sonderlager A* where *Prominenten* were relatively well treated and surveillance was lax, their escape was relatively easy. Still, the Germans were stunned by their disappearance, although they were all recaptured within a month. They were fortunate that this had no fatal consequence. In punishment, they were sent to the *Zellenbau*, to be held in solitary confinement; escape from there was to prove impossible.[34]

Cumberlege made contact with Harry Day and Jack Churchill after their recapture and it is thanks to them that we can at least partially complete the pieces of the puzzle. Churchill only saw Sergeant Steele by mistake when the opposite door to his cell was opened but at least he looked well; he could only see the shadow of Cumberlege on the frosted glass of his cell. He also reported that all four commandos were dressed in blue and white striped convict clothes and ate only low-grade civilian food. Cumberlege wrote a brief report of his activities on 29 January 1945 and smuggled it to Churchill who was last in contact with him on 15 February 1945 before he was transferred to another camp. Messages could be passed to each other once a week, thanks to the Polish spy Alfons Jakubianiec who occupied a cell between them. Churchill was eventually liberated and delivered the last messages we have from the LOCKSMITH party. In one of them, Cumberlege mentioned that Tambanis (Sambanis) had received £1,000 in gold sovereigns.

The LOCKSMITH party had taken with them 4,000 gold sovereigns (equivalent to £20,000 in paper money), 250,000 drachmas and twenty-eight diamonds valued at £965, a considerable sum for the time. The gold was necessary, as rampant inflation in Greece had rendered the drachma nearly worthless. In April 1943 one gold pound was worth 180,000 drachmas. After the war, efforts were made to recover the money, but with little success.

Wing Commander Day was liberated at the end of the war and wrote a letter dated 14 July 1945 to Mr F. Broughton of CW (Casualties) at Queen Anne's Mansions, stating that he had been held at the *Zellenbau* since October 1944. He mentioned that besides his four fellow escapees, he knew of eight other British prisoners held there. He listed:

Lt Cumberlege
Sgt Major J. Steele
Sgt Handley
Sgt Davies (Jan Kotrba)

They were still held in the prison when he was transferred.

Major Sutterall (sic)
Captain Sebastian Williams (sic)

Both taken out from prison at the end of January or beginning of February 1945 and fate unknown.

(These two men were actually Major Francis Suttill (codename PROSPER from the network of the same name) and Captain William Charles Grover-Williams (from the CHESTNUT network). Both were SOE agents captured in France in June and August 1943 respectively and are believed to have been executed at Sachsenhausen on 23 March 1945.)

Sub Lt Falconer
Captain Payne Best

Both removed from prison at the same time as the other two but were now in England.

He added:

While in Sachsenhausen prison I read a note by Lieut Cumberlege which was passed to me secretly & which gave the story of his capture & subsequent history till his imprisonment in Sachsenhausen. In the account he stated, that while under a series of severe interrogations at Vienna, he was forced to sign a document in which he admitted being a saboteur working with some organization in Greece.[35]

Day concluded that prisoners who had been subjected to bad treatment were earmarked for execution as German police officials would be inclined to eliminate any witness who could incriminate them. He also suggested that an attempt should be made to contact Flight Lieutenant Dowse who had taken a lively interest in other inmates.

Dowse could only report that he had no information on the whereabouts of Cumberlege as he had left them on 15 February. He feared that 'he with five others had been taken out of their cells & shot but we have no proof of this'.

Wing Commander Day had been held in two different cells at the *Zellenbau*. He was held in the first cell (no.13) for about four weeks after his recapture. He was handcuffed day and night and schackled to the floor at night. He had only a dirty pallet for a bed and a bucket; rations were limited to 1,500 calories per day and he was not allowed to wash. He left his cell only for interrogation. He was then moved to cell no. 24 where treatment was slightly improved. His furniture now included a stool, a table and a shelf with eating utensils. He could wash every day and shave twice a week. Although a daily period of half an hour exercise in the yard was allowed, this depended on the weather and the will of the guards.

A plea for 'ARTIST'

Lieutenant Colonel Jack Churchill DSO MC had not been part of the 'Great Escape'; neither was he related to Peter Churchill but was a distant cousin of the prime minister. An eccentric who, on occasion, used bows and arrows (in a successful ambush in May 1940), he had led several commando raids until his capture in Yugoslavia in June 1944 during the ill-fated landing operation on the island of Brac (Operation FLOUNCED). He was now held at the *Zellenbau*.

Cumberlege had made contact with former *Abwehr* officer 'Johnny' Jebsen who had been recruited as a double agent, code name ARTIST, by the Double Cross Committee. On his behalf, Cumberlege wrote a special appeal which was smuggled to Jack Churchill:

JOHNY JEBSEN HUN HELD HIGH TREASON CAN D REPEAT D POPOV YSLAV [YUGOSLAV] WARMINSTER (sic) HELP URGENT F.O. KNOW OF J.J. ALL CHARGES AGAINST US ARE BASELESS.

Another letter to his wife was found to contain a concealed message in a similar vein:

JOHNY DEBSEN (sic) HUN HELD HIGH TREASON CAN CHESTER BEATTY OF SELECTION TRUST HELP?

These messages were undoubtedly sent in the hope that Yugoslav double agent Dusko Popov, who was still in excellent standing with German Intelligence, might be induced to intervene on behalf of his friend Johannes 'Johnny' Jebsen. *Abwehr* control officer Jebsen was a personal friend of Popov (codename TRICYCLE), one of the most successful agents used by the Double Cross

Committee. The Yugoslav would later inspire Ian Fleming in his creation of James Bond. Jebsen had no sympathy for the Nazis and was recruited by Popov who had sensed his friend's disillusionment. The German was also enlisted by the XX Committee and proved to be a most valuable source of information. Jebsen was kidnapped in Portugal by Aloys Schreiber and brought across the border hidden in a trunk. According to post-war interrogations, ARTIST had been put at the disposal of a certain 'Hofmeister', who was believed to have been Kaltenbrunner himself but probably was the same Hoffmeister who had extracted the LOCKSMITH commandos' 'confessions'. Jebsen had boasted that he had good connections with Chester Beatty. It is not clear how the Irish-American millionnaire could have interceded to help. It is possible that Mike had sought the advice of Beatty on the technical aspect of blocking of the Corinth Canal as the mining magnate had shown great interest in the work of SOE.

Some sources indicate that Jebsen was arrested for his involvement in financial deals with Rothschild and the smuggling of currencies but, according to Walter Schellenberg, the *Sicherheitdienst* suspected him of working for the British as he had sent conflicting reports. With dismay, London learned of the capture of Jebsen; his knowledge that Popov was a double agent might have compromised the whole FORTITUDE deception, the attempt to draw German forces away from the Normandy landings.

The concern that Cumberlege had expressed for a German fellow prisoner was commendable; he must have realized that the days of Jebsen were numbered and perhaps his own, too. Unfortunately, the call for help reached Allied authorities only at the end of the war when Jack Churchill was liberated. In any case, it was too late for Jebsen who had been executed two or three months before. It is doubtful that they could have found a way to save him. He never revealed his secrets or Dusko Popov would certainly have been arrested and disposed of. Cumberlege's reference to 'all charges against us are baseless' referred to the accusation that they were spies, although the four commandos had been captured in uniform. They had been forced to sign 'confessions' to the contrary. The concern expressed by Cumberlege for his fellow prisoner is nothing short of remarkable, considering the dire straits in which he was. He made no personal plea for help.

Last Message
Entrusted to Jack Churchill, a note addressed to Nancy Cumberlege was smuggled out on 30 January. It read:

> My beloved Nan. I think I have forgotten how to write but will try it for it is really almost the one opportunity of direct contact I will get. Well sweetheart it has been perfectly bloody, no chance to write and always wondering if you are perfectly happy with Master Marcus and Bira. I must

admit I had expected to be able to have heard of you in some way but it really seems there is no hope and I have quit trying to kick against fate. You will be happy darling to hear something of me and please do not worry. I am absolutely fine, a bit thin damn it and never have quite enough to eat. I had not expected anything else anyway. I have forgotten what they mean, things like jam and fresh pastries and sugar cakes! Never mind, our time is coming unless I am mistaken sooner than ever you would expect. I only hope that everything is quite okay with you sweetheart and wonder if you have sufficient coming in for your needs, Fortunately there is always (illegible) allotment which keeps you very kindly thank you! Really that is being such a relief, you can't think; always to have felt that that help was there paving the way for you and others. Well, oh well so long as they haven't struck me off the Navy List altogether. Never forget that my thoughts are continuously with you and his Lordship! The Man from Far will need considerable cosseting on his return.
Abrazos [hugs, in Spanish] and caresses,
Mike

Jack Churchill reached Allied lines and was interviewed by Major Boxshall of SOE on 31 May 1945.

Surviving in the camp had been a matter of luck; British Major Johnny Dodge 'the Dodger', who had also been held in solitary confinement, was suddenly freed on 2 February 1945. British and American prisoners had rescued German officers from execution at the hands of Soviet forces and this was explained as a gesture of goodwill. But it would soon become apparent that, with resistance crumbling in the east, the Germans were desperate to drive a wedge between the Allies.

Dodge was brought to Berlin and given civilian clothes; this was not without some misgivings as he feared the Germans would use it as an excuse to have him shot as a spy. To his bewilderment, he was brought to the Hotel Adlon, the finest in Berlin, where he met Dr Hans Thost of the Foreign Ministry and Paul Schmidt, Hitler's personal interpreter. It is highly probable that the meeting was sanctioned directly by the Führer in the hope of reaching an understanding with the Western Allies and stopping the Soviet tide. The American-born Dodge was in fact a distant relative of Prime Minister Churchill, a fact known to the Germans who hoped he could be used as a conduit to open negotiations. After his failed attempt to escape from Sachsenhausen, the 'Dodger' had been interrogated at the *Zellenbau* and Hans Thost, who was fluent in English, had served as interpreter. Thost, who had lived in England before the war, proved sympathetic to the Englishman and the two men had forged the bond of a friendship that would outlast the war. Dodge was told that Germany would not accept an unconditional surrender and would keep her pre-war frontiers. Later, he was driven to Dresden and Munich; he met with Field Marshal von Kleist and a meeting was also arranged with Himmler but failed to come off.

Dodge was eventually allowed to cross into Switzerland and was interviewed in London on 30 April 1945. He reported that an unknown naval lieutenant (Cumberlege) and Sergeant Major Steele of the Rhodesian Forces were held in the *Straflager* (criminal section) along with Flight Lieutenants Dowse and James, and Lieutenant Colonel Jack Churchill while Captain Peter Churchill and Fusilier Cushing were held in *Sonderlager A*. Conditions were bad but nevertheless prisoners were getting regular Wehrmacht rations and two-thirds Red Cross parcels every fortnight, except Steele (and Cumberlege, Handley and Kotrba). This was the first news of the four LOCKSMITH men since their first and last Red Cross messages. Dodge also noted that an airborne captain named James, not to be mistaken with Flight Lieutenant James, had been held in the *Straflager* and then taken away in October 1944, never to be seen again; ominously, his personal kit was left behind.

When Jack Churchill was liberated, he suggested contacting Captain Alfons Jerzy Jakubianiec. This Polish spy who was held in the next cell to Michael Cumberlege might have some information.

Jakubianiec (who used the alias Georg Kuncewicz, codename KUBA) had worked for the II Section of the Polish General Staff (Intelligence). In September 1939, following the invasion of Poland, he had escaped to Lithuania and then to Stockholm. Polish and Japanese Intelligence Services were collaborating against their common enemy, the Soviet Union. The Japanese Military Attaché, Toshio Nishimura, helped Jakubianiec travel to Berlin where the Pole managed to smuggle out a large quantity of copies of German documents. When Nishimura was transferred to Manchuria, General Makoto Onodera took over and proved equally co-operative, but the German secret service was vigilant and Jakubianiec was arrested on 6 July 1941. During his post-war interrogation, Schellenberg of the *Sicherheitsdienst* described the arrest of Polish officer 'Kunczewiencz' in the Berlin Tiergarten as he handed over a parcel he had brought from Warsaw to a female cook working at the Manchuko Legation. This was Jakubianiec and the parcel contained microphotographs describing the German preparations for the invasion of Russia that, when developed, filled three volumes. Schellenberg claimed to have convinced him to work for German Intelligence in Russia and thereby saved his life, though he lost trace of him in 1945.

It is doubtful that Schellenberg was unaware of the fate of his spy. If he had indeed 'turned' Jakubianiec, why was the Polish officer transferred to Sachsenhausen, unless he had outlived his usefulness? This does cast some doubts on the image Schellenberg tried very hard to paint of himself; after all he could also show a streak of ruthlessness. Efforts to contact the Polish spy after the war came to naught. Jakubianiec, alias KUNCEWICZ, had been executed on 27 February 1945.

Chapter 20

Fate and Justice

Soviet and Polish army units liberated Sachsenhausen on 22 April, but the fate of the four LOCKSMITH commandos remained a mystery. Extensive efforts were now made to find out what had happened to them and to bring to justice any German involved in the mistreatment and death of PoWs. The task was complicated as Sachsenhausen was in the Soviet zone and relations between the Allies had soured. Most of the camp had actually already been evacuated at the approach of the Soviet armies, with the prisoners on a forced 'Death March'. Prisoners dangerous to the state, those who had witnessed executions, as well as a number of Jews and the sick, were liquidated.

There was a brief glimmer of hope when it was learnt that a Sergeant Steele had been liberated, but this was not James Cook Steele but a Sergeant J. A. Steele, captured on Leros in 1943 and liberated from Oflag 79.

Nevertheless, a party led by Lieutenant Colonel G. L. Sprunt of the Prisoners of War and Displaced Persons (PW and DP) Division (Rear Echelon) crossed into the Soviet zone and visited the Oranienburg area on 15/16 March 1946. They were met by Major Oboukoff. At first, the Russian viewed the British party with some suspicion but became quite helpful when the motive of their visit was revealed. Most of the camp records were destroyed intentionally or by bombs and there was little information to be gathered. The victims had been cremated but, although the local Germans were most cooperative, the hope of finding anything more was remote.

Through the Norwegian naval attaché, the Naval Intelligence Division received information that a doctor, Captain Henry Meyer of the United Nations Relief and Rehabilitation Administration (UNRRA), in Shanghai had suggested that two former Norwegian inmates at Sachsenhausen may have some information on Lieutenant Commander Cumberlege and provided their addresses. They were Captain Leif Jensen, Royal Norwegian Army, and Captain Erling Heide, both residing in Oslo. Heide had nothing to contribute but Jensen referred them to a fellow inmate, Captain Arne Simensøn Dæhli, RNNR, who was condemned to death and put in the isolated part (*Zellenbau*) on 15 March 1945. Dæhli did not believe there were British inmates there at the time. In fact, Leif Jensen had been instrumental in organizing the sharing of Norwegian food parcels with the British prisoners at the *Zellenbau;* otherwise they would all have perished from starvation. In March 1945, following pressure from the

Swedish government, Norwegian and Danish inmates were liberated as a gesture of goodwill. This was thanks to the work of Walter Schellenberg of the *Sicherheitsdienst* who managed to influence Himmler to take a softer position. Jensen was at Sachsenhausen until 18 March 1945 and would have been aware of any Briton executed at the crematorium. He believed, erroneously, that Cumberlege had been taken away to Flossenburg and executed there.

Finally, a German witness was found. He was Paul Hermann Schröter from Grabow, now in the Soviet zone. A former inmate at the concentration camp, he travelled to Berlin to be interviewed by Squadron Officer Vera M. Atkins of the Judge Advocate General's (JAG) Branch of the War Crime Sections.

Vera Atkins was a remarkable woman, at a time when few women held responsible positions. Born Vera Maria Rosenberg to a rich Jewish family from Rumania, she became the assistant of Maurice Buckmaster, head of the French section of SOE. SOE had sent some 400 agents to France and a quarter of them had never returned. At the end of the war, she made efforts to discover the fate of the missing agents. A number of them were women Vera Atkins had recruited herself, such as Violette Szabo and Princess Noor Inayat Khan. SOE ceased to exist in January 1946, but she kept the search on by working for the War Crime Sections. She had gone to Berlin to investigate the fate of agents believed to have disappeared at Sachsenhausen and especially Major Francis Suttill also known as PROSPER of the resistance network of the same name. The collapse of the PROSPER network had been the greatest SOE disaster of the war.

Schröter would be thoroughly interrogated by Vera Atkins, travelling to Berlin on three occasions in July and August 1946. A member of a Bible Society, he had been incarcerated for his religious convictions when the society was declared illegal. He made a good impression during his interrogation. Schröter remembered that the four men of LOCKSMITH had arrived at the *Zellenbau* in November or December 1944. His memory was faulty as they had arrived in January 1944; he may have mixed them up with the five escapees who had arrived in October. He admitted that his memory was impaired by the years of mistreatments and could not be relied upon. Two other British officers captured in France were already there, Major Francis Suttill and Captain William Charles Grover-Williams who were also SOE agents. According to Schröter, both men were executed at the end of March; they are believed to have been murdered on 23 March 1945. Junior Commander D. I. Gorrum of the War Office was convinced that the LOCKSMITH party had also been executed at the end of March.

Questioned about the cells where they were held, Schröter confirmed their cell numbers and specified that Handley's cell was number 71 (this had been omitted in the questionnaire). He described the cells as small, 2 metres by 1.5 metres (actually about 2.5 by 2 metres), dark because of small windows with frosted glass and furnished with a bed, a small table, a cupboard, a stool and a sanitary pail. The six men were fed wurzels, a type of beet with a large root, usually used as animal feed, cooked in water and were not allowed to receive their Red Cross parcels. They were very emaciated but their health was reasonably good as they never required the service of a medical officer, though they had skin complaints and sometimes suffered from teeth ailments. Schröter and other inmates would smuggle some items of their Red Cross parcels to them. Every morning the six men were allowed to exercise for fifteen minutes in the yard but precautions were taken so that they could not talk to each other. Other Allied officers who passed through the *Zellenbau* would stay there for about ten weeks but were better fed, being treated as prisoners of war. He remembered specifically one of them, Captain Best, who often shared his food with them.

Curiously, Best made no mention of the LOCKSMITH party in his account.[36] This is surprising since he was on friendly terms with his captors and would most likely have known of the presence of other British prisoners. Schröter remembered that Best was transferred to Bavaria at the end of April; but again his memory was faulty. Best noted everything in his diary and he actually left for Dachau on 20 February. There, he got to know *Korvettenkapitän* Franz Liedig, formerly of the Athens *Abwehrstelle* and therefore well apprised of the LOCKSMITH episode, although it is doubtful that this was ever discussed. Liedig had been incarcerated for his part in the 20 July plot. Both men were lucky to survive the war.

We do not know precisely which cells the four men from LOCKSMITH occupied. There are contradictory testimonies and we cannot be sure exactly how messages were exchanged. Flight Lieutenant H. M. Falconer RAF, an inmate at Sachsenhausen, was later transferred to Dachau but survived. On 13 February 1946 he wrote a statement that Mike Cumberlege had been held in cell 59 (more or less) and Sergeant Steele in cell 6 or 7 (other testimonies put Cumberlege in cell 69 or 70) and a warrant officer who was their wireless operator, Sergeant Handley, was also held. He made no mention of Kotrba. It is possible that Falconer pointed out the location of the cells on the map and his testimony may not be very reliable. Jack Churchill was in cell 6 and had testified that Steele was in the cell opposite to him, which would make him actually in cell 20. Flight Lieutenant James recollected that he had been brought to cell no. 3 in the *Zellenbau*'s Wing A and was a direct neighbour of Cumberlege and his group. It is also quite possible that the prisoners were moved at one time or another to different cells.

Schröter also remembered Colonel Churchill and a prisoner named Daws (Dowse) who helped them as well. Schröter pointed out that Adjutant Heinrich Wessel (*SS-Untersturmführer* Heinrich Otto Wessel) was particularly brutal, usually visiting the *Zellenbau* at night-time and often beating the prisoners and probably witnessing their executions. Of the six SOE men, Captain Williams appears to have been singled out for the most brutal treatment.

About 10 April 1945 Schröter had seen the four members of the LOCKSMITH party being taken away. They were being transported by ambulance to the *Industriehof* to be executed. After their execution, Schröter assisted Petzke, the head camp orderly, in packing their personal effects and these were sent to the Gestapo headquarters in Berlin. He did notice that many articles of clothing, such as underwear and footwear, were missing and their valuables such as watches, etc. had been removed. Their papers, letters, and other personal effects, which could not be used, were taken by the camp boiler-room attendant, Apel, and burned. Schröter added that their garments were brought back to be used by other prisoners and he saw no bloodstains. He suggested that Petzke and the camp barber, Schror, might confirm his testimony, but both men were reported to have tried to reach Silesia and their fate was unknown. Apel was believed to have gone back to his hometown of Kiel, but there is no evidence that he was interrogated. Schröter's testimony was fairly accurate and if a couple of dates appear to have been incorrect there is no reason to believe that it was intentional. He admitted that his memory was not reliable due to the hardships he had endured. He had been an inmate at Sachsenhausen and had no reason to lie; neither was his account motivated by monetary gains as he was only paid 90 DM to cover the three trips he took to Berlin by train.[37]

Willi Feiler, a German communist who survived his incarceration at Sachsenhausen, wrote a detailed description of the camp extermination facilities. Mass murders were committed at the *Industriehof*, a special area where bodies could be disposed of by cremation. Prisoners could be driven into a sandpit where they would then be machine-gunned. In May 1943 he witnessed about eighty to a hundred British and American airmen, who were held at the *Sonderlager*, sent to the sandpit and the firing began. He could hear screams but could only make out the name of cities such as St Louis, Detroit, New York, London or Bristol. They were probably shouting their own names or names of their loved ones with their address in the hope that someone would perhaps inform their relatives of their death. Some prisoners shouted 'God save the king'. To cover their executions, it was then recorded that they had 'escaped'.

Next to the sandpit, a *genickschussbaracke* (neck shooting barrack) was built. It consisted of three rooms where prisoners could be disposed of quietly and without arousing their suspicions. This was supposed to be an infirmary and, in the first room, the prisoners were undressed; in the second room an SS man disguised as a doctor 'examined' them and they were then sent to the third room where another doctor weighed them and measured them but, as the prisoner stood on the height-gauge, a slide opened in the wall behind him and another SS man standing in a narrow hallway would shoot him in the neck. The opposite wall consisted of narrow white ribbons of cloth stretched taut at top and bottom giving the appearance of a solid white wall. Behind the ribbons was a block of wood which received the bullets. Loud music would be played to cover the sound of the gunshots. Since prisoners were told to undress during the 'medical examination' it was therefore not surprising that their clothing bore no trace of blood. The exit of the third room led to a chute to the crematorium. In the autumn of 1943 a gas chamber was built next to the neck-shooting barrack, to provide a more 'humane' way of killing a large number of prisoners.[38]

The majority of the victims of the camp were Russian prisoners of war. Soviet political commissars were specially earmarked for vicious treatments.

The information collected by Vera Atkins was passed on to Mr F. W. Kemp of CW (Casualties) who had succeeded Mr Broughton and he would have the delicate task of informing Nancy Cumberlege of the fate of her husband.[39] Relatives of Steele, Handley and Kotrba were informed accordingly, though it was noted that Eileen Kotrba was now pregnant and appeared to have found solace elsewhere.

Anton Kaindl

At the end of the war camp commandant *SS-Standartenführer* Anton Kaindl fled to the British zone and was arrested on 14 May at the town hall of Plön as he was carrying false papers in the name of Anton Rieger. Recognized as the commandant of Sachsenhausen, he was held in custody until it was decided to send him to the Soviets for prosecution as most of the victims of the camp were Russians.

Rudolf Hoess, head of Amt D/I which was responsible for the administration of the concentration camps, testified that, at the end of January 1945, he received a telephone call from *Gruppenführer* Müller, head of Amt IV RHSA (Gestapo), later confirmed by telegram, requesting a list of potentially dangerous inmates in the concentration camps so that these could be executed before the evacuation of the camps. This order was immediately transmitted to the various camp commandants, including Kaindl. When Hoess later enquired if it had been carried out, the adjutant at Sachsenhausen replied that this had been done immediately. Hoess did not know who figured on the lists but it is certain that the executions in February 1945 were a direct result of this order.[40] In 1947 Hoess, who had been camp commandant at Auschwitz, was convicted by a Polish tribunal and hanged on the site of his infamous crimes.

Vera Atkins had interrogated Kaindl thoroughly about the fate of the six men held at the *Zellenbau* but had failed to extract an admission. Kaindl was born in Munich on 14 July 1902 and, after service with the 3rd SS Division *Totenkopf*, was appointed to Sachsenhausen in 1942. British authorities soon gave up on trying the Sachsenhausen camp commandant and his followers and recognized that the Russians, who had been the chief victims of this camp, had perhaps better claims. In June 1946 about thirty persons connected to war crimes at

Sachsenhausen were transferred from the British zone to Soviet custody at Helmstadt on the demarcation line.

Anton Kaindl and fifteen of his associates were tried by a Soviet Military Tribunal (23 October–1 November 1947).

The following exchange occurred during the trial:

Public Prosecutor: What kind of extermination was committed in your camp?

Kaindl: Until mid-1943, prisoners were killed by shooting or hanging. For the mass exterminations, we used a special room in the infirmary. There was a height gauge and a table with an eye scope. There were also some SS wearing doctor uniforms. There was a hole at the back of the height gauge. While an SS was measuring the height of a prisoner, another one placed his gun in the hole and killed him by shooting in his neck. Behind the height gauge there was another room where we played music in order to cover the noise of the shooting.

Public Prosecutor: Do you know if there was already an extermination procedure in Sachsenhausen when you became commandant of the camp?

Kaindl: Yes, there were several procedures. With the special room in the infirmary, there was also an execution place where prisoners were killed by shooting, a mobile gallows and a mechanical gallows which was used for hanging three or four prisoners at the same time.

Public Prosecutor: Did you change anything in these extermination procedures?

Kaindl: In March 1943, I introduced gas chambers for the mass exterminations.

Public Prosecutor: Was it your own decision?

Kaindl: Partially yes. Because the existing installations were too small and not sufficient for the exterminations, I decided to have a meeting with some SS officers, including the SS Chief Doctor Heinz Baumkötter. During this meeting, he told me that poisoning of prisoners by prussic acid in special chambers would cause an immediate death. After this meeting, I decided to install gas chambers in the camp for mass extermination because it was a more efficient and more humane way to exterminate prisoners.

Public Prosecutor: Who was responsible for the extermination?

Kaindl: The commandant of the camp.

Public Prosecutor: So, it was you?

Kaindl: Yes.

Public Prosecutor: How many prisoners were exterminated in Sachsenhausen while you were commandant of the camp?

Kaindl: More than 42,000 prisoners were exterminated under my command; this number included 18,000 killed in the camp itself.

He confirmed that when the Soviet Army reached the Oder river on 1 February 1945 preparations were made for the evacuation of the camp. Müller, the chief of the Gestapo, had ordered that prisoners considered particularly dangerous as well as those unable to walk, were to be selected for execution. He had instructed *Untersturmführer* August Höhn to carry out his orders and, from 1 February to the end of March 1945, some 5,000 inmates had been murdered.

Kaindl was found guilty of war crimes and condemned to life imprisonment.[41] He was shipped to the Vorkuta Gulag, above the Arctic Circle in Siberia. He died a few months later.

Was Kaindl a monster? The answer is a complex one. Captain Best, who had been his prisoner before being transferred to Dachau on 20 February 1945 and had known him well, wrote kind words about him. Yet, it can hardly be denied that the camp commandant bore responsibility for the executions of many prisoners, even though he may just have followed orders.

Kurt Eccarius

SS Hauptscharführer Kurt Eccarius, who was in charge of the *Zellenbau*, was also tried at the same time by the Soviets and admitted that some forty *Zellenbau* inmates had been murdered in 1944-45 and that he had himself participated in the killing of fourteen of them. He testified:

> In February 1945, I was involved in the shooting of Captain Cumberleigh (sic) and four English soldiers. They had been imprisoned for about two years. The same day the Polish Army Captain Kuzewitz (sic, Kuncewicz, this was the alias used by Jakubianiec) was also shot'.[42]

He spoke freely of the execution of the Communist Party leader König at about the same time and, at the end of the same month, the murders of SOE agents Grover-Williams and Suttill at the crematorium. In the notebook, Suttill was marked as having gone to the crematorium on 23 March. Only thirteen prisoners were left at the *Zellenbau* when the camp was evacuated.

Earlier, when grilled by his British captors at Camp Tomato (the interrogation centre located near Linden), he merely replied that Cumberlege and his men had been 'sent to Berlin'. He obviously lied to avoid incriminating himself. After all, some prisoners such as Major Dodge had indeed been sent to Berlin and survived; Eccarius could plead ignorance of their subsequent fates. He did remember Cumberlege and that he had been sent to Greece with his three men in the spring of 1942 (actually the winter of 1943) and had come to

Sachsenhausen via Vienna which was substantially correct. He claimed that they had been fed SS rations but this was a brazen lie; they had been on a starvation diet and had only survived so far thanks to food parcels smuggled by other prisoners.

In another interrogation, he remembered that at one time Dr Baumkötter had examined Cumberlege and sent him to the dentist. He also remembered that the English prisoner had gold teeth.

Eccarius described that the prisoners assigned to the *Zellenbau* would arrive with an *Einlieferungschein* (receipt) signed by Kaindl himself. To his British interrogators he used Cumberlege as an example:[43]

Einlieferungschein

Der Cumberlege, Michael, geboren... (Understandably he did not remember his date of birth.)
Engländer, wird in Einzelhaft genommen (British, solitary confinement.)
Vergünstigung: SS Kost, Rauchen, Lesen, Freistunde (Privileges: SS rations, smoking, reading, free time) (all apparently lies.)
Darf mit anderen 3 nicht zusammen kommen (not allowed contact with the other three men).

Signed: Kaindl

Eccarius stated that he received a verbal order from the camp adjutant, Wessel, to prepare Cumberlege and his three men for transfer to Berlin. *Unterscharführer* Hackmann took them to the *Kommandantur*. This was in autumn 1944 and he remembered that Cumberlege had taken a grey canvas rucksack with him.

He had obviously lied to the British except for some minor details. The time was wrong and contradicted by his later testimony in Soviet hands when he had given the date of their execution as February 1945. It is quite possible that the prisoners were told that they would be transferred to avoid a possible resistance. After all, Godwin and his men had resisted when the Germans had made the mistake of telling them that they would not need their kits where they were going.

We can only hope that the end came swiftly for Mike and his three companions.

A German inmate, Hans Appel, found a notebook with handwritten notes indicating that Kuncewicz had been sent to the crematorium on 27 February 1945. The author of this notebook is unknown and it was probably copied from an official document. Possibly this was done by an inmate who had access to the registration files and realizing their importance, had made a copy. It was delivered to the Russians and we now have an approximate translation of it. If accurate, and if we accept the statement by Eccarius, then the members of the LOCKSMITH team were murdered on that date.[44]

Born on 5 March 1905 in Coburg, Bavaria, Eccarius had joined the Nazi Party in 1932 and the SS in 1933. He was married and had three young children. He had arrived at Sachsenhausen in the summer of 1939 and had been put in charge of the *Zellenbau*. He had admitted his role in the murder of 18,000 Soviet prisoners of war in the autumn of 1941 and a number of prisoners of different nationalities, including ninety-six Dutch military personnel on 2 May 1942. The Soviets had, perhaps, means of extracting 'confessions' which the Western powers lacked, at least officially. This could be excused since the bulk of prisoners murdered at Sachsenhausen were Russians. It should not cast doubt on the guilt of Kaindl and his men; they may have had moments of doubts and perhaps kindness, but they were the willing executioners who allowed the system to exist and thrive.

Condemned to life imprisonment and forced labour at the Vorkuta Gulag in the Arctic Circle, Eccarius survived, but many of his fellow inmates, including Kaindl, did not. He was repatriated in 1956 along with German prisoners of war to West Germany following a deal brokered by Chancellor Konrad Adenauer. He found his freedom but his troubles were not over, for in 1962 he was indicted for the shooting of six prisoners of war during the Sachsenhausen 'Death March' and sentenced to four years. Another accusation was levelled at him related to the execution of 13,000 Soviet prisoners of war in the *Genickschussanlage* (neck-shooting facility) in 1941 and he was sentenced to eight-and-a-half-years' imprisonment in 1969, but served only two years.

The former inmate Schröter, who appeared to have been an honest man, mentioned Eccarius as the man in charge at the *Zellenbau,* but pointed out that it was *Unterscharführer* Lux who was particularly brutal towards the prisoners; Eccarius was the one who treated them the most fairly. This is also confirmed by Captain Best who mentioned that, on the date of his departure from the camp, Eccarius brought him extra bread and tobacco to make sure that he had enough rations for the trip. Yet, at his Soviet trial, Eccarius had confessed to have participated himself in some of the murders at the *Industriehof*, including those of Mike Cumberlege and his men.

A Question of Dates

There will always be an element of doubt as to the exact date Cumberlege and his men were executed. Do we believe Eccarius who had nothing to lose when he admitted his part in their death or Schröter who had nothing to gain? If we accept Eccarius' version then the 'Russian' notebook seems to suggest that 27 February is the date, since he related that Cumberlege and his men went to their death at the same time as the Polish spy Jakubianiec, alias Kuncewicz. Schröter in his version gives the date as 9 or 10 April; we know that he had good intentions, but mixed up dates on at least one other occasion when he talked about the departure of Best from Sachsenhausen. In this instance, we have to believe Best's diary is a more reliable source than Schröter's memory. Schröter himself admitted that his memory was unreliable as he had suffered from many privations. Eccarius' testimony is reinforced by that of the Norwegian naval reserve captain, Arne Simensøn Dæhli, who did not believe there were any British prisoners left at the *Zellenbau* on 15 March. However, if we accept the Norwegian's version then the 'Russian' notebook which dates the death of Francis Suttill as 23 March is invalid and by the same token casts some doubts at the date of Kuncewicz' death.

How dependable is the 'Russian' notebook? Who wrote it? Was it written in haste? From the text, it must be dated from April 1945, a 'James Stawle' is listed as no.14, it is almost certain that this refers to James Steele. Since his fate is not recorded, it gives credence to Schröter's version that he was murdered on 9 or 10 April. Did the author copy the information faithfully or did he make mistakes? The notebook is perhaps our best source. But unless an official document can be found, and even these are not without errors, we can only be certain of the uncertainty of the dates.

During the last days of the war, several notorious prisoners would be disposed of. On 6 April Hans von Dohnanyi, one of the most famous figures of the German resistance, was convicted by a summary court with Kaindl acting as one of the three presiding judges; he was executed on 8 or 9 April at Sachsenhausen.

In November 1945 Captain Yuri 'Yurka' Galitzine of AG3 (VW War Crimes) who was investigating the deaths at various concentration camps was informed by the War Crimes Commission that a German was being accused at Nuremberg of murdering Sergeant Major Steele.[45] This German was none other than Ernst Kaltenbrunner, the dreaded chief of the Security Police or *Reichsicherheitshauptamt* who had been captured by an American patrol on 12 May 1945. He had tried to pass himself off as a doctor but, while in custody; his mistress found him, called him by name and rushed to hug him, sealing his fate.

The Schellenberg interrogation

In the preliminary interrogations leading to the Nuremberg trials, Lieutenant Colonel Smith W. Brookhart Jr, of the US Army, had grilled Kaltenbrunner on 10 November and had asked him about Hitler's *Kommandobefehl* of 18 October 1942 which ordered the execution on the spot of British and Allied commandos, even if caught in uniform. The chief of the RHSA had professed complete ignorance. One of the great difficulties encountered by the prosecutors was that they could find few documents incriminating Kaltenbrunner. When questioned about the murder of the fifty escapees from Stalag Luft III following the 'Great Escape', he vehemently denied any knowledge of the affair.

A few days later Brookhart interrogated Walter Schellenberg, head of the Intelligence Section of the *Sicherheitsdienst (Amt VI),* and presented him with a document that he was asked to identify.[46] Schellenberg had little sympathy for Kaltenbrunner and proved most cooperative.

Brookhart: I show you another document (377-(b)), being a *Schutzhaftbefehl*, for one James Cook Steele, British subject, dated January 1944, and ask you if you can identify the document.[47]
(The document was handed to the witness)
Schellenberg: No, I never saw this before. I only know that this is an old form. The letterhead reads 'Secret State Police' and below 'Reich Main Security Office IV C 2' and then the file number. The stamp below is the State Police Stamp of Vienna, and it was authenticated by a certain *Kriminalrat*. I can't tell the name of the *Kriminalrat*, but there are discrepancies in this document.
Brookhart: Discrepancies from what?
Schellenberg: On the heading.
Brookhart: Do you mean changes?
Schellenberg: No, there is the heading of the RHSA and the stamp is from Vienna.
Brookhart: But isn't it signed in the name of Dr Kaltenbrunner representing the RHSA?
Schellenberg: Yes, it would be possible, I think, that the order must have been issued during the residence of Kaltenbrunner in Vienna.
Brookhart: Not according to the date.
Schellenberg: Yes, he could have been in Vienna at that time for a visit.
Brookhart: Do you know whether this was the ordinary form of *Schutzhaft* arrest document?
Schellenberg: I can't say that exactly. I only know that there were protective custody orders. But I don't know the form. I don't know whether this was the last form. The form changed frequently.
Brookhart: Were all of such protective custody orders done in the name and on the authority of the chief of the RHSA?
Schellenberg: I can't say that exactly. However, in all important cases it was certainly so. There was another category, however, in which the chiefs of the department could issue protective and preventive custody orders for imprisonment.
Brookhart: Do you know who determined whether it was necessary to have the approval of the chief of the RHSA for arrest, and under what conditions it was the authority of the local police?
Schellenberg: That was not all centralized for the head of the RHSA to determine, but it was rather loosely constructed according to a policy

which is unknown to me. There were regulations which changed often during the war, depending upon the intelligence received and the telephone and radio information. However, everything had to have permission granted after a certain time from Berlin headquarters.

So it was clear that a document had been found incriminating Kaltenbrunner and this concerned Sergeant Steele. Most probably the chief of the RHSA had also signed the arrest papers for Cumberlege, Handley and Kotrba, but these were never found. From this exchange, it was obvious that the prosecution was preparing charges against him for his upcoming trial at Nuremberg.

Justice at last
The Austrian Kaltenbrunner had become the head of the RHSA in 1943, following the murder of Reinhard Heydrich by SOE-trained Czech commandos. As such he was head of the *Sichertheitspolizei* which combined Gestapo, the *Kriminalpolizei* and the *Sichertheitsdienst*, the intelligence service headed by Schellenberg. Schellenberg did not like Kaltenbrunner and it was said that even Himmler feared him.

It is noteworthy that in the preliminary interrogation of Kaltenbrunner the case of Sergeant Steele was not raised. The intention of the prosecution was probably to reserve this exhibit for the trial.

The Nuremberg trial began on 20 November 1945; the document shown to Schellenberg was part of the evidence used against Kaltenbrunner. This was item 1574-PS and it stated that a warrant for protective custody had been issued for Sergeant James C. Steele on the grounds that he had been proven guilty of activities to the detriment of the German Reich, and that there was reason to expect that he would, if released, commit acts prejudicial to the Reich.[48]

Was it a coincidence that Kaltenbrunner had been in Vienna at this time or did he take a particular interest in the men from LOCKSMITH? We know that Kaltenbrunner, when interrogated prior to his trial at Nuremberg, claimed that he was a Balkans expert. He was known to have always taken a particular interest in *Amt VI E*, the department dealing with the Balkan countries. Although this department, located in Vienna, was technically under the direct command of Schellenberg, Kaltenbrunner had considered it as his own and Schellenberg had not disputed it. We know that the chief of the RHSA frequently took an interest in meeting his foreign captives in person. He may have been particularly interested in the men who had attempted to block the Corinth Canal. Schellenberg stated that Kaltenbrunner was responsible for all the *Schutzhaft* of important persons. The LOCKSMITH party must have caught his attention. The bits of information that Cumberlege managed to pass confirm that the four commandos were transferred from Vienna to Sachsenhausen in January 1944.

Why were the commandos not executed within a short time of their capture?

Hitler's *Kommandobefehl* acknowledged that they could be kept alive as long as their interrogation could yield results. We know from other examples that even the Führer's orders were not always obeyed to the letter. According to General Lahousen who testified in Nuremberg on 30 November, the *Abwehr* had also objected to the application of the *Kommandobefehl* and the *Abwehr III* division was particularly interested in interrogating the commandos. The objection was not entirely altruistic as the action might have exacted reprisals from the Allies on their own Brandenburg units who were engaged in special operations similar to those carried out by British commandos. We do not know precisely at what time the LOCKSMITH party was transferred from the *Abwehr* to the *Sicherheitsdienst*, which was less inclined to observe the Geneva Convention.

Certainly the evidence relating to Sergeant Steele was only a minor item in the list of accusations directed at the former chief of the RHSA and it was not used in the trial itself. But a statement from Martin Sandberger, Group Leader VIa of the RHSA, was produced by the prosecution in April 1946:[49]

> In February, 1945, I was told by group leader *SS Standartenführer* Steinle that he had to represent Schellenberg at the daily Section Chief meetings. On that occasion, Müller (Section IV) presented to Kaltenbrunner a list of persons who were in confinement in or close to Berlin for Kaltenbrunner to decide if they were to be transported to Southern Germany or if they were to be shot, because the Soviet Armies were closing in on Berlin. Steinle did not know who these people were. Kaltenbrunner made his decisions in an extremely hasty and superficial manner and Steinle expressed his indignation to me about the frivolity of the procedure. I assumed that Kaltenbrunner had ordered a number of shootings, because if evacuation had been ordered, there would have been no talk about the frivolity.

It is probable that the four members of LOCKSMITH were on this list as Sachsenhausen was thirty kilometres from Berlin.

Did the chief of the RHSA issue the actual order for the executions of the four men? No proof was ever found but it is not improbable.[50] This was further confirmed by the testimony of Rudolf Hoess, former commandant at Auschwitz (15 April 1946):

> This was shortly before the end of the war, and shortly before Northern and Southern Germany were separated. I shall speak about the Sachsenhausen camp. The Gestapo Chief, *Gruppenführer* Müller, asked me to see him one evening and told me that the *Reichsführer* (Himmler) had ordered that the camp at Sachsenhausen was to be evacuated at once.

I pointed out to *Gruppenführer* Müller what that would mean. Sachsenhausen could no longer depend on any other camps for accommodation except, perhaps, a few labour camps attached to the armament works that were almost filled up anyway. Most of the detainees would have to be lodged in the woods somewhere. This would mean countless thousands of deaths and, above all, it would be impossible to feed these masses of people. He promised me that he would once more discuss the matter with the *Reichsführer*. He called me back and told me that the *Reichsführer* had refused to rescind the order and demanded that the commandants should carry out his order immediately. At the same time Ravensbrück was also to be evacuated in the same manner but it could no longer be done. I do not know whether camps in Southern Germany were cleared or not, since we, the Inspectorate, had no longer any connections with Southern Germany.

At Nuremberg, Walter Schellenberg painted a somewhat different picture. According to him, Himmler had actually ordered the camps not to be evacuated and allowed for their inmates to be liberated by the advancing Allied armies. This was part of his softening attitude during the last months of the war when he had entertained the idea of making a deal with the Western powers through Swiss and Swedish contacts. This had already resulted in certain gestures of goodwill. Over 1,200 Jewish inmates from the Theresienstadt concentration camp in Austria were given passage to Switzerland, and Scandinavian prisoners were being released from Sachsenhausen in the custody of the Swedish Red Cross. But the evacuation order was countermanded by *Gruppenführer* Müller, head of the Gestapo. When Schellenberg inquired on whose authority his order was overridden, Müller referred him to Kaltenbrunner who in turn replied that it came from the direct order of Hitler. According to Schellenberg's recollections the discussion had taken place on 10 April. If one believes Schröter's version, this was the very day the four members of LOCKSMITH had been executed.

Since Müller worked under Kaltenbrunner, the latter could not evade responsibility. Despite his repeated denials, the chief of the RHSA did not survive his victims very long. He was found guilty of war crimes at Nuremberg and hanged on 16 October 1946.

An anonymous writer wrote the following tribute in *The Log* (Spring 1946):[51]

During the past twelve months we have been glad to learn of the return of O.P's who had been prisoners of war, but up to the present there has been no such happy news of Lieut.-Cmdr C. M. B. Cumberlege, DSO, R.D., R.N.R., who, in March last year, was known to be in the Sachsenhausen Concentration Camp at Oranienburg, some twenty miles north-west of Berlin. Most of the prisoners had been recovered from this camp at the end of February in face of the Russian advance, but Cumberlege was not among them. It is known that several Naval personnel were cold-bloodedly murdered by the S.S. at the camp in April, and witnesses to the shooting of all these except Michael have been found.

The complete story of Cumberlege's achievements in Crete and on the mainland will probably never be published but we know it is one of thrilling, daring and dangerous adventure. His last act as a free man was an amazing piece of sabotage on the mainland, on the successful completion of which his party got into touch by wireless with our people and arranged a rendezvous at sea. At the arranged time they put off in their rubber dinghy but at the rendezvous they found only German patrol craft to greet them. After ten days in Athens he was sent first of all to Mauthausen Concentration Camp near Vienna where for eight months he was kept in solitary confinement and treated most brutally. A correspondent who knew Cumberlege intimately writes: 'He knew the risks and what the outcome might be if he were caught, but he loved Greece and the Greeks and the months he spent ashore were wonderful and made anything that might happen later more than worthwhile. I know no other case of such varied qualities combined in one person. He was truly Elizabethan in character – a combination of gaiety and solidity and sensitiveness and poetry with daring and adventurousness and great courage. We hope and pray that he'll return.'

Rear Admiral Claude Cumberlege (Retired) wrote from Juan-Les-Pins to the Admiral Commanding Reserves requesting a summary of the services of his son during the war 'for the benefit of my remaining children'. Admiral Charles E. Morgan replied in a letter dated 17 January 1947 giving him details of Mike's career and concluded with 'I had the pleasure of meeting your son on several occasions at Alexandria and I always had the greatest admiration for the splendid manner in which he was carrying out his most dangerous work.'

In December 1941 Morgan himself was the victim of 'insidious means'; he had been the commanding officer of the battleship HMS *Valiant* when she was crippled at Alexandria by Italian human torpedoes. By a curious coincidence, in 1945, he was called upon to pin the Italian Gold Medal on the chest of Luigi Durand de la Penne, the man who had sunk his ship. Mike would have approved. Yesterday's enemies were now friends. It was time to forgive, but not to forget.

Chapter 21

Conclusion

Blocking waterways proved to be extremely difficult in wartime, at least with insidious means.

We have seen that the Corinth Canal was effectively blocked by the Germans in 1944; so was the Suez Canal in 1956 and 1967 by the Egyptians. We can observe that the only times that major canals were effectively blocked it was done by regular means and with the blessing of the government in power. In the case of the Corinth Canal, the Germans wanted to deny the use to the Royal Navy which a few days later would be occupying the area. The Suez Canal was blocked in 1956 by scuttling a number of ships to prevent an Anglo-French force from re-occupying the area in the wake of the nationalization of the waterway. The canal was again blocked in 1967, following the Third Arab-Israeli war, as it was feared that Israel might be able to use it and in the mistaken belief that the international community would put pressure on the Jewish state to evacuate the area. For six years, the canal would become a no man's land separating Egyptian and Israeli Forces until a new war would liberate the area and re-open the waterway.

Canals proved to be very resilient to outside interference. From air attacks or other means, when damage actually occurred, clearance was made in a matter of days. To effectively block a canal it would have been necessary to sink a large ship in it. For the Corinth Canal, this proved to be impossible as sailings of large ships were made during daytime and air attacks on the area were confined to night-time when the risk of interception by enemy fighter forces was limited. In 1944 the situation had changed dramatically and Allied air forces could bomb the area with relative impunity, but the need to block the canal had passed. It was now necessary to prevent the Germans from carrying out wholesale destruction as SOE and the Greek resistance attempted anti-scorching operations; but these were no easy tasks either.

Other canals were on occasion bombed or mined from the air, but the results were limited and even when an occasional ship was sunk, the shallow waters of the waterways involved made the salvaging of the vessel relatively easy. The Panama Canal proved to be a very difficult target, as sabotage does not appear to have been seriously considered and air attack meant the necessity of a Japanese aircraft carrier coming within range, an almost impossible task after the Battle of Midway. The use of a submarine task group turned out to be equally prohibitive, due to the difficulty of training with special aircraft.

Sabotage did not provide a better solution. It was recognized that limpets could be used but would cause relatively small damage and only a minor inconvenience to the enemy. The Corinth Canal was mined twice, the first time by a magnetic mine borrowed from the Fleet Air Arm, and the second time by a magnetic mine designed specifically for the requirement of Lieutenant Cumberlege. In both instances the mines failed. In the first case, it is possible that the mine from the FAA was defective and given away for that very reason. In the second, either the original design was faulty – the hurry to deliver the mines may have prevented adequate testing – or they were damaged in transit. We know that Cumberlege was aware of the defects before the operation was carried out but carried on in the hope that he would be proved wrong. The desire to inflict maximum damage to the enemy in the end turned out to be counter-productive. Limpets were not used as it was feared that the enemy would increase security and make the main attempt more difficult, so that in the end no effective act of sabotage took place. Although limpet attacks became frequent during the summer of 1943, it would not have been easy to sink a ship in the canal as limpet delay mechanism could only be set for a few hours. Limpets would have to be applied immediately before the sailing of a ship and the short passage of the canal made it impossible to insure that the explosion would occur during the transit.

The steep cliffs of the Corinth Canal made them prone to landslides but at the same time offered some protection from a low-level air attack. We have seen that limpet mines were inadequate for the purpose because of their relatively small charge of explosives and the problem of timing the explosion due to the short length of the canal.

As with all special operations, it took time to prepare and when it was finally ready the main purpose of the mission – to disrupt supplies to *Panzerarmee Afrika* – had disappeared. But the main problem of carrying out Operation LOCKSMITH was the lack of a suitable mine. The mine had to be just the right size: small enough to be easily transported, and yet large enough to destroy the target.

The final product appears to have been a marvel of design as it could be disguised as a petrol tin and the counter-mine would provide additional destructive power. But time was of the essence and the magnetic mechanism appears to have been inadequately tested and fragile. The specification that it should explode only within five feet of a hull was probably too restrictive. Cumberlege realized that the mine itself could not inflict enough damage to prevent the salvaging of the vessel and he depended on the RAF to complete the destruction. This was easier said than done, at this stage of the war, for Allied bombers could only attack the canal by night and it is doubtful whether they could deliver an accurate low-level attack to achieve this purpose.

It is certain that if the canal had been closed during the months preceding the Battle of El Alamein it would have had a direct effect on the Axis supply situation on that front. However, we have to recognize that ships could have been re-routed along the west coast of the Peloponnese, though at greater risk. But already in late-August 1942, supplies were only trickling to North Africa, not only because of depredations from British bombers and submarines, but also because there were few supplies to be sent, the priority being given to the war with Russia. But it is undeniable that the blocking of the Canal would have put an unbearable strain on traffic in the Aegean and made the Axis position there untenable. This, we have already seen, was recognized by none other than Admiral Riccardi, the Commander-in-Chief of the Italian Navy.

When the operation was finally carried out, Cumberlege and his men could not take a direct part in it as none could pass for Greeks. It was certainly frustrating to have come so far yet be unable to participate in the final leg of the operation. They had to rely on members of MIDAS 614 who may not have had the training required to complete it satisfactorily.

Michael Cumberlege had been a strong proponent of the operation, but his two attempts at the canal had failed because the weapons were defective. His perseverance was commendable but unrewarded. He was willing to have a third try but his detailed reports sealed his fate and that of his companions. His wish to roam the Aegean and attack enemy patrol boats was never fulfilled. He felt responsible for the life of the three men who had volunteered to join him and his subsequent incarceration in solitary confinement must have borne heavily upon him.

The four men who had embarked on the submarine *Papanicolis* were well aware of the dangers that awaited them, but they had volunteered for a mission and never faltered. They completed their mission even though fortune did not smile upon them and gave their lives for their country and the freedom of Greece.

Steele, Handley and Jan Kotrba were awarded the Military Medal in November 1946.

The following appeared in the *London Gazette* of Tuesday, 3 December 1946:

The KING has been graciously pleased to approve the following Reward and awards.

For great gallantry, and determination of the highest order in clandestine operations behind the enemy lines in Greece in January and February, 1943:

Bar to the Distinguished Service Order. Acting Lieutenant-Commander Claude Michael Bulstrode CUMBERLEGE, DSO, R.D., Royal Naval Reserve (Retired). (This Appointment to be dated 21 February, 1944.)

Many years later, Marcus Cumberlege would recollect his experience in meeting King George VI at Buckingham Palace and accepting the DSO and Bar awarded to his father:

> I remember I was at prep school at Stubbington House in Hampshire (a kind of naval college for small boys – with all the discipline, sport, Latin, Greek and chapel – when I was called to the headmaster and told I had to go up to London to meet the King, my mother would meet me at Waterloo station and take me to Buckingham palace. For a few days the masters were very nice to me, and I wasn't beaten. We arrived at the palace in a taxi (at least they have hardly changed) and in fear and trepidation we joined the queue of lucky widows lining up to get a medal (dad won two DSOs, so we were doubly proud). After about an hour we were at the front of the queue at the entrance of a huge, barely furnished room, where a little man with a straight back stood in the distance. 'Who will take it madam, you or the boy?' the usher asked. 'You take it, Marcus,' said my mother, 'after all, he was YOUR fawther' – she had a strong Canadian accent. She looked very attractive in her black suit with one of those Jackie Kennedy hats with a veil. I was wearing my usual grey jacket, white shirt, striped school tie, grey knee-length shorts, grey socks and black shoes. My knees started to knock together, I turned to her and said 'You better do it, Mum, I'm feeling sick.' She did it. We marched up to the funny man with the nice smile; he stretched forward, pinned it on her chest somewhere near the left shoulder, and gave her a kiss. I don't remember whether he squeezed my hand or just clasped it. We were out of the room and glad to be so. Five years later (that all happened in 1947 when I was eight) the poor chap died himself, which I have always thought was rather sad, as he was A GOOD KING.[52]

Sixty-five years later, the poet would write:

> *MEIN VATER LEBT*
> Mike was a long time in the hut
> for his final interrogation
> by the German officers
> before his release.
>
> When he finally came out
> and I took him in my arms –
> the thin young man in the pale brown sweater –
> I knew at last death is an illusion.

Mein Vater lebt, I proudly announced
to the plump female with the horsewhip
who hadn't wanted to believe me,
as we turned and walked downhill.

'You must stick to your agreements
from now on, papa' I warned him,
'no more unexplained disappearances
into the nebulous atrophy of war.'

Although it was a dream,
I still feel him in my arms,
that warm young muscular body,
glad to be in the land of the living.

Written on my seventy-third birthday.
Marcus Cumberlege

Epilogue

May 2014. Seventy-one years have elapsed since the four LOCKSMITH saboteurs were captured. The author has had the privilege of returning to Boufi cove, this time with Marcus Cumberlege and his daughter Eunice Cumberlege-Ravassat. We stroll in silence along the beach. The blue sky is melting in the Aegean Sea. It is a solemn moment for all.

Abbreviations, Pseudonyms and Codenames

12-land	Germany
18-land	Turkey
22-land	Great Britain
32-land	Italy
35-land	Yugoslavia
41-land	Greece. Note that the expression 41-landers was used to describe Greeks.
95-land	USSR
18,904	Code name for ISLD agent Lieutenant Commander Noel Rees, vice-consul in Smyrna, aka HATZIS.
A Force	A department in charge of deception but also included MI9 in the Middle East.
A/D3	Director of Mid East Group of SOE (MO4). At first, Colonel George Pollock was in command but Terence Maxwell replaced him from 15 August 1941 (although Pollock was not informed before the first week of September). On 13 August 1942 Maxwell was replaced by Lord Glenconner, who was himself replaced in 1943 by Major-General William Stawell.
A/DH	Terence Maxwell who took over SOE Cairo from Pollock.
A/H44	Commander Zangas RHN, appointed by Kanellopoulos as his personal representative at Smyrna.
A/H92	Major Ioannis Tsigantes, leader of MIDAS 614.
A/H100	Lieutenant Vassilios Zakynthinos of MIDAS 614, aka MIKY.
A/H101	Lieutenant Fotios Manolopoulos of MIDAS 614
A/H106	Dimitrios Gyftopoulos of MIDAS 614, aka GYPSY.
A/H114	Spyros Kotsis of MIDAS 614.
A/H118	Colonel Napoleon Zervas, head of EDES.
A/H120	Captain Alexandros Levides RHN, aka AHCXX.
ABWEHR	German Intelligence Service
AJAX	Major David Pawson (D/H 62).
ALEXANDER	Lieutenant Commander Ioannis Abatzis of Operation FLESHPOTS.
ANIMALS	Cover plan for the invasion of Sicily.

ANZAC	Australian and New Zealand Army Corps during the Great War. Although the term was not officially used in the Second World War, it still appeared in some documents.
APOLLO	Ioannis Peltekis, head of the YVONNE organization who also used the pseudonym of GEORGE BARAS, DEBARRED or GOD (THEOS) and sometime referred in British documents as 'a/m'.
ARES	Ares Veloukhiotis aka Nicolas Sclavounos, pseudonyms of Athanasios Klaras, the Greek communist leader who, with Colonel Zervas, co-operated with Myers and Woodhouse to blow up the Gorgopotamos bridge.
B6	Greek Section at MO4 (SOE Cairo).
BATH	Island of Samos.
BCIS	Balkan Counter-Intelligence Service (or Section)
BdS	*Befehlshaber der Sicherheitspolizei und des Sicherheitsdienstes* (Head of the Security and Secret Police)
BOB	Sergeant Bob Morton who seconded Don Stott.
BONZOS	German PoWs recruited by SOE.
BREVITY	Operation led by Major Kiphonides (code name KOMNINOS), who was to take over all political aspects of the Tsigantes organization and to make contact with right-wing elements, including the 'six colonels'.
BULLS	The Turkish Police.
CAM	Christos Gogas aka Captain Harris, also code name for Rhodes.
CAPITOL	Reginald 'Rex' Leeper
CD	Assistant to the Minister of Economic Warfare (SOE). In sequence: Sir Frank Nelson, Sir Charles Hambro and Major General Sir C. McV. Gubbins (Gubbins, then Brigadier, had joined SO2 on 18.11.1940 as Director of Operations and Intelligence.)
CHRIS	Major Christopher M. Woodhouse.
CLAUDIUS	Thomas Bowman, former vice-consul in Athens, in SO2, became Assistant to Sebastian.
CONEY ISLAND	Antiparos
CORK	Megara (Attica).
COSTA	SOE Wireless Station in Athens. It transmitted only during 20-29 July 1942 before being discovered by the Germans.
COTILLION	Operation to block the Levkas Channel.
CUTHBERT	Panayotis Kanellopoulos, Greek politician.
DIAMOND	Diamantis Arvanitopoulos (aka Kipriadis).

D section	A branch of SIS concerned with sabotage in peacetime. Later amalgamated with MI(R) by SOE.
D/E33	Theodoros Liakos, wireless operator.
D/E34	Matthaeou Andronikos, wireless operator.
D/H	Major George F. Taylor.
D/H24	Captain Alfred W. Lawrence of the Royal Tank Regiment, also referred in some documents as Captain D. Lawrence, who was to assist McNabb in organizing resistance in the Peloponnese. He had himself escaped from Greece on 31.07.1941.
D/H26	Reginald G. Barwell, SOE agent in Athens, in charge of purchasing caiques.
D/H41	Captain Richard O'Brien McNabb, New Zealand Engineers, reported arrested in Athens ca. June 1942.
D/H52	Captain Nicholas G. L. Hammond;, he sailed with Mike Cumberlege on *Dolphin II* and *Athanassios Miaoulis* in 1941.
D/H62	Major David Pawson; in charge of the Smyrna section. Reputed to have a bad temper but to be one of the best men in the Middle East. He was captured in the Dodecanese in September 1943 (also known as AJAX).
D/H71	Lieutenant Commander Francis Grant Pool, in charge of Para-Naval activities in the Middle-East for SOE from February 1941.
D/H89	Lieutenant Claude Michael Bulstrode Cumberlege. Note: during the re-organization of Force 133 in January 1944, the D/H symbols were abolished.
D/H109	Major (later Lieutenant Colonel) E. G. Boxshall (1899-1984) in charge of the Balkans Section. Born in Bucharest. At SOE London's Rumanian desk during the war.
D/H113	Major (later Lieutenant Colonel) Julian A. Dolbey. His real name was Count Julian Dobrski. In November 1942 he was assigned to Force 133 in Cairo.
D/H131	Captain Francis Noel-Baker, GSO2 (Political) in the Greek Section, later replaced by Major A. F. M. Mathews.
D/H200	Lord Glenconner, head of SOE Cairo (1942-1943), see also A/D3.
D/H203	Captain (later Major) Jack Smith-Hughes of Operation STILLETO.
D/H263	Major Alan W. Paton (Codename DRAX) who replaced Pawson at the head of SOE Smyrna after the latter was captured in October 1943.
D/H267	Lieutenant Samuel Beckinsale of *Armadillo*.
D/H273	Harry Paterson, SOE agent assigned to the Smyrna branch.

D/H315	Major Christopher M. Woodhouse, second in command to Eddie Myers during the Gorgopotamos operation.
D/H336	Lieutenant Colonel John M. Stevens who succeeded D/HA (Pirie) as Head of B6 (Greek Section). Stevens was later succeeded by Lieutenant Colonel McMullen, Lieutenant Colonel Budge and finally Lieutenant Colonel Graves.
D/H366	Brigadier C.M. Keble, Chief of Staff SOE Cairo.
D/H394	Brigadier E. C. W Myers RE, who organized the attack on the Gorgopotamos viaduct.
D/H533	Captain (later Major) Michael Ward who was in charge of SOE Liquidations in Greece and tried to find out the fate of the LOCKSMITH party.
D/HA	Ian Pirie, head of Greek Section until ca. December 1942.
D/HG6	Captain R. Menzies (aka SUSSEX) who organized the Salonika demolitions in 1941.
D/HG14	Pamela Lovibond, the very capable secretary to David Pawson in Smyrna who used to run things in his absence. She had been Ian Pirie's secretary in Athens. After the war, she married David Pawson.
D/HG15	Marshall, accountant of Athens Light and Power, recruited by SOE.
D/HG16	Christos Gogas, later known as Captain Chris Harris aka THE CODE MASTER. Greek-born in Istanbul, he was commissioned in the British Army as sergeant interpreter in the Middlesex Regiment.
D/HG17	Spyromiliou (personal representative of Tsouderos).
D/HG21	Elli Papadimitriou, an early recruit of SOE, opponent of the Metaxas regime.
D/HG26	Constantin Papaconstantinou, one of the early SOE recruits.
D/HG29	Alexis Ladas used as courier between Tsouderos and Kanellopoulos infiltrated in Greece with ODYSSEUS in November 1941.
D/HG50	Alexandros Zannas, head of the Greek Red Cross (a former Minister for Air), he gave considerable aid to British escapers. Arrested after the Atkinson debacle and sentenced to a jail sentence of 18½ years of which he served 20 months in an Italian jail before he was liberated at the armistice.
D/HG51	Lieutenant John Campbell. He carried out several para-naval operations with HMS *Hedgehog*.
D/HG60	Commander Ioannis Toumbas RHN, participated in the destruction of the Salonika installations. Later distinguished himself as the commanding officer of the RHN destroyer *Adrias*.

D/HP	Colonel George Pollock was Director of Mid East Group of SOE (MO4) 1940-1941. Maxwell replaced him from 15 August 1941 (although Pollock was not informed before the first week of September.)
D/HV	Lieutenant Colonel James S.A. Pearson, head of SOE Balkan section.
DIAMOND	Diamantís Arvanitopoulos. Radio operator who used the cover name of Kostas Kipriadis for Operation ISINGLASS.
DNI	Director Naval Intelligence Division (Vice Admiral John Henry Godfrey until dismissed in October 1942 and replaced by Captain, later Rear Admiral, Edmund Rushbrooke).
DPA	Director of Policy and Agents (Masterson). From 20 November 1942 it was re-organized by Maxwell and the control of agents transferred to DSO. DPA then stood for Director of Political Advisers.
DRAX	Major Alan W. Paton (D/H263) who replaced Pawson at Smyrna after the latter was captured in October 1943.
DSC	Distinguished Service Cross.
DSM	Distinguished Service Medal.
DSO	Directorate of Special Operations known formerly as G(R). One of three directorates established by Maxwell in Cairo (it amalgamated SO2). Nominally responsible for all agents in Greece. The initials were also used by the Defence Security Officer, Egypt and for the Distinguished Service Order.
DSP	Director of Subversive Propaganda.
DURBIN	Lieutenant, later Captain, Atkinson of the ill-fated Antiparos episode, see also ROBIN.
E-boat	Enemy boat, usually describes fast motor torpedo boats.
EAM	Greek National Liberation Front. Εθνικό Απελευθερωτικό Μέτωπο, translit. *Ethniko Apeleftherotiko Metopo*. The political branch of the communist resistance movement.
EDDIE	Colonel, later Brigadier, Eddie Myers. He organized the Gorgopotamos operation.
EDES	National Republican Greek League founded by Colonel Napoleon Zervas. Εθνικός Δημοκρατικός Ελληνικός Σύνδεσμος, translit. *Ethnikos Dimokratikos Ellinikos Syndesmos*)
ELAS	Greek People's Liberation Army controlled by the Communist Party (KKE). Ελληνικός Λαϊκός Απελευθερωτικός Στρατός, translit. *Ellinikós Laïkós Apeleftherotikós Stratós*, ΕΛΑΣ.
ELAN	Greek People's Liberation Navy controlled by the Communist Party (KKE).

ELKS	Escapers.
EMPERORS	E. Graham Sebastian (aka CLAUDIUS), adviser on Greek affairs to H.M. Ambassador at Cairo, and Thomas Bowman (aka TIBERIUS).
ETON	Athens.
FAA	Fleet Air Arm.
FILM	Caique.
FLEAS	The Turkish Police.
FLESHPOTS	Operation to contact Kanellopoulos and carry out sabotage to disrupt the Corinth Canal traffic.
FORCE 133	A name for SOE in the Middle East effective January 1944. This force covered Greece, Rumania and Bulgaria; Brigadier B. K. B. Benfield DSO MC became head of Force 133 on 14 March 1944 and later of Force 140.
FORMULA	MO4 Smyrna.
FOX	David Pawson, also the codename of Lieutenant Commander Papachristou who headed a Greek resistance organization which helped the evacuation of military, air and naval personnel.
GFP	*Geheime Feldpolizei*, German Field Police, equivalent of British Field Security Police, often referred as the Gestapo of occupied territories.
G(R)	Operation Branch of SOE later became DSO.
GSO	General Staff Officer.
GYPSY	Warrant Officer Dimitrios Gyftopoulos of MIDAS 614.
H.B.	J. G. Beevor, 1942-43 Assistant to Sir Charles Hambro; later on the SOE Planning Staff.
HARLEM	Codename for Antiparos.
HATZIS	Noel Rees, vice-consul in Smyrna. Worked for MI6 and organized MI9 based in Smyrna. Frequently at odds with SOE.
HHMS	His Hellenic Majesty's Ship.
HIS	Hellenic Intelligence Service led by Captain Konstas RHN and later by Captain Cortessis RHN.
HMAS	His Majesty's Australian Ship.
HMS	His Majesty's Ship.
ISLD	Inter-Services Liaison Detachments (as SIS or MI6 were known in the Middle East) under the leadership of Sir David Petrie.
JOHNSON	Major Tsigantes aka KEPHALLONITIS.
KEW	Khioste caique base (Turkey).
KIP	Ioannis Lekkas, a henchman of Tsouderos. Landed in Greece in October 1941 (Operation FLESHPOTS).
KOMNINOS	Major Kiphonides of the BREVITY mission.

LEIGH	Michael Parish of MI9. Captured during the Leros campaign.
LEPHTERIS	Police Officer Parisis who took over MIDAS 614 after the death of Tsigantes, aka ZIRELIS.
LOCKSMITH	Operation to block the Corinth Canal using special mines devised by Lieutenant Cumberlege.
LOOE	Peloponnese.
LUTON	Antiparos.
M/DH	Colonel Guy Richard Tamplin, MO4 (SOE Middle East) Director of Special Operations, Balkans. Died of heart attack on 6 November 1943.
ME102	SOE training school in Middle East.
MEW	Minister of Economic Warfare in charge of SOE. The position was filled by: – Ronald Cross (03.09.1939-15.05.1940) – Hugh Dalton (15.05.1940-22.02.1942) – Roundell Cecil Palmer, 3rd Earl of Selborne (22.02.1942-23.05.1945)
MI6	Another name for the Secret Intelligence Service (SIS) or ISLD as it was known in the Middle East.
MI9	Military Intelligence department in charge of communications with PoWs and organizing escapes. MI9 Mediterranean was based in Cairo under Lieutenant Colonel A. C. Simonds and part of A Force, headed by Colonel Dudley W. Clarke.
MI (R)	Military Intelligence (Research), a branch of the War Office under Lieutenant Colonel Holland, was to organize guerillas in occupied countries. Later amalgamated with Section D by SOE.
MIDAS 614	Organization led by Major Tsigantes.
MIKY	Lieutenant Vassilios Zakynthinos of MIDAS 614.
MO4	A name for SOE in the Middle East, later re-organized as Force 133. SOE in Cairo was constituted in September 1941 and amalgamated three groups by Maxwell who took command on 15 August 1941 of SO1 and SO2 (D in charge of subversion and sabotage in the Balkans, MI (R) in charge of organizing guerrillas in occupied territories, GSI (K) in charge of subversive propaganda aimed at Italian troops in Africa). On 21 August 1942, Lord Glenconner took over command; his chief of staff was Lieutenant Colonel, later Brigadier, C. M. Keble and Colonel Guy Tamplin took over DPA from Masterson, Pirie became Head of Greek Country Section.
MORTLAKE	One of the W/T sets at AMM HQ in occupied Greece.

NARA	National Records and Service Administration, aka as the National Archives (Washington DC).
NICO	EAM (Greek National Liberation Front).
NID	Naval Intelligence Division.
NIKO	W/T station operated by ODYSSEUS. First contact was made on 18 June 1942; the original set was seized by the Germans on 18 July 1942 but was replaced in August.
NOAH'S ARK	Operation to harass German troops when they were retreating from Greece.
NOIC	Naval Officer in charge.
ODYSSEUS	Gedeón Angelopoulos aka Gerasimos Alexatos (D/HG21), a smuggler used as a courier by SOE.
OIC	The Admiralty Operation Intelligence Centre.
OSS	Office of Strategic Services, American Intelligence organization formed during the Second World War and led by Colonel 'Wild Bill' Donovan; after the war became the CIA.
PANTELIDES	Captain Miltiadis Kanaris who became head of MIDAS 614 in March 1943.
PARIS	aka Town 330, Smyrna.
PHILON or PHILNUT	Nikos Karabasas, wireless operator of Operation FLESHPOTS.
PIUS	Anthony Simonds, head of MI9 in the Middle East.
PROMETHEUS	Organization founded by Colonel Evripidis Bakirtzis (PROMETHEUS I) and then taken over by Commander Koutsoyannopoulos (PROMETHEUS II).
PWE	Political Warfare Executive. In October 1942, the head of the PWE mission in Cairo was Mr Vellacott, a former headmaster at Harrow. Initially known as SO1 and part of SOE, it was gradually removed from it.
RA	Royal Artillery.
RAF	Royal Air Force.
RAN	Royal Australian Navy.
RD	Reserve Decoration, awarded to officers of the Royal Naval Reserve with over 15 years of service.
RDF	Radio Detection Finding (radar).
RE	Royal Engineers.
RHAF	Royal Hellenic Air Force.
RHN	Royal Hellenic Navy.
RHSA	*Reichsicherheitshauptamt* or Reich Main Security Office which included the Gestapo, the Police and the Intelligence Service (SD).
RN	Royal Navy.

RNR	Royal Naval Reserve.
RNVR	Royal Naval Volunteer Reserve.
ROBIN	Lieutenant, later Captain, Atkinson of the ill-fated Antiparos episode, see also DURBIN.
RUDE	Aegean Islands.
S.1	Major Henry McL. Threlfall of the Scandinavian Section who initiated the ill-fated attempt to block the Kiel Canal.
SARAH	Codename of Katina Logotheti who worked for Lieutenant Commander Emmanuel Vernikos RHNR.
SAS	Special Air Service.
SBS	Special Boat Section (Special Boat Squadron from March 1943), belonging to the SAS.
SCUM	The Italians.
SD	*Sicherheitsdienst*, German Intelligence Service of the SS, rival to the *Abwehr*. It was run by Reinhard Heydrich, and, after his assassination, by Ernst Kaltenbrunner who was hanged at Nuremberg.
SIM	*Servizio Informazioni Militare*, the Italian Intelligence Secret Service led by Colonel, later General, Cesare Amè for most of the war.
SIME	Security Intelligence Middle East, responsible both for military and civil security (equivalent to MI5) under Colonel R. J. Maunsell since 7.12.1939.
SIS	British Secret Intelligence Service under Admiral Sir Hugh Sinclair until his death in November 1939, then under Colonel, later Sir, Stewart Menzies (C); his chief assistant was Colonel Claude Dansey who had no use for SOE although he was supposed to work as liaison between SIS and SOE and act as arbiter in disputes between the two services.
SO	Head of MEW and SOE. The position was filled by: – Ronald Cross (03.09.1939-15.05.1940) – Hugh Dalton (15.05.1940-22.02.1942) – Roundell Cecil Palmer, 3rd Earl of Selborne (22.02.1942-23.05.1945)
SO1	Section of SOE in charge of propaganda (aka PWE for Political Warfare Executive), later became known as DSP.
SO2	Section of SOE in charge of guerrilla warfare and sabotage.
SO3	Section of SOE in charge of planning.
SOE	Special Operations Executive was under Hugh Dalton (Minister of Economic Warfare, replaced by Lord Selborne in February 1942) and its executive directors were:

	– Sir Frank Nelson (until 1942).
	– Sir Charles Hambro, (until August 1943)
	– Major General (Sir) Colin Gubbins.
	The organization was divided in SO1, SO2 and SO3.
SPHINX	Code name of M. Spentidakis who was landed in Crete by the submarine HMS *Parthian* in July 1940. Also codename used by the Cretan emissary Papadoconstantakis sent by Prime Minister Tsouderos to entice Kanellopoulos to join the Greek government in exile.
STATION 333	W/T station operated from November 1941 until 2 February 1943 by the PROMETHEUS II organization.
SUGAR	Colonel Epaminondas Tselos. He belonged to the Kanelopoulos organization.
TANZA	Section N of Advanced HQ A Force.
THURGOLAND	Operation to block the Corinth Canal using limpets to be carried out by MIDAS 614, organization led by Major Tsigantes.
TIBERIUS	E. Graham Sebastian, former Consul-General in Athens then adviser on Greek affairs at the British Embassy in Cairo. He was to maintain contact with all British Intelligence organizations working in Greece, including MI9. His assistant was Bowman.
TICK	Code name of Colonel Stamatios Mantikas of Operation KEATS (Mytilene).
TIGER	Major Jimmy Corfe (MI9).
TNA	The National Archives located in Kew, London. The NA is an amalgamation of the Public Record Office and the Historic Documents Commission.
TOADS	SOE agents.
TOBY	Major Georgios Diamantopoulos of Operation ERUPTION, he used a variety of code names:
	TOM for Operation BIZARRE
	BILL for Operation PAN
	FRED for Operation BARBARITY
	JACK for Operation BREVITY
TOM BROWN	Colonel John M. Stevens.
TUCKSHOP	ISLD Smyrna.
U-boat	Submarine, from the German *Unterseeboot*. During the Second World War, the term was generally used to describe Axis submarines.
USSME	*Ufficio Storico Stato Maggiore dell'Esercito* (Italian Army Archives).

USMM	Ufficio Storico Della Marina Militare (Italian Navy Archives).
V/CD	Vice Chief of SOE: Major General C. Gubbins DSO MC (1943).
VC	Victoria Cross, the highest decoration for gallantry awarded in the UK, Commonwealth and the Empire.
WEAZEL	Captain Donald Stott DSO. He carried out the destruction of the Asopos bridge and later made controversial contacts with the Gestapo in Athens.
WELLS	Kuşadası (Turkey).
Y service	British wireless interception service.
YAK	Led by Peter Fleming, this mission was to slow down the German adavance in Northern Greece in 1941.
YORK	Çeşme (Turkey).
YVONNE	W/T station of the organization led by Ioannis Peltekis (APOLLO). It claimed to have carried out sabotage on some 58 Axis vessels in the Piraeus area in 1943-1944 and provided valuable intelligence on Axis shipping.
Z27	Leonidas Parisis, policeman recruited by Tsigantes to be his bodyguard and who succeeded Manolopoulos at the head of MIDAS 614. He also used the pseudonyms of ELIAS ZIRELIS and LEPHTERIS.
ZINC	Code name of Lieutenant Zathis of Operation KEATS (Mytilene).
ZIRELIS	Police Officer Parisis, aka LEPHTERIS.
ZP	Foreign Office.

Appendix B

Personalities

Abatzis, Ioannis	Lieutenant Commander (RHN) of Operation FLESHPOTS.
Arvanitopoulos, Diamantis	Radio operator of Operation ISINGLASS. Aka Kostas Kipriadis and code name DIAMOND. Executed by the Italians in 1943.
Atkinson, George	Captain. Leader of Operation ISINGLASS. Executed by the Italians in 1943.
Barwell, Reginald G.	SOE agent in Athens. In 1941, he purchased a fleet of caiques for SOE use.
Ben Shaprut, Shmuel	Jewish Haganah member, participated in the first Corinth Canal attempt.
Cumberlege, Cleland	Army Major. Cousin of Mike Cumberlege, took part in the first operation to block the Corinth Canal. Killed in action in 1941.
Cumberlege, Claude Michael Bulstrode	Lieutenant RNVR RD DSO & Bar, later Lieutenant Commander. Worked for SOE and MI9. Attempted to block the Corinth Canal in 1941 and 1943. Leader of the LOCKSMITH team.
Cunningham, Sir Andrew B.	Admiral Commander-in-Chief of the Mediterranean Fleet.
Glenconner, Lord	Head of SOE in the Middle East (August 1942-1943).
Gogas, Christos	Greek SOE agent who earned a commission in the British Army and was known as Captain Harris. Operated from Smyrna. Accused of communist sympathies by the Foreign Office and ISLD.
Hammond, Nicholas Geoffrey Lemprière	British scholar of Ancient Greece. Distinguished SOE officer. In 1941 he escaped from Crete with Mike Cumberlege.
Handley, Thomas E.	Radio operator of the LOCKSMITH team.
Harris, Capt. Chris	Captain, see Christos Gogas.
Kanellopoulos, Panayotis	University Professor respected for his political views. SOE hoped that he could rally Greek

	Resistance but he was forced to flee to the Middle East after the ISINGLASS fiasco. Became Defence Minister in the Tsouderos government and eventually Prime Minister.
Kostika, Shlomo	Jewish Haganah member, participated in the first Corinth Canal attempt.
Kotrba, Jan	Czech member of the LOCKSMITH team. Before the war, he had been on sailing trips with Mike Cumberlege
Kotsis, Spyros	Member of MIDAS 614. Met the LOCKSMITH party in February 1943. Took over MIDAS 614 when Kanaris was captured.
Leeper, Rex	British Ambassador to the Greek government in exile.
Levides, Alexandros	Captain RHN. Worked with MIDAS 614. Involved in Naval sabotage but had to escape to the Middle East in January 1943. Captured in 1943 and briefly suspected of having betrayed MO4 to the Germans. The culprit turned out to be Lieutenant Levitis of Operation CISTERN.
Manolopoulos, Fotios	Lieutenant (Reserve) in the Greek Army in exile. Carried out Operation LOCKSMITH in March 1943. Escaped to the Middle East.
Maxwell, Terence	Head of SOE in the Middle East August 1941-August 1942.
Morton, Bob	New Zealander Sergeant, friend of Donald Stott.
Pawson, David	SOE agent worked in Greece 1940-1941. Head of Smyrna Branch 1942-1943, until his capture during the Leros fiasco.
Pearson, James	Lieutenant Colonel, head of SOE Balkan section in London.
Peltekis, Ioannis	Codename APOLLO. Head of YVONNE, one of the most successful resistance organizations of the Second World War.
Perkins, Donald	Worked for SOE Greek Section in London.
Philipps, J. F.	British Army captain of the Devonshire Regiment. His rifle shot is credited to have blown up the Corinth Canal bridge during the German airborne assault in April 1941.
Pirie, Ian	Head of SOE in Greece (1940-1941), then head of MO4 B6 (Greek Section) based in Cairo.
Pollock, George	Head of SOE in the Middle East until August 1941.

Psaros, Dimitrios	Colonel, head of the EKKA Greek resistance group. Murdered by the communists in 1943.
Rees, Noel	ISLD agent, vice-consul on the island of Chios in 1941, later head of the Smyrna Branch.
Saunders, Ernest Frank	Able Seaman, participated in the first Corinth Canal attempt. Killed in action in 1941.
Sideris, Koulis	Captain of *Aghia Varvara*, the caique used during the LOCKSMITH operation.
Stawell, William	Head of Force 133 (SOE in the Middle East) from 1943 on.
Steele, James C.	Sergeant and right hand man of Mike Cumberlege during Operation LOCKSMITH.
Stott, Donald	New Zealander Sergeant, later Captain. Participated in the destruction of the Asopos Bridge. In 1943, he held controversial talks with the Germans in Athens.
Tselos, Epaminondas	Principal aide of Kanelopoulos. SOE hoped he would organize the Greek Resistance. Quarrelled with Tsigantes of MIDAS 614.
Tsigantes, Ioannis	Head of MIDAS 614. Killed by the Italian police on 14 January 1943.
Turle, Charles Edward	Rear Admiral, Naval Attaché in Athens (1940-1941). Blamed for the failure to block the Corinth Canal in April 1941.
Tyson, J. T.	Lieutenant of the Royal Engineers. In April 1941 he prepared the Corinth Canal bridge for demolition.
Veloukhiotis, Ares	Aka Nicolas Sclavounos, pseudonyms of Athanasios Klaras, the Greek communist leader who with Colonel Zervas co-operated with Myers and Woodhouse to blow up the Gorgopotamos bridge. Known for his cruelty. Killed in 1945.
Ward, Michael	Major, went on an SOE mission in Greece in 1943. After the war in charge of liquidations of SOE accounts in Athens. Investigated the fate of the LOCKSMITH party. Died in Athens in 2011.
Zervas, Napoleon	General, head of EDES (Republican) resistance organization. Participated in the attack on Gorgopotamos. In 1944, under communist pressure, he was forced to flee to Corfu.

Appendix C

Traffic in Corinth Canal from 16 May to 22 June 1941

This list, which is certainly incomplete, is based on Admiral Vittorio Tur's report, the war diaries of *Comando Gruppo Navale Italiano Egeo Settentrionale*, of *Supermarina*, of Admiral Hans-Hubertus von Stosch (*Befehlshaber Griechenland*) and other sources.

Date	Vessel	Ton	Destin.	Remarks
16 May	*Ichnusa*	1241	Piraeus	Italian minesweeper
16 May	*Sirio*	642	Piraeus	Italian torpedo boat
16 May	*Sagittario*	642	Piraeus	Italian torpedo boat
16 May	Unidentified flotilla[54]	?	Piraeus	Italian minesweepers
17 May	*Alicante*	2140	Piraeus	German freighter
17 May	*Maritza*	2910	Piraeus	German freighter
17 May	*Procida*	1843	Piraeus	German freighter
17 May	*Castellon*	2086	Piraeus	German freighter
17 May	*Santa Fé (ex-French)*	4627	Piraeus	German freighter
17 May	*Curtatone*	967	Piraeus	Italian torpedo boat
17 May	*Monzambano*	967	Piraeus	Italian torpedo boat
17 May	*Castelfidardo*	967	Piraeus	Italian torpedo boat
18 May	*Boeo*	185	Piraeus	Italian tug
18 May	*MAS-538*	29	Piraeus	Italian E-boat
18 May	*MAS-539*	29	Piraeus	Italian E-boat
18 May	*MAS-534*	29	Piraeus	Italian E-boat
18 May	*MAS-535*	29	Piraeus	Italian E-boat
18 May	*Ardenza*	193	Piraeus	Italian tug
18 May	*Rovigno*	113	Piraeus	Italian minelayer
18 May	*Albona*	113	Piraeus	Italian minelayer
18 May	*V.117 Argentario*	86	Piraeus	Italian minesweeper
18 May	*V.178 Margherita*	100	Piraeus	Italian minesweeper
18 May	*V.182 San Giuseppe*	108	Piraeus	Italian minesweeper
18 May	*V.203 Carmelo Padre C.*	91	Piraeus	Italian minesweeper
18 May	*RD-9*	216	Piraeus	Italian minesweeper
18 May	*RD-17*	201	Piraeus	Italian minesweeper

18 May	*R.187 La Nuovo Maria Luisa*	35	Piraeus	Italian minesweeper
19 May	*Alcione*	679	Piraeus	Italian torpedo boat
19 May	*Aldebaran*	679	Piraeus	Italian torpedo boat
19 May	*Cefalo*	302	Piraeus	Italian fishing vessel[53]
20 May	*V.178 Margherita*	100	Piraeus	Italian patrol boat
20 May	*V.182 San Giuseppe*	108	Piraeus	Italian patrol boat
20 May	*V.203 Carmelo Padre C.*	91	Piraeus	Italian patrol boat
20 May	*V.219 Nicolina Madre*	179	Piraeus	Italian patrol boat
29 May	*Albatros*	404	Tripoli (Syria)	Italian sailing vessel
29 May	*Diana*	1764	Rhodes	Italian sloop
29 May	*Quintino Sella*	935	Taranto	Italian destroyer
31 May	*Tinos*	2826	Piraeus	German freighter
31 May	*Bellona*	1297	Piraeus	German freighter
31 May	*Savona*	2120	Piraeus	German freighter
31 May	*Strombo*[55]	5232	Dardanelles	Italian tanker
1 June	*Annarella*	5999	Dardanelles	Italian tanker
1 June	*Dora C.*	5843	Dardanelles	Italian tanker
1 June	*Calatafimi*	967	Piraeus	Italian torpedo boat
1 June	*Castelfidardo*	967	Piraeus	Italian torpedo boat
1 June	*Calino*	5000	Salonika	Italian freighter
1 June	*Lupo*	679	Taranto	Italian torpedo boat
2 June	*FL.B-405*	43	Piraeus	German rescue boat
2 June	*FL.B-426*	43	Piraeus	German rescue boat
2 June	*FL.B-430*	43	Piraeus	German rescue boat
3 June	*Achaia*	1778	Piraeus	German freighter
3 June	*Albaro*	2104	Constanza	Italian tanker
3 June	*Diana*	1764	Taranto	Italian sloop
4 June	*Alberta*[56]	3357	Constanza	French tanker
4 June	*Trapani*	1855	Piraeus	German freighter
4 June	*Livorno*	1829	Piraeus	German freighter
4 June	*Spezia*	1825	Piraeus	German freighter
6 June	*Addis Abeba*	614	Taranto	Italian freighter
7 June	*Tinos*	2826	Catania	German freighter
7 June	*Bellona*	1297	Catania	German freighter
7 June	*Savona*	2120	Catania	German freighter
7 June	*Utilitas*	5342	Constanza	Italian tanker
7 June	*Alberto Fassio*	2289	Constanza	Italian tanker
8 June	*Le Cid*	248	Beirut	French minesweeper
8 June	*Urano*	5512	Constanza	Italian tanker
9 June	*Caldea*	2703	Patras	Italian freighter

10 June	*Spezia*	1825	Patras	German freighter
10 June	*Trapani*	1855	Patras	German freighter
10 June	*Bellona*	1297	Patras	German freighter
10 June	*Achaia*	1778	Patras	German freighter
10 June	*Viminale*	8657	Piraeus	Italian freighter
10 June	*Argentina*	5014	Piraeus	Italian freighter
11 June	*Aldebaran*	679	Patras	Torpedo boat
11 June	*Diana*	1764	Leros	Italian sloop
11 June	*Tampico*	4958	Constanza	Italian tanker
11 June	*Vesta*	3351	Rhodes	Italian freighter
12 June	*Viminale*	8657	Brindisi	Italian freighter
12 June	*Argentina*	5014	Brindisi	Italian freighter
12 June	*Giorgio*	4887	Constanza	Italian tanker
13 June	*Annarella*	5999	Corinth	Italian tanker
13 June	*Dora C.*	5843	Corinth	Italian tanker
13 June	*Five unidentified vessels*		Patras	Fishing vessels
14 June	*Fertilia*	986	Prevesa	Italian freighter
14 June	*Hercules*	632	Piraeus	Italian tug
15 June	*Pietro Micca*	1371	Taranto	Italian submarine
15 June	*Diana*	1764	Taranto	Italian sloop
19 June	*Genepesca II*	1200	Piraeus	Italian freighter
19 June	*Padenna*	1589	Piraeus	Italian freighter
19 June	*Boeo*	185	Patras	Italian minesweeper
20 June	*Maritza*	2910	Patras	German freighter
20 June	*Città di Napoli*	5418	Patras	Italian freighter
20 June	*Thessalia*	2875	Piraeus	German freighter
20 June	*Macedonia*	2874	Piraeus	German freighter
20 June	*Beilul*	620	La Spezia	Italian submarine
21 June	*Calino*	5000	Patras	Italian freighter
22 June	*Trapani*	1855	Piraeus	German freighter
22 June	*Livorno*	1829	Piraeus	German freighter
22 June	*Spezia*	1825	Piraeus	German freighter
22 June	*Francesco Crispi*	7600	Bari	Italian freighter
22 June	*Galilea*	8040	Bari	Italian freighter
22 June	*Castellon*	2086	Catania	German freighter

Traffic in Corinth Canal
from June 1942 to 7 August 1942

(Source: OIC document in DEFE3/893, TNA)

JUNE 1942

Date	Ship	Ton	Destination	Remarks
4 June	*Contarini*	1417	Dodecanese	Italian freighter
10 June	*Ossag*	2793	Crete	German tanker
12 June	*Monstella*[57]	5311	Crete	Italian freighter
19 June	*Motia*	2473	Dodecanese	Italian freighter
19 June	*Aprilia*	3412	Dodecanese	Italian freighter
24 June	*Bucintoro*	1273	Dodecanese	Italian freighter

June total: 6 ships for 16,679 grt.

JULY 1942

Date	Ship	Ton	Destination	Remarks
2 July	*Alberto Fassio*	2289	Tobruk	Italian tanker
11 July	*Rondine*	6077	Tobruk	Italian tanker
12 July	*Alba Julia*	5701	Istanbul	Italian freighter
17 July	*Asmara*	7192	Dodecanese	Italian freighter
17 July	*Minerva*	1905	Crete	Italian freighter
18 July	*San Andrea*	5077	Crete	Italian tanker
20 July	*Potestas*	5237	Crete	Italian tanker
20 July	*Calino*	5000[58]	Dodecanese	Italian freighter
20 July	*Adriana*	4346	Piraeus	Italian freighter
21 July	*Stige*	1342	Crete	Italian freighter
22 July	*Vesta*	3351	Dodecanese	Italian freighter
24 July	*Hermada*	4421	Dodecanese	Italian freighter
25 July	*Cagliari*[59]	2322	Crete	Italian freighter
27 July	*Scillin*	1000?[60]	Tobruk	Italian tanker
28 July	*Milano*	4028	Benghazi	Italian freighter with troops

28 July	*Aventino*	3794	Benghazi	With troops
30 July	*Camperio*	6382	Benghazi	Italian freighter
31 July	*Italia*	5203	Benghazi	Italian freighter
31 July	*Tergestea*	5890	Benghazi	Italian freighter

July total: 19 ships for 80,557 grt.

AUGUST 1942

Date	Ship	Ton	Destination	Remarks
1 August	*Tagliamento*	5448	Benghazi	Italian freighter
1 August	*Arca*	2222	Crete	Italian tanker
1 August	*Sportivo*	1598	Tobruk	Italian freighter
2 August	*Abruzzi*	680	Crete	Italian tanker
2 August	*Bottiglieri*	883	Benghazi	Italian freighter
2 August	*Stige*	1342	Crete	Italian tanker
5 August	*Foscolo*	5059	Benghazi	Italian freighter

August total (to 7 August): 7 ships for 17,232 grt.

Appendix E

Use of Corinth Canal
by U-boats

U-77 (*Kapitänleutnant* Heinrich Schonder) on 7 April 1942 (Salamis to La
Spezia).

U-371 (*KL* Waldemar Mehl) on 1 July (Salamis to Pola).

U-97 (*KL* Friedrich Bürgel) on 20 August (Salamis to La Spezia).

U-77 (*KL* Heinrich Schonder) on 25 August (Salamis to Pola).

U-565 (*KL* Wilhelm Franken) on 31 August (Salamis to La Spezia)

U-83 (*KL* Hans-Werner Kraus) on 31 August (Salamis to La Spezia).

U-453 (*KL* Freiherr Egon Reiner von Schlippenbach) on 17 September (Salamis
to Messina).

U-375 (*KL* Jürgen Könenkamp) on 24 September (Salamis to Pola)

U-561 (*KL* Heinz Schomburg) on 30 September (Salamis to La Spezia).

U-371 (*KL* Waldemar Mehl) on 12 October (Salamis to Pola).

U-617 (KL Albrecht Brandi) on 8 February 1943 (Salamis to Pola).

U-593 (*KL* Gerd Kelbling) on 24 April (Salamis to Pola).

The Cairo Questionaire concerning the Corinth Canal

(addressed to David Pawson on 26 May 1942).[61]

1. Position and number of sentries.
2. Areas not patrolled in the vicinity of canal.
3. Position where dredgers are anchored at night.
4. Are dredgers guarded?
5. Are the crews of dredgers Greek?
6. Map giving paths and roads around canal.
7. Position where the canal sides are on approximately the same level as the canal itself.
8. Where is it possible to scale the sides of the canal? Would it be easy?
9. What are the defences of the entrances to the canal? Other than AA defences?
10. What are the arrangements for lighting:
    the canal
    its entrances.
11. What areas are least lit?
12. Are vessels searched before entering the canal?
13. What are the arrangements for mine-spotting in the canal?
14. Are there any arrangements for making smoke along the canal?
15. What is the use of the pipe line that runs along the north bank of the canal?
16. What is the diameter of this pipe?
17. Where does it lead to?
18. What is the construction of the railway bridge which crosses the middle of the canal? (Full details required).
19. What are the guards on this bridge?
20. Do the trains run to a timetable?
21. If so, at what time do the trains cross?
22. Are vessels transiting the canal towed or do they proceed under their own power?
23. Are there any areas with barbed wire or booby traps in them?
24. Are the Greeks in the village around the canal allowed to move about freely?
25. Is there a curfew?
26. What signals are exhibited from the signal masts at each end of the canal to indicate that a ship has permission to enter the canal?
27. Is a pilot compulsory for ships entering the canal?

Appendix G

Schemes Proposed by Major Tsigantes

1. Sinking a shaft near the north bank with the object of blowing the bank into the canal. This was an unlikely project owing to the number of tools and large quantity of explosives required.
2. Drilling into the side of the lining wall by personnel lowered from the top and inserting explosives in the drills. Again the large quantity of explosives required would probably make the project impracticable.
3. Lowering a camouflaged mine (magnetic or otherwise) into the canal from the top of one of the banks. This was the project most likely to meet with success but the past unreliability of all magnetic mines jeopardized the scheme. Furthermore the canal was unlikely to be blocked by this method for more than three weeks.
4. Running a suitably loaded submarine past the boom into the canal and sinking it as a blockship. It would, however, be almost impossible to pass the boom, and the scheme involved almost certain loss of the crew, let alone the destruction of a submarine.
5. Limpeting at Piraeus or Patras of ships known to be passing through the canal. But it would be most difficult to time this operation, and here again the canal was unlikely to be blocked for more than three weeks. This objection applied also to limpeting from a caique which purposely fouled a ship at either entrance to the canal and used the opportunity to attach a limpet to it.
6. Sinking a blockship in the canal. The difficulties of passing a blockship into adjacent waters were, however, believed to be insurmountable and passage into the canal would be impossible owing to the thorough examination carried out.
7. Bribery of a suitable skipper to blow up his ship in the canal during its passage. This was probably the easiest method, but blockage beyond three weeks would be unlikely, owing to the fact that the thorough searching would probably limit the amount of explosives able to be used.
8. Another version of (3) above, in which a camouflaged mine would be dropped by a cargo ship or caique before the passage of a subsequent

214 Target Corinth Canal 1940–1944

ship. This scheme would be subject to similar disadvantages to those already mentioned.

9. Blowing the railway bridge into the canal, preferably when a train was passing over. It was, however, believed impossible to prepare the bridge for demolition owing to extraordinarily strong guard. In any case the closing of the canal was unlikely to exceed three weeks by which time the bridge and the train could be removed.

10. Bribing a dredger skipper either to drop a mine into the canal or to sink his ship. Again the closing of the canal was unlikely to exceed three weeks.

11. Blowing the road bridge into the canal. This would be subject to the same difficulties as (9) above.

Appendix H

Limpets and Naval Sabotage in the Second World War

The SOE preferred method of sabotaging enemy ships was by the use of limpets.[62] These small mines (10lb of high explosive) could be affixed to the hull of a vessel thanks to magnets.

We have seen that the first sabotage attempt of the war may have been that of the British *Tintern Abbey* in January 1940, probably carried out by an *Abwehr* agent. The first use of plastic explosives, developed by the Czechs but supplied by the British, was made by Corsican Sub Lieutenant Claude André Péri of the French Naval Reserve on 10 May 1940, the same day the German attack on the West began. He managed to affix a limpet onto the hull of the German supply ship *Corrientes* anchored at Las Palmas, Canaries. The explosion damaged the vessel but she did not sink and the Germans did not suspect sabotage and attributed it to a 150mm shell fired by an enemy cruiser from outside the territorial waters.

In 1941 a resistance group in Tunisia, organized by the lawyer André Mounier and *Commandant* Jean Breuillac, was supplied with limpets by SOE. The targets were Italian ships engaged in phosphate and iron ore traffic. Swimmers managed to sabotage two vessels. *Achille* sank in shallow waters at La Goulette (9 June 1941) but two limpets affixed to the hull of *Sirio* failed to explode and were found in Naples. Two weeks later, the Belgian swimmer François Vallée was captured while attempting to blow up the freighter *Proserpina* and this led to the collapse of the network. Lieutenant Victor Attias belonged to this organization and managed to escape to Malta. He was selected by Mike Cumberlege for Operation LOCKSMITH but his release from the Free French Forces could not be secured.

The Italians were the first to use human torpedoes. These torpedoes were manned by two frogmen and carried in their warhead some 600lb of high explosives. The warhead could be detached under the keel of an enemy ship and the explosion was enough to cause massive damage. Their greatest successes were achieved at Gibraltar and Alexandria, crippling in the latter the last battleships of the Mediterranean Fleet, *Queen Elizabeth* and *Valiant*. The method was effective but required careful planning and a long period of training for their crew. Later in the war they used limpet mines similar to the British model. The limpet just required a good swimmer to carry it. They met with success at Algiers and, during the months preceding the Italian armistice, combat swimmer Luigi Ferraro single-handedly managed to affix limpets to four merchant ships lying at Mersin, Turkey. Fortunately, only one was damaged, when the limpet exploded at sea. None of the limpets on the other ships exploded due to failures of their delay mechanism.

The delay mechanism problem was not confined to Italian limpets. British-made limpets occasionally failed. A shipment tested in Egypt in 1944 found all the limpets defective and Greek saboteurs complained frequently of their failure to detonate. For the underwater swimmers or folbot (kayak) crews, the problem could be a frustrating experience. But the limpets were cheap to produce and liberally distributed.

Another variant of the limpet mine was the miniature torpedo. This was actually a limpet mine with a small motor and screw which enabled two or three to be launched simultaneously from a folbot at different targets. The miniature torpedo used a contact mechanism instead of a delay fuse. Its weakness was that it was difficult to aim unless relatively close to the target and thus the folbot crew had only a minute or so to escape from the area. The miniature torpedo was used only once, at Crotone in September 1942, and it failed to explode. The folbot crew was captured and its use abandoned.

Among the most successful attacks carried out by folbots were the ones at Bordeaux by ten British commandos in 1942, Operation FRANKTON, and those carried out by Norwegian saboteurs led by Max Manus. In the Far East theatre there were similar operations against Singapore shipping (Operations JAYWICK and RIMAU). Greek saboteurs were not supplied with folbots and used swimmers instead, or bribed sailors or workers who had access to their intended victims (a list of their achievements follows in Appendix I).

A fuse delay was activated and the first types would normally explode after an hour. Later, more sophisticated fuses were introduced but the delay depended greatly on the water temperature. Saboteurs would be able to select from a number of fuses, their colour indicating the length of time. In 1942 the limpets delivered in Greece had three- or nine-hour delay fuses and three-day delay fuses.

In 1944 fuses used by the APOLLO group were described thus:

Red had a delay ranging from three hours at 30° C to six hours at 5°C. (In
    1941 the Red fuse was about an hour, the Green fuse about 12 hours).
Orange 6 to 12 hours at the same temperatures.
Yellow 10 to 20 hours.
Green 17 to 34 hours.
Blue 25 to 67 hours.
Violet 2.5 days to 8.5 days.

These delays could not be depended on for accuracy. A 15° deviation could be expected as well as a deviation of two hours.

Since the passage of the Corinth Canal could be made in as little as twenty-five minutes, it was difficult to achieve a well-timed explosion. Also the 10lb of explosives were not judged sufficient to sink a large ship and this had resulted in the development of a new type of magnetic mine by Mike Cumberlege.

Ships Sunk or Damaged by SOE and Greek Saboteurs

According to a report compiled by SOE at the end of the war, 900 activities, of which nearly 253 were sabotage of ships, were carried out in the Aegean.[63] Some 53,000 tons of enemy shipping were damaged and 13,000 tons were sunk (forty-eight vessels). Harbour installations were also damaged and a five-day strike in Piraeus was successfully organized. In land and sea operations SOE used 695 British personnel in Greece.

In addition 206 craft totalling 8,900 tons were enticed or captured.

Two para-naval fleets and a few military missions carried out 300 missions, travelling some 300,000 miles, including over twenty-five submarine operations. They landed 1,700 tons of stores and 164 agents and evacuated 550 British stragglers. They captured forty-six vessels, killed 160 Germans and took 190 prisoners. They lost only a 6-ton caique. Sixteen joint operations were carried out resulting in thirteen caiques sunk; twenty-one aircraft and 200,000 gallons of petrol were destroyed.

The list below is not definitive but gives an approximate view of sabotage activities in Greece during the war. The authenticity of the claims cannot always be verified.

Naval sabotage before APOLLO (May 1941 – May 1943).

30.05.41	Bulgarian *Knyaguinya Maria Louisa* (3821 grt) was set afire in Piraeus. She blew up and the explosion sank the Rumanian *Jiul* (3127 grt), the German *Alicante* (2140 grt) and the Italian *Albatros* (404 grt). According to ODYSSEUS (via Station 333), this was done by a communist group but it is unlikely. American sources indicate that it was actually by former RHAF personnel who had disclosed their intention before the deed. The claim that she was sunk by Wellington bombers is not supported by German documents.
21.08.41	At 2100 hrs, while anchored at Skaramanga, the Italian tanker *Strombo* (5232 grt), already damaged by torpedoes from the

	submarines *Parthian* and *Torbay,* was damaged by an explosion which completed her destruction. It is not clear if this was due to sabotage or if she drifted onto a mine.
Early Nov 1941	The destroyer *Vasilefs Georgios* was sabotaged, without explosives, while in dry-dock (via Station 333).
04.11.41	An unidentified 5,000-ton transport was sabotaged by limpet and sunk on her way to Libya (via station 333).
25.02.42	*Eleni Kanellopoulos* (464 grt) was lost by an explosion (sabotage?).
26.05.42	An Italian ship was sabotaged in Piraeus with two limpets with nine hour delay but they failed to explode (via Station 333).
28.05.42	A limpet with three days delay was attached to a German tanker in Piraeus (via Station 333).
11.06.42	The German *Plouton* (4,500 tons) was reported damaged and dry-docked. Electrical installation (?) of *Ardenna* destroyed (via Station 333). The destroyer *Vasilefs Georgios* (German *ZG-3 Hermes*) was reported operational.
13.06.42	An Italian ship loaded with lorries, was limpeted by a swimmer in Piraeus (via Station 333).
26.06.42	The Italian tanker *Avionia* caught fire and was destroyed as it was loading cans of benzine in the harbour of Heraklion (accident or sabotage?). There were no victims.
29.06.42	The Italian tankers *Albaro* and *Celeno* were limpeted at Perama. At 1930 hrs a bomb exploded on the starboard side of *Celeno* causing a gash of 40cm by 20cm. The *Albaro* hull was examined and a device was found attached 50cm above the waterline and removed. There were no casualties.
End of June 42	A small tanker was limpeted at Heraklion at the end of June 1942; the work was done by a communist who had been supplied with limpets by Major Chris M. Woodhouse.

05.07.42	According to Station 333, two tankers were limpeted near St George's Bay, Keratsini; one bomb exploded and the tanker was towed to the Shell facilities to pump out the rest of the fuel, the second tanker apparently sailed undamaged. This appears to refer to the action of 29/30 June.
08.12.42	Station 333 reported that three of their best swimmers and limpeteers were caught ten days before by an officer of the gendarmerie, Velisarios Dimou, and handed over to the Italians. They were Koutsoyannopoulos, Pasrakis and Mylonas and all three were executed.
03.01.43	In Piraeus, a limpet was discovered attached to the stern of *Città di Alessandria* and successfully removed. The culprits were arrested.
04.01.43	At 0100 hrs, a searchlight was sabotaged at Salamis. At 2330 hrs, *Hermada* was limpeted, causing an important leak astern, she was docked for repairs on 7 January. Station 333 believed this was the work of naval Captain Levidis who worked for MIDAS 614.
06.01.43	At Salamis an attempt to sabotage a searchlight failed, the saboteurs coming by boat. One saboteur was severely wounded and captured but later died of wounds.
08.03.43	An attempt to sabotage a searchlight at Selinia (Salamis) failed but the attackers made good their escape.
15.03.43	A patrol boat was sunk by an explosion in the engine room at Chania (SKL).
26.03.43	An attempt at sabotage searchlight at Salamis was made but the saboteurs were fired upon and repulsed.
11.04.43	An Italian postal boat was captured by Greek partisans in the Volos area.

Naval Sabotage claims by APOLLO and others
(June 1943 – October 1944)

12.06.43	At 1205 hrs, an explosion shook *Città di Savona* and she sank in shallow waters (2-3m below her keel), sixty-nine horses were drowned (APOLLO claimed 120 horses drowned) and forty-three saved. She was repaired and sailed from Piraeus on 14 August for Missolonghi.
08.07.43	The Greek caique *Aghios Dimitrios* in German service suffered an explosion aft and sank in Piraeus.
10.07.43	*Celeno* (initially reported as *Salerno*) damaged by sabotage.
11.07.43	A Greek-manned dredger sank in the Corinth Canal (the cause was not reported); however shipping was not obstructed.
11.07.43	At Perama an unidentified 5,000-ton vessel (probably *Celeno*, see 10.07.43) and dry-dock were limpeted. An Italian 500-ton iron motor-schooner, loaded with military stores for Crete, was sunk at Aghios Georgios.
14.07.43	*Konstantin Louloudis* mined in Chalkis, and anchored south of the bridge. Later reported to have been torpedoed twice (by HMS *Taurus*). (APOLLO reported that the caique *Evangelistria* (Piraeus 1027) under Captain Koulouras sailed from here (Piraeus?) on 12 July with German/Italian spies for Rhodes then Cyprus.)
15.07.43	At 1915 hrs, *Celeno* was damaged by explosion and docked in Georgios harbour (Italian zone). The ship was not seaworthy.
05.08.43	At 0015 hrs, *Tanais* (Greek crew, German Flak crew) was confirmed limpeted forward but damage was slight (according to Italian sources the explosives were placed on board), a small hole was made in her hull (30 x 50 cm).
09.08.43	At 2020 hrs, *Ardenna* (German crew) was limpeted, the explosion occurring in a compartment filled with sand for ballast. She was repaired and sailed on 8 September 1943 for Zante.
11.08.43	Italian sources reported that a Greek ship carrying ammunition was seriously damaged by a magnetic mine through sabotage.

	(APOLLO reported that the caiques *Aghios Georgios* (Syros 542) and *Aghios Sozon* (Spetsai 1057) were ready to sail for the Turkish coast and suspected them to work for the Germans.)
13.08.43	*Cherso* at Eleusis was claimed damaged by use of explosive coal.
14.08.43	The tug *Taxiarchis* damaged by use of explosive coal.
21.08.43	At 0630 hrs, the Italian salvage vessel *Cyclops* was limpeted, she had a hole 50 x 50cm, took a list and sank in shallow waters. The vessel had an Italian captain but a Greek crew. She was, however, patched up and returned to service the same day.
22.08.43	At 0005 hrs, *Orion* (707 grt) was rocked by an explosion at the Vasiliadis Works; she had a large hole under the waterline on the port side and sank in shallow waters (*Orion* was confirmed sunk but later raised). She was alongside the German patrol boat *GA-01* which was not damaged. She was sabotaged by 22-year-old Antonios Arvanitis who had been recruited by Niko Adam. Arvanitis was captured on 3 September 1943 and executed on 9 October 1943.
23.08.43	The salvage ship *Cyclops* (800 tons) was limpeted.
30.08.43	At 0435 hrs, sea-going tug *W24* of 250 tons was sunk by limpet at the Salamis Arsenal but reported raised on 3 September 1943. A floating crane was damaged in same attack. There were no casualties. The saboteur Niko Adam was arrested while attempting to sabotage *Santa Fé* at Eleusis. Two more collaborators were also arrested (reported on 5 September). Another saboteur, Lieutenant Peter Doannidis RHNR, was forced to flee to the Middle East.
03.09.43	The tug *Titan* was damaged (tug *Hercules* was also damaged by same explosion). A 2,000-ton vessel was claimed sabotaged, result unknown and an 800-ton sloop carrying ammunition was claimed sunk.
17.09.43	The Italian crew of the destroyer *Francesco Crispi* was provided with explosives to sabotage their vessel; she was out of action for two months. Not confirmed by KTB Admiral Aegean.

01.11.43	A 200-ton caique was claimed sunk and an Italian destroyer and tug destroyed in dock. No confirmation in KTB *Seeverteidigung Attika.*
13.11.43	At 1400 hrs, *Pier Luigi* (2575 grt) was limpeted in No.2 hold and abandoned at 1700 hrs. She sank in 16 fathoms in Suda Bay (see ADM223/24). No confirmation from KTB *Seeverteidigung Attika.*
26.11.43	An 8000-ton ship was claimed sunk 10 miles from Suda but it was not known if this was the result of Allied action or sabotage as a ship of similar size had been sabotaged in Piraeus.
30.11.43	A floating dock was reported sunk by submarine near Skiathos (this referred to HMS *Torbay*'s action of 22.11.43).
18.12.43	*Boccacio* was known to have sunk twenty days before (reported on 9 January 1944). It was uncertain if this was through Allied action or sabotage.
22.12.43	The caique *Buona Fortuna* (100 tons) was sunk at Noukaria (two Germans killed).
24.12.43	An unidentified 80-ton caique was sunk at Perianos Koufounisis.
10.01.44	Info only: *Drache* was reported to have sailed with one battalion and landing craft *F-366* and *F-367*, with two caiques and two destroyers.
15.01.44	Three large caiques were reported sunk at Amorgos.
18.01.44	At 1345 hrs, the tug *HP-16* was sunk about 30 miles from the coast; the cause could not be determined. Three Germans were drowned or missing.
22.01.44	An unidentified 200-ton caique loaded with petrol was sunk at Nikouria.
23.01.44	Two motor-lighters were sabotaged.
24.01.44	Info only: an air raid on Piraeus destroyed tug *HP-52* and *Centauros*. At 0205 hrs, the tug *HP-52* was actually reported sunk on a mine between New-Perama and Aghios Georgios.

26.01.44	The caique *Kal-177* of 140 tons was sabotaged in the Gulf of Corinth.
05.02.44	Info only: a ship of 800 tons sank south of Syros.
07.02.44	The tanker *Poppi* of 350 tons was sabotaged.
08.02.44	A limpet was affixed to *Tanais* but without result.
18.02.44	*Tanais*, *Terema* and *Burgas* were limpeted without results.
19.02.44	Information only: *Leda* (ex-*Leopard*) was reported sunk at Leros. *Città di Savona* also sank at Leros when an aircraft fell on her and exploded her ammunition cargo. *Petrola* (ex-*Capo Pino*) sank at Suda Bay. *Oria*, to avoid a submarine attack, hit a rock at the Saronicos; 4,000 Italians and eighty Germans were claimed to have drowned.
20.02.44	A limpet was discovered attached to a steamship in Piraeus harbour and removed in time (DEFE3/641/298).
21.02.44	Drillings discovered in gears of the German submarine chaser *UJ-2153*, believed to have been sabotaged at Skaramanga.
26.02.44	Info only: the destroyer *Francesco Crispi* arrived at Piraeus seriously damaged.
04.03.44	*Luxenburg* (4,700 tons) was damaged by sabotage and dry-docked; this was confirmed by RAF reconnaissance.
05.03.44	Info only: *Crispi* reported sunk by RAF in three minutes near Heraklion.
06.03.44	A 30-ton caique was sunk at Paroikia, Paros (no details).
14.03.44	A 25-ton caique was sunk at Naousa, Paros and a 120-ton caique loaded with petrol at Naxos.
26.03.44	The Piraeus restaurant owner Emmanuel Parlamas who was an important source of shipping information for the APOLLO group, was arrested by the Germans. He was executed on 8 September 1944.

03.04.44	In Piraeus, the floating crane *Patras* was reported damaged by an explosion, sabotage was suspected.
12.04.44	A 100-ton caique sunk at Naxos and a 25-ton caique west of Naxos.
05.05.44	*Gunther* of 40 tons was sabotaged by 21-year-old Georgios Tavlarios of the YVONNE organization (he survived the war).
09.05.44	The tug *Samson* was sabotaged.
12.05.44	The tug *HP-13* was slightly damaged by limpet.
13.05.44	*Panagista* of 60 tons was sunk by sabotage while en route from Piraeus to Poros; seventeen Germans drowned.
14.05.44	*Aghios* Georgios of 80 tons was sunk at Piraeus but raised on 17 May.
26.05.44	At 1200 hrs, the tug *San Cataldo*, *HP-55*, was damaged at Piraeus by an explosion in the engine room and was beached.
June 44	The motor-vessel *PI-195* of 200 tons was sabotaged and sunk. One man also informed that he had sabotaged salvage ship *Aghios Nikolaos* but APOLLO had not been informed beforehand and could not verify. During this month, 29-year-old Ioannis Mavromatis, one of the most important collaborators of Peltekis (he had organized the sabotage or attack on forty-six enemy vessels and had also worked for PROMETHEUS II), was arrested by the Gestapo. He managed to escape to the Middle East.
01.06.44	The 'pirate' vessel *Poppi* was captured and the next day also the *Charalambos*. Another partisan boat was captured on 11 June. Troops were sent to Spetsai and Hydra.
02.06.44	A 200-ton motor vessel sabotaged. At 1920 hrs, the transport *Gertrud* (1960 grt) was wrecked by a heavy explosion forward in the harbour of Heraklion, she was a total loss (DEFE3/647/130). At 2200 hrs, the caique *Evangelistria* was sunk by limpet mine in Piraeus, the crew was saved.
07.06.44	The caique *Aghia Paraskevi* (*PI-678*) of 40 tons was destroyed by sabotage at Piraeus.

08.06.44	At 1000 hrs, the tug *HP-6* was limpeted but the explosives were found and defused by the team of KL (W) Müller (*Sperrwaffenkommando*).
16.06.44	Motor vessel *PI-413* of 170 tons destroyed by sabotage.
22.06.44	The motor vessel *Katina* (*KAL-182*) of about 100 tons was destroyed by sabotage.
26.06.44	A new caique of 300 tons was sabotaged at Perama.
01.07.44	APOLLO's chief saboteur and five collaborators were arrested.
02.07.44	Unknown saboteurs made an attempt on *Morosini* with little damage (the explosives were removed but seven Germans were killed or wounded). On 4 July, this was corrected stating it was APOLLO's men.
05.07.44	A 100-ton F-lighter was claimed sunk at Molos, Paros (twenty Germans killed).
06.07.44	The caique *PI-182* was sabotaged.
29.07.44	The 22-year-old Georgios Mastorakis was arrested and executed on 08.09.44. He was reported to have successfully sabotaged a ship and a caique. Another saboteur known only as 'Athanassios' and who had participated in the sabotage of sixteen ships, was forced into hiding.
03.08.44	*Carola* was damaged by explosion and took a list at 1330 hrs but had only minor damage (despite all the ammunition on board) as the fire was fought energetically. The next day, she sailed escorted by the destroyer *TA-19* with 300 tons of ammunition and stores for Leros.
20.09.44	An 800-ton ship was sabotaged east of Paros.
23.09.44	A 1,000-ton ship was sabotaged at Dekouso (three Germans killed, eleven wounded).
08.10.44	The floating dock with destroyer *Crispi* was claimed to have been sunk by limpets.

12.10.44	Sinking of *John Knudsen*. Both floating dock and *John Knudsen* were sabotaged by a team which included Vassilios Kiparissiotis, Georgios Roussos and others. Not confirmed by *Hafenkommandant Piraeus* but this appears likely. Explosions sank *John Knudsen* before she reached her blocking position.

Naval sabotage was not confined to the Greek resistance. During the night of 17/18 June 1944, the Royal Marine Boom Patrol Detachment (RMBPD) sent three canoes (kayaks) *Shark*, *Salmon* and *Shrimp* manned by six Royal Marines to attack shipping in Portolago, Leros. They were led by Lieutenant J. F. Richards RM, and this was known as Operation SUNBEAM A.

The three canoes were launched from the motor launch *ML-360* and the attack was made with limpets. In the early hours of 18 June 1944, the KFK boat (*Kriegsfischkutter* or coastal water cutter) *GD-91* and the salvage tug *Titan* blew up and sank. The two destroyers *TA-14* (ex-Italian *Turbine*) and *TA-17* (ex-Italian *San Martino*) were badly damaged respectively by two and five explosions. *TA-17* would be later destroyed by the YVONNE organization while docked in Salamis.

The Kiel Canal

The Corinth waterway was not the only canal to be targeted by SOE.

During the Second World War the Kiel Canal (or Kaiser Wilhelm Canal, as it was also known), linking the Baltic to the North Sea was extensively used by the German Navy and thus became a strategic objective. Following their training in the relatively quiet waters of the Baltic, U-boats would frequently pass through the canal before sailing for patrols in the Atlantic. The alternative would have been to use the Kattegat, but its shallow waters made it especially vulnerable to enemy mining. The Germans had been the first to make extensive use of magnetic mines, the first 'secret weapon' introduced during the Second World War. They quickly became a major nuisance in the approaches to British ports as they were being laid in large numbers by German bombers and destroyers during the winter months of 1939-40. The problem was partly solved by the de-magnetization of ships or 'de-gaussing'.

By April 1940 the Royal Air Force was ready to turn the tables and the shallow waters of the Baltic and North Sea were to prove inviting targets as thousands of mines would be sown until the end of the war. Bomber Command is reported to have mined the Kaiser Wilhelm Canal three times in 1940. During the night of 14/15 May, four mines were observed to have been dropped in the canal but were cleared the next day without any trouble. However, the narrowness of the waterway made it a difficult target and magnetic mines dropped could usually be observed and thus swept in a relatively short time. Six mines were actually laid in May, five in June and another four during the night of 27/28 December 1940. No further mining was attempted before 1944. The Kiel Canal was closed after a collision between the Danish *Silkeborg* (1800 grt) and the Finnish *Inga* (1929 grt) on 17 December 1940. The Finnish ship sank, blocking a number of merchant ships as well as two destroyers, two U-boats and two minesweepers which were seeking passage. Traffic was only partially restored at the end of the year but it took several months before it returned to normal. The battleships *Bismarck* and *Tirpitz* were to move to the Baltic but could only do so after the last part from *Inga* was removed on 5 March.

In the winter of 1942 Major Henry Threlfall of SOE German section was sent to Stockholm under the cover of assistant to the Naval Attaché, Henry M. Denham, a personal friend of Michael Cumberlege. He was approached by a certain Blackman who was serving as a steward on a Swedish merchant ship.

This man proposed to use a Swede named Lindström, reputed to be a very reliable friend, to plant explosives on a German ship loading iron ore at Lulea. The ship would be using the Kiel Canal and, hopefully, be sunk in the middle of it.

According to Threlfall, in an interview he gave for a book on SOE, the ship was reported to have been sunk but outside the canal after having made the passage.

Unfortunately, Threlfall's memory was seriously at fault. In fact, after money and explosives had been provided, the 'reliable' friend quickly informed the German consul in Göteborg of the machination (30 July 1942). Blackman and Lindström were arrested by the Swedish police and Threlfall had to make a quick exit from Sweden. Later Denham would write that he had been unaware of the sabotage attempt and was abruptly informed that his 'assistant' had left Sweden. The Naval Attaché was severely admonished by Admiral Godfrey, Director of Naval Intelligence, for having failed to control Threlfall.[64] The failure of Threlfall's mission does not appear to have affected his standing at SOE where he became head of the Hungarian Section and carried out a successful mission in Eastern Europe.

At SOE headquarters the setback did not discourage planners from studying another scheme against the Kaiser Wilhelm Canal. In July 1943 a new plan was initiated which would later develop into Operation KINDLE. It was similar in concept to Threlfall's but it tried to tackle the main obstacle which was how to time the bomb to detonate at the desired time. Lieutenant C. A. Broberg RNVR submitted the initial plan. It was proposed to have an agent attach a limpet mine to a ship, preferably loaded with iron ore so that it would sink quickly. The ship would have to be a Swedish or Danish ship. This could be done while the vessel was proceeding in an east-west direction and waiting for entry near the Kiel light vessel. The agent would have to pass himself for a member of the ship's crew and plant the mine unobserved.

Later, as the plan evolved, it was thought that it would be easier to plant the limpet in Copenhagen or Stockholm, the latter being the preferred location as, if caught, the agent would at least be in neutral hands. Ideally the limpet could be planted when the ship was in ballast (empty) and, if placed three feet under the waterline, this would ensure that when the vessel was loaded, the limpet would then be eight feet or more below the waterline and thus more difficult to find. Usually limpet mines used a timing device but this mine was to use a firing device which would be a 'sympathetic detonator'. The agent would wait till the ship was in a suitable spot in the canal and then drop in the water a small hand-grenade-type bomb which would detonate the mine in sympathy. The most suitable spot was determined to be 1,000 yards north-northeast of the Gruenenthal Bridge. How all this could be done without arousing the suspicion of the rest of the crew was not solved. It was hoped that the explosion would be attributed to an air-laid mine. Otherwise, to deflect the suspicions that would fall on the crew members, leaflets would be left pretending that the operation had been carried out by the 'Red Circle', a German resistance organization which had been crushed by the Gestapo. In May 1944 the operation appeared to find traction and an agent was apparently sent to Copenhagen but was arrested by the Gestapo shortly after his arrival. He managed to escape but the plan appears to have been shelved in August 1944.

The RAF came back into the game when a suitable mine was developed for use in the canal; this was the Mk I-IV and later the Mk VII. During the night of 12/13 May 1944 the canal was mined by thirteen Mosquito bombers of No.8 Group, one minesweeper was sunk and the waterway was blocked until 16 May. Nine Mosquitos from the same bomber group again mined the canal on 5 October 1944, blocking it until 11 October. But, two days later, the minesweeper *Steinbutt* was mined despite repeated sweeps. The wreck temporarily prevented ships of over 1,000 tons from making the passage.

Two more attempts were made in 1945. During the night of 28 February/1 March lone Mosquito of 627 Squadron managed to lay his two mines in poor visibility. Two nights later, six Mosquitos of the same squadron dropped twelve mines. No casualties occurred but there was serious disruption of traffic. This was the last attempt, as the collapse of Germany was now a matter of time and the need to block the Kiel Canal no longer existed.

Endnotes

1   *NID - Corinth Canal* (ADM223/480, TNA).

2   *SOE activities in Greece 1940-1942* by Ian Pirie (HS7/150, TNA).

3   P.70 (ADM199/806, TNA).

4   *SOE activities in Greece 1940-1942* by Ian Pirie (HS7/150, TNA).

5   See *Signals concerning the blocking of the Corinth Canal*, pp. 68-9 (ADM199/806, TNA).

6   See Appendix C for a list of Axis vessels using the Canal in the weeks following the occupation.

7   *Memorandum on Corinth Canal* pp.72-4 (ADM199/806, TNA).

8   Hammond wrote a detailed account of his escape from Crete and this section borrows heavily from it. See *Memories of a British Officer serving in Special Operations Executive in Greece 1941* in Balkan Studies (1982, Volume 23 (1)). Mike Cumberlege's report for this period does not appear to have survived.

9   Undated copy of letter from Mike Cumberlege to John Pendlebury's father (BSA).

10 ADM199/806, TNA, p.61.

11 The tankers were *Luisiano, Picci Fassio, Cassala, Alberto Fassio, Albaro, Berbera, Meteor, Romagna, Celeno, Clizia, Maya* and *Devoli* (T1022/2545, NARA).

12 *'Crete'* undated [ca. September 1941(HS5/678, TNA).

13 *Hide and Seek* by Xan Fielding (Secker & Warburg, London, 1954).

14 Captain Frank Macaskie of 2nd Leicestershire Regiment volunteered to return to Greece and arrange the extraction of evaders. With Alexis Ladas as interpreter, he arrived in November 1941 but, the following February, on their return trip, both men were captured by the Italians on the island of Kythnos.

15 See *Operation LOCKSMITH, Appendix E* (HS5/533, TNA).

16 Nikolaos Manzaris was born in Damala in 1893. His first wife died in 1920 and he remarried in 1923. In 1918 he had emigrated to Australia but returned to Greece ten years later. He was fluent in English and this was an asset to the LOCKSMITH mission. Nikolaos had five children and died on 11 December 1964. His son Panayotis, born 1941, was interviewed by the author in May 2013.

17 *Esame della situazione strategica in Mediterraneo - 18 Febbraio 1943* (T821/140, NARA).

18 At this time Ewen Montagu was busy planning the deception scheme known as *'The Man who never was'* (Operation MINCEMEAT). A body with false

papers was released by submarine (HMS *Seraph*) off the Spanish coast to induce Spanish Intelligence to believe that a plane had crashed in the sea. It was to act the part of an emissary carrying important papers indicating that the Allies intended to land in Sardinia and in Greece. It was hoped that the papers would find their way into Axis hands and lead them to believe that Sicily was not the actual target. The Spanish authorities did not disappoint and the Italians and Germans were provided with copies of the documents before they were returned to the British.

19 A dredger from the Corinth Canal company was reported sunk by sabotage and then raised on 28 July 1943; it is not clear if the sinking was accidental or if it had been mined. The Greek resistance does not appear to have claimed this action, so it is possible that the dredger detonated a mine.

20 We must remember that the Pagona 'leak' in December 1942 had also reached Italian authorities in Xylocastro and there may have been a connection with this visit. Sambani's house was near the beach, about two kilometres south-west of Boufi Cove.

21 Liedig was under suspicion and was investigated by the SD (or *Sicherheitsdienst* run by the Gestapo, the rival Intelligence service of the *Abwehr*) for his dealings with the Greek Nikolopoulos, a notorious trafficker in arms and currencies. He left the *Abwehr* and served as executive officer of the light cruiser *Köln*. Following Operation WALKYRIE, the July 1944 plot to assassinate Hitler, he was arrested and imprisoned in a succession of concentration camps. Unlike most of the conspirators, Liedig would survive the war.

22 Among the caiques used by the *Abwehr* in Athens were *Aghios Nikolaos* (v.351), *Evangelistria* (both common names in Greek caiques), *Spiridon K, Aghios Dimitrios* and *Taxiarchis*.

23 Interview of Panayotis Manzaris by the author with the assistance of Kostas Thoctarides (24 May 2013).

24 Although Mike was captured before Panayotis' christening, the latter had received the gold earring (24 carat according to him) and melted it to make it a finger ring. Panayotis later gave it to his own son but it was stolen when he was doing his military service.

25 The two Greeks made the mistake of showing off by going on a buying spree and were arrested by the EAM Andartes but the latter more interested in getting a share of the spoils and released them after collecting some of the money. Philippopoulos later applied for compensation from SOE. He admitted that, with his partner Bisias, he had appropriated the 2,000 gold sovereigns but claimed that he had been blackmailed by an individual named Mitsopoulos who extorted 65 sovereigns while the Andartes got another 300 sovereigns. He was then held in a concentration camp by ELAS where he spent the remainder. Understandably, his claim was rejected by SOE who considered him as dishonest if not a traitor.

26 Captain Harris was Greek (his real name was Christos Gogas) but had been commissioned in the British Army. In 1944 he was accused by the Greek General Staff of being an EAM sympathizer; the charge was found to be groundless and quickly withdrawn. Yet in his reports Harris did not hide his sympathies for left-wing elements.

27 The *Smyrna Sitreps (Situation Reports)* show that German deserter Max Gerhardt who had helped APOLLO, escaped to Smyrna and was sent to Cyprus in July 1943. Another German deserter Olaf Richter, who had also been recruited by APOLLO, escaped at the end of November 1943.

28 His son Marcus, born on 23 December 1938. Bira was their Siamese cat!

29 The two other saboteurs were Antonios Arvanitis and Costantinos Kapoutsides. Peltekis in an undated report but most likely written about September 1944, mentioned that five saboteurs had been executed including Niko Adam (APOLLO file, Benaki Museum).

30 Laskarina Bouboulina (1771-1825) was a Greek heroine of the War of Independence. Born on Hydra Island, she later moved to Spetses and organized a fleet to combat the Turks.

31 They could have landed on 17 October but this was a Tuesday and considered a bad omen in Greece as the Fall of Constantinople in 1453 had occurred on this day of the week.

32 Operation CICERO was one of the *Abwehr*'s most successful operations. Elyesa Bazna, the Turkish valet of the British ambassador in Ankara, provided the German Secret Service with invaluable information from the personal safe of his master. Initially, he was paid in Turkish notes but then insisted on being paid in British pounds, and the German Secret Service obligingly paid him with the counterfeit notes.

33 The story of Odette Sansom was filmed as *Odette* in 1950 with Anna Neagle in the title role and Trevor Howard playing the role of Peter Churchill. Odette and Peter were married after the war but later divorced. Maurice Buckmaster who had led the SOE French Section appeared briefly in the movie.
    Peter Churchill was twice landed by submarine in Vichy France, the first time by HMS *P.36* and the second time by HMS *Unbroken*. cf. *The Spirit of the Cage* by Peter Churchill (Hodder & Stoughton, 1954).

34 The five men survived the war. In 1968 Germany paid the British government £1,000,000 as a compensation for victims of Nazi persecution. Thirteen British survivors of Sachsenhausen, including Harry Day, Sydney Dowse, Jack Churchill and Peter Churchill, filed a claim to the government to get a share of this sum. They were assisted by Airey Neave MP, who had himself escaped from Colditz during the war and was later murdered by the INLA. Nancy Cumberlege was approached for advice but the claim was resisted by the government (see FCO46/50 and other files in the same series).

35 *Letter from Wing Commander Day to Mr. F. Broughton dated 14 July 1945* (ADM1/28910).

36 See *The Venlo Incident* (Hutchinson, London, 1949).

37 *Interrogation of Paul Schröter* (HS8/882, TNA).

38 *Testimony of Willi Feiler* (WO309/2040, TNA).

39 *Letter from Mr Kemp to Nancy Cumberlege dated 30 August 1946* (ADM1/28910).

40 *Statement of Rudolf Hoess of 20 May 1946* (WO309/438, TNA).

41 The death penalty had been abolished in the Soviet Union on 26 May 1947. *SS Untersturmführer* Heinrich Wessel, born on 13 April 1904, was not one of the fifteen men but he was brought to trial in Verden, West Germany, and given a sentence of seven and half years.

42 '*Im Februar 1945 wurden mit meiner Beteiligung der englische Hauptmann Cumberleigh und mit ihm zusammen 4 englische Soldaten erschossen. Sie saßen etwa 2 Jahre im Gefängnis. Am gleichen Tage wurde auch der Angehörige der polnischen Armee Kapitän Kuzewitz erschossen.*'
Citation taken from page 37 of *Todeslager Sachsenhausen / Zsgest.* by Fritz Sigl. - Berlin : SWA-Verl., 1948.*5*

43 See *Sachsenhausen Concentration Camp, Germany: killing and ill-treatment of allied nationals* (WO309/853, TNA).

44 I am indebted to Francis Suttill, son of Major Francis Suttill of SOE, for the information on the so called 'Russian' notebook, the Eccarius interrogations and several sections of this chapter.

45 Prince Galitzine belonged to an old Russian family which had emigrated to England following the Bolshevik Revolution. In 1939 he had joined the Royal Northumberland Fusiliers and became an intelligence officer.

46 *Interrogation of Walter Schellenberg - 14 November 1945* (M1270/18, NARA). Schellenberg had captured SIS agents Best and Stevens during the Venlo Incident (see earlier section in this chapter). At Nuremberg he received a sentence of six years for war crimes against humanity but was released in 1951 for health reasons. He died in 1952 from a liver ailment.

47 The *Schutzhaftbefehl* was a protective custody order usually directed at enemies of the state, this could only be issued by the Gestapo. The document was actually dated 19 January 1944; a translated copy can be found in *C. S. M. James Cook Steele Personnel File* (HS9/1410/3, TNA).

48 *Nazi Conspiracy and Aggression. Vol. II.* USGPO, Washington, 1946, pp.575-84 *http://www.ess.uwe.ac.uk/genocide/Kaltenbrunner.htm*

49 Document 3838-PS which became Exhibit USA 800.

50 The Trial of German Major War Criminals, One Hundred and Sixth Day: Friday, 12 April, 1946 (Part 9 of 12) in *http://www.nizkor.org/hweb/imt/tgmwc/tgmwc-11/tgmwc-11-106-09.shtml*

51 *The Log* was the magazine published by the Nautical College attended by Mike in his youth. My thanks to Robin Wright for unearthing this extract.

52 Email from Marcus Cumberlege to the author (7 September 2012).

53 This list is probably incomplete and some movements may be off by a day.

54 Possibly this was the *3^Squadriglia Dragamine: R-14, R-46, R-59* and *R-112* (Third Minesweeping Squadron).

55 On 3 June *Strombo* was torpedoed near Cape Helles by the submarine HMS *Parthian* but managed to reach Istanbul. She was again torpedoed on 10 July 1941 by the submarine HMS *Torbay* but again managed to reach Salamis towed by the torpedo-boat *Monzambano* and then by the Italian salvage vessel *Hercules*.

56 *Alberta* was torpedoed by the submarine HMS *Torbay* on 6 June and beached on Rabbit Island, near Cape Helles, at the entrance of the Bosphorus; the wreck was finished off by gunfire from the same submarine on 10 June.

57 Sunk on 30 August 1942 by HMS *Rorqual*.

58 Actually 5186 grt, mined and sunk on 10 January 1943.

59 This must be an error: she had already been sunk by HMS *Taku* on 6 May 1941.

60 Actually 1579 grt, she was sunk with heavy loss of life by HMS *Sahib* on 13 November 1942. It was a tragic error as she carried a large number of British PoWs.

61 See *Reports, Various: Military, Political and Civil* (HS5/687, TNA).

62 The limpet mine was a small bomb of about 10lb (4.5kg) with a size of approx 10in x 5in x 5in (about 25cm x 13cm x 13cm); it had a magnet to attach it to a ship's hull.

63 *Report of SOE activities in Greece and the Islands of the Aegean Sea* (HS8/428, TNA).

64 See *Inside the Nazi Ring* by Henry Denham (Holmes & Meier, New York, 1984).

Primary Sources

NATIONAL ARCHIVES, LONDON

ADM1/15803	RM Boom Patrol Detachment - Operation SUNBEAM A
ADM1/12771	Operation AGREEMENT
ADM 1/28910	Lt Cdr C.M.B. Cumberlege: Operation LOCKSMITH
ADM 116/4367	Azores and Cape Verde Island: plans for proposed occupation (1940)
ADM 199/255	Mediterranean and Red Sea Area: intelligence and enemy reports (1940-1942).
ADM 199/414	Mediterranean Command: war diaries (1941)
ADM 199/415	Mediterranean Command: war diaries (1941)
ADM 199/621	Losses of HM Ships and other vessels by enemy action: reports.
ADM 199/800	Defence of Crete (1940-1941)
ADM 199/806	Naval operations in Mediterranean: reports (1941)
ADM 199/810	Mediterranean Operations 1941
ADM 199/1220	Submarine Patrol Reports (HMS *Taku* 09-12-42 to 01-01-43)
ADM 199/1429	F.O.L.E.M war diaries (August–December 1944)
ADM 199/1850	Submarine Patrol Reports (RHN *Papanicolis* 07-01-43 to 23-01-43)
ADM 199/2226	War diary summaries: situation reports–April 1941
ADM 207/13	815 Squadron diary–October 1939-December 1941
ADM 223/47	OIC Merchant shipping available to the Axis
ADM 223/77	Telegram messages 5 May-22 July 1941
ADM 223/89	Report of Mediterranean Operational Intelligence Centre
ADM 223/480	Special Operations Executive: Part 1
ADM 234/560	British Mining Operations 1939-1945 (Vol.1)
ADM 234/561	British Mining Operations 1939-1945 (Vol.2)
AIR 20/5471	Proposed attack on Corinth Canal
AIR 25/795	ORB No. 201 Group RAF (1939-1942)
AIR 27/397-400	ORB No. 38 Squadron
AIR 27/613-615	ORB No. 70 Squadron
AIR 27/994	ORB No. 148 Squadron
AIR 40/1857	Levant reports of escapees and friendly aliens
AIR 41/19	*The RAF in the Maritime War (Vol 6): The Mediterranean and Red Sea* (10 June 1940-14 May 1943)
AIR 51/234	Target files Greece: Korinthos (Corinth) Canal (May 1943-February 1944)

DEFE 3/862	Signal Intelligence (ULTRA) March-April 1943
DEFE 3/868	Signal Intelligence (ULTRA) July 1943
DEFE 3/893	Intelligence from intercepted German, Italian and Japanese radio communications (June 1941-November 1942)
FCO 64/50-52	Claims from prisoners of war detained in the Sonderlager at Sachenhausen
FCO 64/71	Parliamentary Commissioner for Administration Sachsenhausen enquiry into Nazi persecution and criticisms of the Foreign Office
FCO 79/86-87	Parliamentary Commissioner for Administration cases: question of naming officials in reports (Sachsenhausen concentration camp enquiry)
FO 371/48356	Corinth Canal 1945
FO 371/48935	Communications from Lt Cdr Cumberlege
FO 371/58849	Clearance of the Corinth Canal and reconstruction of Piraeus harbour
FO 1012/734	War crimes: alleged murder of British naval personnel
FO 1093/339	War crimes: account by Sigismund Payne Best of imprisonment in Sachsenhausen concentration camp and personal descriptions of the accused
HS 5/294	Plan to block Corinth Canal
HS 5/305	Greece and the Aegean – FO Policy and directives to SOE
HS 5/340	Midas Reports and Claims
HS 5/341	Midas Reports, etc.
HS 5/346	SOE activities in Greece – WASHING-LOCKSMITH
HS 5/347	SOE activities in Greece – WASHING-LOCKSMITH
HS 5/363	SOE activities in Greece – Personnel
HS 5/365	Casualties: individual cases A-Z
HS 5/416	Operations LOCKSMITH and BUCKRAM
HS 5/441	Transport and shipping; losses
HS 5/450	SOE Greece – Sea operations
HS 5/491	Interrogations – March-September 1943
HS 5/497	SOE Greece – Reports, Various
HS 5/501	SOE Greece – Reports, Various, PROMETHEUS I and PROMETHEUS II
HS 5/509	Greek organization, evacuation and re-organization of Balkans section in Istanbul
HS 5/524	SOE activities in Greece – FLESHPOTS, ISINGLASS
HS 5/531	Missions LOCKSMITH/THURGOLAND
HS 5/532	Mission: LOCKSMITH
HS 5/533	Missions LOCKSMITH/THURGOLAND; personnel including Corporal J. Kotrba; arrest of LOCKSMITH party; missing documents

HS 5/535	Captain R. J. Stott (WEAZEL)
HS 5/547	Record of APOLLO
HS 5/568	MIDAS enquiry: activities of Major Tzigantis and Mission MIDAS 614
HS 5/678	SOE Crete – Operational Policy
HS 5/687	SOE Greece – Reports, Various, Smyrna, etc.
HS 5/688	Major Pirie collection of reports
HS 5/689	Major Pirie collection of reports
HS 5/711	SOE Greece – Reports, Various, Smyrna, etc.
HS 5/713	SOE Greece – Reports, Various, Niko, Odysseus, etc.
HS 5/748	Miscellaneous, London SO files
HS 6/630	Prisons, internment and concentration camps: Sachsenhausen, Emsland Oranienburg, Gusen (Mauthausen)
HS 7/150	SOE activities in Greece 1940-42 (chapters 1-6) by Major Ian Pirie
HS 7/151	SOE activities in Greece 1940-42 (chapters 7-18) by Major Ian Pirie
HS 7/172	MI9 Activities in Eastern Med 1941-45
HS 7/212 to 271	SOE war diary (1940-43)
HS 8/216 to 225	SOE Weekly Progress Reports (1940-43)
HS 8/453	SOE – Greek para-naval Claims
HS 8/880	SOE Security – War Crimes
HS 8/882	SOE Security – Interrogations
HS 9/653/6	Sergeant Thomas Handley Personnel File
HS 9/1410/3	CSM James Cook Steele Personnel File
HS 9/1430/6	Francis Alfred Suttill Personnel File
HS 9/1596/8	William Charles Frederick Grover-Williams Personnel File
HW 1/22	BONIFACE report of 15 August 1941
HW 1/70	ULTRA – French tankers and Corinth Canal
HW 1/3239	ULTRA – Corinth Canal
HW 19/Various	ULTRA *Abwehr* Decrypts
KV 2/977	Walter Sensburg file (*Abwehr* Athens)
KV 2/3568	Schreiber, alias Schier
PREM 13/2274	Question of compensation for Service survivors of Sachsenhausen concentration camp: correspondence with Airey Neave MP
WO 106/3224	Greece - General – April-December 1940
WO 193/628	SOE – Intelligence Reports - 20 January-31 May 1941
WO 201/69	Corinth Canal: reports on attack by German parachute troops 1941
WO 201/2747	Events at the Corinth Canal in April 1941

WO 201/2750	Report of German paratroops attack on Corinth Canal April 1941
WO 201/2756	SOE operations in Greece and the Aegean Islands
WO 204/9135	Re-opening of the Corinth Canal
WO 204/12897	German Intelligence Activities in Greece, Crete and the Greek Islands
WO 204/12952	Greece: Axis Intelligence Organisation and Activities
WO 208/3253	Summary of MI9 Activities in the Eastern Mediterranean
WO 208/3391	Caique operations: enemy captures (1942-43)
WO 208/4519	Intelligence war diary (Greece), 1939-46.
WO 208/5584	Special Interrogation Reports on Allied prisoners of war: Greece
WO 309/352	German orders to kill captured Allied commandos and saboteurs
WO 309/353	German orders to kill captured Allied commandos and saboteurs
WO 309/437	Sachsenhausen-Oranienburg concentration camp
WO 309/438	Sachsenhausen-Oranienburg concentration camp
WO 309/439	Sachsenhausen-Oranienburg concentration camp, Germany: killing and ill-treatment of Allied nationals
WO 309/493	Sachsenhausen and Neuengamme concentration camps, Germany: killing and ill-treatment of Allied nationals
WO 309/1589	Sachsenhausen concentration Ccmp, Germany: ill-treatment and possible death of British naval personnel
WO 309/1620	Sachsenhausen
WO 309/2050	Special Interrogation Reports – Oranienburg
WO 309/2217	Ill Treatment of Allied PoWs and Internees at Sachsenhausen
WO 373/27	Combatant Gallantry Awards. Middle East (Greece and Crete).
WO 373/61	Escape and Evasion and Special Operations. 26 Aug 1941-29 Sept 1942

NATIONAL ARCHIVES, WASHINGTON [NARA]

M1270/9	Preliminary interrogation of Ernst Kaltenbrunner
M1270/18	Preliminary interrogation of Walter Schellenberg
RG99/226/54	History of OSS Cairo
T501/252	*PG 41031/3: Anlagenband 2 zum Kriegstagebuch Nr.3 Militärbefehlshaber Griechenland /Ia - 20 Nov 1942–18 Nov 1943*

T821/140	*Esame della situazione strategica in Mediterraneo (18 Febbraio 1943)*
T1022/1930	*Marinegruppenkommando Süd* (1944)
T1022/2550	*Admiral Süd-Ost Aegäis* 1941
T1022/2580	KTB *Marinebefehlshaber Griechenland* 1941
T1022/2634	KTB *Küstenschutzflottille Attika* (1942-44)
T1022/2669	KTB *Seevertidigung Attika* (1942-44)
T1022/4023	KTB *Admiral Aegäis* 1943 (1/1/1943 – 31/7/1943)
T1022/4024	KTB *Admiral Aegäis* 1941

IMPERIAL WAR MUSEUM, LONDON [IWM]

13345 05/75/1	Private Papers of Major Michael Ward OBE
7347 76/150/1	Private Papers of Lord Glenconner

UFFICIO STORICO DELLA MARINA MILITARE, ROME [USMM]
Supermarina – Diario di guerra 1940-1943
Supermarina schacchieri esteri (Morea) (cartella 13/319): *Canale di Corinto*
Supermarina schacchieri esteri (Morea) (cartella 15): *Relazione sulla missione in Morea (11 Maggio–18 Giugno 1941)* [diary of Admiral Tur]
Notiziie Belliche Delle FF.AA. (Egeo) Giugno 1940-Luglio 1942
Archivio LII – *Supermarina Diari di guerra* (cartelle 67 & 68)
Archivio LII – *Diari di guerra Comando Gruppo Navale Italiano Egeo Settentrionale* (cartella 48)
Archivio 37   Torpediniera *Castelfidardo* (cartella C9)
          Torpediniera *Lupo* (cartella L7)
          Torpediniera *Monzambano* (cartella M11)
          Torpediniera *Sagittario* (cartelle S1, S2)
          Torpediniera *Sirio* (cartella S10)
Supermarina Sbarramenti: Mine magnetiche - Dragamine (cartella 8, b8/f232) *Argomento: Torpedini inglese a forma di latta di petrolio*

UFFICIO STORICO DELLO STATO MAGGIORE DELL'ESERCITO [USSME]
Diario di guerra Generale Amé (SIM) (Aprile 1943)

HELLENIC NAVAL ARCHIVES, ATHENS [HNA]
RHN Submarine *Papanicolis* file.
Corinth Canal 1947-48, operational file 18/48.

BENAKI MUSEUM, ATHENS [BM]
Papers of APOLLO and MIDAS.

BRITISH SCHOOL AT ATHENS [BSA]
Pendlebury papers.

The following websites have been used:

Axishistory.com
Fold3.com
Marinearchiv.de
Palyam.org
Uboat.net
Warsailors.com
Wikipedia
and many others.

Select Bibliography

Ansel, Walter, *Hitler and the Middle Sea*, Duke University Press, Durham, 1972.

Auty, Phillips and Richard Clogg (eds), *British Policy towards Wartime Resistance in Yugoslavia and Greece,* MacMillan Press, London, 1945.

Bailey, Roderick, *Forgotten Voices of the Secret War: An Inside History of Special Operations in the Second World War*, Edbury, London, 2009.

Bauer, Yehuda, *From Diplomacy to Resistance: A History of Jewish Palestine 1939-1945*, Varda Books, Skokie, 2001,

Beesly, Patrick, *Very Special Admiral – The Life of Admiral J.H. Godfrey, CB,* Hamish Hamilton, London, 1980.

Beevor, Antony, *Crete, the Battle and the Resistance*, Penguin, London, 1992.

Beevor, John Grovesnor, *SOE – Recollections and Reflections 1940-1945*, The Bodley Head, London, 1981.

Beker, Cajus, *The Luftwaffe War Diaries*, Ballantine, New York, 1966.

Best, Captain S. Payne, *The Venlo Incident*, Skyhorse Publishing, New York, 2009 (reprint of 1949 edition).

Bragadin, Marc'Antonio, *The Italian Navy in World War Two*, USNI, Annapolis, 1957.

Brown, Anthony Cave, *'C' – The Secret Life of Sir Stewart Menzies*, MacMillan, New York, 1987.

– *The Secret War of the OSS*, Berkeley, New York, 1976.

– *The Last Hero - Wild Bill Donovan*, Times Bks, New York, 1982.

Bryer, Robin, *Jolie Brise,* Secker & Warburg, London, 1982.

Buckley, Christopher, *Greece and Crete 1941*, Efstathiadis Group, Athens, 1984 (first published in 1952).

Butler, J. R. M., *Grand Strategy – Volume II: September 1939-June 1941,* HMSO, London, 1957.

Carroll, Tim, *The Great Escape from Stalag Luft III*, Pocket Books New York, 2004.

– *The Dodger,* Mainstream Publishing, Edinburgh, 2012.

Cavallero, Ugo, *Comando Supremo – Diario 1940-1943 del Capo di S.M.G.*, Cappelli, Rome, 1948.

Churchill, Capt. Peter Morland, *The Spirit of the Cage,* Hodder & Stoughton, London, 1954.

Cooper, Artemis, *Cairo in the War 1939-1945*, Hamish Hamilton, London, 1989.

Cunningham, Admiral A. B., *A Sailor's Odyssey*, E.P. Dutton, New York, 1951.

Damer, Sean and Ian Frazer, *On the Run*, Penguin Books, Australia, 2007.

Denham, Henry, *Inside the Nazi Ring,* Holmes & Meier, New York, 1984.

Ewer, Peter, *Forgotten Anzacs – The Campaign in Greece, 1941*, Scribe, Melbourne, 2008.

Farran, Roy, *Winged Dagger,* The Elmfield Press, UK, 1973.

Fielding, Xan, *Hide and Seek*, Secker & Warburg, London, 1954.

Foot, M. R. D., *SOE - An Outline History of the Special Operations Executive*, The Folio Society, London, 2008.

Foot, M. R. D. & J. M. Langley, *MI9 – Escape and Evasion 1939-1945*, Bodley Heag, London, 1979.

Fournet, Vice Amiral Dartige du, *Souvenirs de guerre d'un amiral 1914-1916*, Plon, Paris, 1920.

Gerolymatos, André, *Guerilla Warfare & Espionage in Greece 1940-1944,* Pella Publishing, New York, 1992.

Gill, Anton, *The Great Escape,* Headline Books, London, 2002.

Golla, Karl-Heinz, *The German Fallschirmtruppe 1936-1941*, Helion & Company Ltd, Solihull, 2012.

Grundon, Imogen, *The Rash Adventurer: The Life of John Pendlebury*, Libri, London, 2007.

Halder, Franz, *The Halder war diary 1939-1942*, Presidio Press, Novato, 1988.

Hammond, Nicholas, *Venture into Greece – With the Guerillas 1943-1944*, William Kimber, London, 1983.

  – Memories of a British Officer serving in Special Operations Executive in Greece 1941 [Article in Balkan Studies, Volume 23 (1), Thessaloniki, 1982].

Hampshire, A. Cecil, *Undercover Sailors*, William Kimber, London, 1981.

Harris, Alan, *Courage Endured*, Alan Harris, Kwelera, South Africa, 2011.

Heckstall-Smith, Anthony & H. T, Baillie-Grohman, *Greek Tragedy 1941*, W.W. Norton, New York, 1961.

Helm, Sarah, *A Life in Secrets - Vera Atkins and the missing agents of WWII,* Little, Brown London, 2005.

Hinsley, F. H. & et al, *British Intelligence in the Second World War*, [5 volumes] (HMSO, London, 1979-1990.

Holt, Thaddeus, *The Deceivers – Allied Military Deception in the Second World War*, Skyhorse Publishing, New York, 2007.

Jager, Charles, *Escape from Crete – The Pirating of the 'Aghia Irini'*, Floradale Productions Sydney, 2004.

James, B.A. 'Jimmy', *Moonless Night*, Leo Cooper, London, 2001.

Kédros, André, *La résistance grecque (1940-1944)*, Robert Lafont, Paris, 1966.

Kotsis, Spyros, *ΜΙΛΑΣ 614,* Athens, 1976.

Kurowski, Franz, *Jump into Hell*, Stackpole Books, Mechanicsburg, 2010.

Lodwick, John, *Raiders from the Sea*, Naval Institute Press, Annapolis 1990 (reprint of *The Filibusters: The Story of The Special Boat Service* published in 1947).

Mackenzie, Compton, *Gallipoli Memories*, Cassel, London, 1929.
– *First Athenian Memories*, Cassel, London, 1931.
– *Greek Memories*, Chatto & Windus, London, 1939.
– *Aegean Memories*, Chatto & Windus, London, 1940.
– *Wind of Freedom* (London: Chatto & Windus, 1943).

Mackenzie, William J. M., *The Secret History of SOE*, St Ermin's Press, London, 2000.

Macintyre, Ben, *Double Cross – The True Story of the D-Day Spies*, Bloomsbury, London, 2012.

Macmillan, Harold, *The Blast of War*, Macmillan, London, 1967.

McClymont, W. G., *To Greece (Official History of New Zealand in the Second World War)*, Department Internal Affairs, Wellington, 1959.

McKay, C.G., *From Information to Intrigue – Studies in Secret service based on the Swedish Experience, 1939-1945*, Frank Cass, London, 1993.

Marks, Leo, *Between Silk and Cyanide*, Free Press, 2000.

Mason Walter Wynne, *Prisoners of War – Official History of New Zealand in the Second World War*, Dept Internal Affairs, Wellington, NZ, 1954.

Masterman, John C., *The Double Cross System*, Avon, New York, 1972.

Mattesini, Francesco, *Corrispondenza e Direttive tecnico-operative di Supermarina, Vol. 2, I Tomo, Gennaio 1941 – Giugno 1941*, Ufficio Storico della Marina Militare, Rome, 2001.
– *Le direttive tecnico-operative di Superaereo, Vol.1, II Tomo, Aprile 1940-Dicembre 1941*, Stato Maggiore Aeronautica Ufficio Storico, Rome, 1992.

Montanari, Mario, *L'Esercito Italiano nella Campagna di Grecia*, Stato Maggiore dell'Esercito, Rome, 1999.

Medlicott, W.N., *The Economic Blockade – Vol. 1 & 2*, HMSO, London, 1952.

Miller, Russell, *Code name Tricycle*, Pimlico, London, 2005.

Montagu, Lt Cdr Ewen, *Beyond Top Secret U*, P. Davies, London, 1977.

Myers, E. C. W., *Greek Entanglement*, Rupert-Hart Davies, London, 1955.

Neave, Airey, *Saturday at M.I.9*, Pen & Sword, London, 2010 (reprint of 1969 edition).

Ogden, Alan, *Sons of Odysseus*, Bene Factum Publishing, London, 2012.

Panagiotakis, George I., *Documents from the Battle of Crete and the Resistance*, Heraklion, 2000.

Papastratis, Procopis, *British Policy towards Greece during the Second World War 1941-1944*, Cambridge, 2008.

Parish, Michael Woodbine, *Aegean Adventures 1940-1943*, The Book Guild, London, 1993.

Playfair, I. S. O. & Al, *The Mediterranean and the Middle East* (Vol.1 & 2), HMSO, London, 1956.

Popov, Dusko, *Spy/Counterspy*, Grosset & Dunlap, New York, 1974.

Rogers, Anthony, *Churchill's Folly – Leros and the Aegean*, Cassell, London, 2003.

Roskill, Stephen W., *The War at Sea (4 volumes),* HMSO, London, 1965.

Saunders, Tim, *Crete – The Airborne Invasion*, Battleground, London, 2008.

Shores, Christopher & Al, *Air War for Yugoslavia, Greece and Crete,* Grub Street, London, 1987.

Sigl, Fritz, *Todeslager Sachsenhausen. Ein Dokumentarbericht v. Sachsenhausen-Prozeß*, SWA-Verlag, Berlin, 1948.

Simpson, Michael (ed.), *The Cunningham Papers Vol .I*, Navy Records Society, Greenwich, 1999.

Sinclair, D. W., *19 Battalion and Armoured Regiment – Official History of New Zealand in the Second World War,* Dept Internal Affairs Wellington, 1954.

Smith, E.D., *Victory of a Sort – The British in Greece 1941-1946*, Robert Hale, London, 1988.

Smith, Sydney, *Wings Day*, Collins, London, 1968.

Sweet-Escott, Bickham, *Baker Street Irregular*, Methuen, London, 1965.

Tsatsos, Jeanne, *The Sword's Fierce Edge*, Vanderbilt University Press, Nashville, 1965.

Lupinacci, Pier Filippo, *La Difesa del Traffico con l'Albania, La Grecia e l'Egeo,* Ufficio Storico della Marina Militare, Rome, 1965.

Waller, Douglas, *Wild Bill Donovan*, Free Press New York, 2011.

Ward, Michael, *Greek Assignments: SOE 1943-1948,* Zeno Books London, 1992.

West, Nigel, *Secret War – The Story of SOE*, Hodder & Stoughton London, 1992.

Wilkinson, Peter, *Foreign Fields – The Story of an SOE Operative*, I.B. Taurus, London, 1997.

Wilkinson, Peter and Joan Bright Astley, *Gubbins & SOE*, Pen & Sword Books, London, 2010 (first published by Leo Cooper in 1993).

Woodhouse, C. M., *The Apple of Discord*, Hutchinson, London, 1948.
  – *The Struggle for Greece 1941-1949* (Hurst, London, 2002 (reprint of 1976 edition).

Woollams, Fred, *Corinth and all that,* A. H & A. W. Reed Wellington, 1945.

Index

Fleet Air Arm, 29, 37, 59, 74, 87, 187, 197
Fleming, Ian, 51, 168
F-lighters, 86–7
Foca, 25
Force 133, 147, 151–2, 154, 194, 197–8, 205
Formidable, HMS, 29, 58
Foscolo, 98, 210
Foster, Group Captain, 62
Fotini, 51
Fournarakis (brothers), 75
Fournet, Adm. Dartige du, 3–4
Freeman, Air Chief Marshal Sir Wilfrid, 88
Freyberg, Gen. Bernard Cyril, 55
Fuerst, Walter, 128
Funkspiel, 141, 145

G (R), 64
GA-01, 222
GA-02, 132
GA-03, 132
GA-04, 133
GA-05, 132
GA-06, 132
GA-08, 132
GA-09, 132
GA-26, 132
GA-43, 132
GA-51, 129
GA-52, 131
GA-53, 115, 132
GA-54, 129
GA-55, 115, 132
GA-57, 131–2
GA-59, 115, 132
GA-62, 131–2
GA-67, 129
GA-68, 115
GA-69, 132
GA-78, 155

GA-79, 155
Galatas, 80–1, 107, 110, 130
Galilea, 208
Galilei, Galileo, 27
Galitzine, Capt. Yuri, 180, 234
Galli, Lt. Gianluigi, 77
Gamelin, Gen. Maurice, 164
GD-91, 227
Gelli, Lt Cdr. Ugo, 46
Genepesca II, 208
Geniere, 98
Georgatos, Mayor Angelos, 149
George I, King of Greece, 2
George II, King of Greece, 5, 16, 37, 72, 99, 118, 148
George VI, King of England, 189
Gerhardt, Max, 233
Gertrud, 225
Gestapo, x, 95, 100–101, 108, 112, 117, 139, 145, 149–51, 161–2, 174–5, 177, 182–4, 197, 200, 202, 225, 230, 232
Giamalvia, V., 17
Giannacopoulos, Miltiadis "Aristides", 91
Giannakea, Christos, 121
Giannakea, Eleni, 121
Giskes, Hermann, 141
Giuseppina Ghirardi, 49
Glenconner, Lord Christopher Grey, 15, 89, 92, 100, 138, 148, 192, 194, 198, 203
Glenearn, HMS, 52
Glezos, Manolis, 71
Gloucester, HMS, 54
GM-59, 132
GM-61, 132
GM-66, 132
GM-68, 132
Godfrey, Adm. John Henry, 11–12, 32–3, 59, 93, 95, 138, 196, 229
Godwin, Sub Lt. John, 163–4, 178

Holmes, Sherlock, 14
Hood, HMS, 9
Hotspur, HMS, 52
Houghton, Capt. Joseph B.G., 160
HP-6, 226
HP-13, 225
HP-16, 223
HP-52, 223
Huddart, Lt. J.S., 76
Hyacinth, HMS, 36
Hydra, destroyer, 7
Hydra, island, 51, 80, 96, 104–106,
    115, 118, 129, 131, 135, 145, 154,
    225, 233
HYDRO, 9

Iatrides, Miltos, 105
Ichnusa, 44–5, 206
Illustrious, HMS, 19–20
Imperial, HMS, 57
Inga, 228
Instancabile, 119
Ionia, 125
Irene, 21, 51
Irene Vernikos, 81
Isandanis, 78
Isis, HMS, 52
ISLD, 64, 67, 76, 83, 99–100, 138,
    192, 197–8, 201, 203, 205
Ispmi, 61
Italia, 125, 210
Iwanow, Jerzy Szajnowicz, 73

Jackal, HMS, 66
Jadwiga, HMS, 19
Jakubianiec, Alfons Jerzy, 165, 170,
    177, 179
James, Lt. Bertram A., 165, 170, 173,
    180
Jantina, 50
Janus, HMS, 55
Jebsen, Johannes, 167–8

Jennings, Cdr. A.E., 127, 144
Jensen, Capt. Leif, 171–2
Jiul, 47, 218
John Knudsen, 155, 157, 227
Jolie Brise, 32
Jung, Lt Cdr., 44
Juno, HMS, 58
Junon, 160

Kaindl, Col. Anton, 160, 175–80
Kal-177, 224
Kalamaki, 84, 100–101, 148, 156
Kalamata, 43, 52, 90, 124, 134
Kaltenbrunner, RHSA Chief Ernst,
    149, 161–2, 168, 180–4, 200
Kanaris, Capt. Miltiadis, 122–3, 149,
    199, 204
Kanellopoulos, Panayotis, 73, 76, 79,
    90–1, 118, 192–3, 195, 197, 201,
    203
Kapetanides, 102, 121
Kapoutsides, Costantinos, 233
Karabasas, Nikos, 73, 199
Karayianni, Lela, 75
Karlovolos, Konstantinos, 113
Karvounis, Dr, 17
Karystos, Euler, 122
Kashmir, HMS, 58
Kasos Strait, 24, 54, 57
Katina, 200, 226
Katsonis, 144
Katt, Emilius, 134
Kavallar, Lt., 45
Keble, Brig. Mervyn, 89, 119, 135,
    195, 198
Kelevini, 96
Kelly, HMS, 58
Kemp, F.W., 175, 234
Khan, Noor Inayat, 172
Kiel Canal, 32, 200, 228–30
Kilkis, 29
Kimberley, HMS, 55